and insinuate that a person's circumstances in the world are a mark of character. But Ryan notes that this inhospitable system of beliefs appears to be developing a few cracks, and that sharing is perhaps not altogether alien to the American tradition.

Dr. William Ryan, a clinical psychologist by training, received his Ph.D. from Boston University and is currently a professor of psychology at Boston College. Since the mid-1960s, he has been active in welfare rights and in prison reform, helping to organize the Citizen Observer Program in Walpole Prison in 1973. His previous books include *Distress in the City* and *Blaming the Victim*.

Also by William Ryan

BLAMING THE VICTIM
DISTRESS IN THE CITY (Editor)

EQUALITY

EQUALITY

William Ryan

 PANTHEON BOOKS / NEW YORK

Copyright © 1981 by William Ryan
All rights reserved under International and Pan-American Copyright
Conventions. Published in the United States by Pantheon Books,
a division of Random House, Inc., New York, and simultaneously
in Canada by Random House of Canada Limited, Toronto.
Manufactured in the United States of America
First Edition

Library of Congress Cataloging in Publication Data

Ryan, William, 1923–
Equality.

Includes index.
1. United States—Social policy. 2. Equality. 3. Equal pay for equal work—
United States. 4. Equality before the law—United States. 5. Sex discrimination
in employment—United States. I. Title.
HN65.R92   305   80-8655
ISBN 0-394-50493-3

Grateful acknowledgment is made to the following for permission to reprint
previously published material:

George Allen & Unwin (Publishers) Ltd. and Barnes & Noble Books: excerpt
from *Equality* by R. H. Tawney, 1964. Reprinted by permission of George Allen
& Unwin (Publishers) Ltd. and Barnes & Noble Books, a division of Littlefield,
Adams & Co., Inc.

Commentary: excerpt from "The Idea of Merit" by Paul Seabury. *Commentary*,
December 1972. Reprinted by permission: all rights reserved.

Irving Kristol: Excerpt from "About Equality" by Irving Kristol appeared in
Commentary, November 1972. Reprinted by permission of the author.

The Public Interest: excerpt from "On Meritocracy and Equality" by Daniel
Bell, *The Public Interest,* no. 29 (fall 1972). Reprinted by permission of the
author. Copyright © 1972 by National Affairs, Inc.

For my wife, Phyllis, who, in the cause of justice and equality, has given lavishly of the strength of her mind and soul and has exhausted the powers of her body. With love for her, with admiration of her, and with pride in her, I dedicate this book to the courageous woman who, for thirty years, has been a loving companion in all that we have done.

Rabbi Tarfon used to say: You are not required to complete the task; but neither are you free to desist from it.—*Pirke Avoth (Sayings of the Fathers)*

Contents

Acknowledgments

One of the points I attempt to make in the following pages—that human products are the consequence of collective, rather than individual, effort—became acutely apparent to me as I turned to writing these words. I cannot begin to acknowledge all those whose influence has contributed to the shaping of this book—whose books I have read, who have taught me and whom I have taught, who have shared in the significant actions of my life. I came to realize that none of the ideas in this book were born inside my head. My hope is that I have made a contribution in organizing and linking these ideas in a way that will be useful.

Among the many colleagues, students, and friends who have worked on these ideas with me, who have read earlier drafts, who have challenged, stimulated, and enlightened me, I wish especially to thank Ali Banuazizi, Jack Beatty, Donald Benders, James Breeden, Barbara Carmen, Joseph Gannon, Marian Glaser, Thomas Glynn, Bernard Kramer, Ramsey Liem, Brinton Lykes, Lois Masur, Edward O'Donnell, John Osler, James Riley, Ellen Winner, and William Zimmer.

My daughter Elizabeth provided a brilliant analysis of early draft material that helped me immeasurably in rethinking and reorganizing my work; to her, my loving paternal gratitude. A friend and former colleague, Lynne Ballew, generously contributed her editorial skill, piercing intelligence, and awesome knowledge to the task of carefully reading and writing all over the first complete draft of the book. Her help was invaluable, as I hope she will recognize in reading the final version.

What I have come to think of as "the Pantheon people" have kept this project afloat for many years. The work of James Peck and Jonathan Cobb on earlier drafts benefited me and the book tremendously. Susan Gyarmati patiently shepherded me through the agonies of the final restructuring and rewriting. André Schiffrin—to my mind the model of what a publisher should be—with tactful encouragement and understanding, provided constant support through the six long years I have spent in constructing this book.

Finally, the brief lives of Martin Luther King and George Wiley have provided a constant model of what it means to give oneself completely to the cause of equality. I hope this book reflects some sparks from their lives.

To those I have named, and to all my other unnamed collaborators, my profound thanks.

Equality

1

The Equality Dilemma

FAIR PLAY OR FAIR SHARES?

I How Do I Know I'm Up if Nobody Else Is Down?

Thinking about equality makes people fidgety. Insert the topic into a conversation and listen: voices rise, friends interrupt each other, utter conviction mingles with absolute confusion. The word slips out of our grasp as we try to define it. How can one say who is equal to whom and in what way? Are not some persons clearly superior to others, at least in some respects? Can superiority coexist with equality, or must the one demolish the other? Most important, are the existing inequalities such that they should be redressed? If they are, what precisely should be equalized? And by whom?

We feel constrained by the very word—to deny equality is almost to blaspheme. Yet, at the same time, something about the idea of equality is dimly sinful, subject to some obscure judgment looming above us. It is not really adequate to be "as good as." We should be "better than." And the striving for superiority fills much of the space in our lives, even filtering into radio commercials. Listen to a chorus of little boys singing, "My dog's better than your dog; my dog's better than yours." They are selling dog food, it turns out, and apparently successfully, which must mean that a lot of people want very much to have their dogs be better than your dogs. Their *dogs*!

This passing example suggests how far it is possible to carry the competition about who and whose is better. The young voices sing fearlessly. There is little danger that some fanatic will leap up and denounce the idea of one dog's being superior to another or quote some sacred text that asserts the equality of all dogs. In regard to people, however, we do hesitate to claim superiority or to imply inferiority. No commercials announce, "My son's better than your son" or "My wife's better than yours" or, most directly, "I'm better than you." That we remain reticent about flaunting such sentiments and yet devote ourselves to striving for superiority signals the clash of intensely contradictory beliefs about equality and inequality.

We all know, uneasily but without doubt, that our nation rests on a foundation of documents that contain mysterious assertions like "all men are created equal," and we comprehend that such phrases have become inseparable components of our license to nationhood. Our legitimacy as a particular society is rooted in them, and bound and limit our behavior. We are thus obliged to agree that all men are created equal—whatever that might mean to us today.

But our lives are saturated with reminders about whose dog is better. In almost all our daily deeds, we silently pledge allegiance to inequality, insisting on the continual labeling of winners and losers, of Phi Beta Kappas and flunkouts, and on an order in which a few get much and the rest get little.

We re-create the ambiguity in the minds of our children as we teach them both sides of the contradiction. "No one is better than anyone else," we warn. "Don't act snotty and superior." At the same time we teach them that all are obliged to get ahead, to compete, to achieve. Everyone is equal? Yes. Everyone must try to be superior? Again, yes. The question reverberates.

As a nation we grow more troubled about many issues that in large part touch on questions of equality, although they are not defined in such terms.

Consider several examples:

• Regarding racial equality there is swelling bitterness as one side calls for affirmative action and the other side curses reverse discrimination—and both are attending to the same phenomenon.

• Then there is the astonishing failure to achieve rapid passage of the equal rights for women amendment. The simple sentence that was supposed to become the twenty-sixth amendment is so innocuous as to be almost banal, almost like the casual correction of an oversight. At first there was no dispute, no controversy; rapid ratification seemed certain. The process started just that way. Then, suddenly, the equal-rights amendment was becalmed. The obvious had somehow become obscure, the undisputed controversial; the simple sentence was scribbled over with complicated interpretation and exegesis. "Are you *against* equal rights for women?" one asks, aghast. "Of course not! But it's not as simple as it seems. You don't understand . . ."

• Even events that have been lumped together under the cliché "middle-class tax revolt" have the flavor of perceived violations of principles of equality. Although such events as the passage of Proposition 13 in California, which drastically cut back property taxes, were facilely interpreted as protests against "big government," what the voters themselves said to interviewers does not support this interpretation. It seems clear that voters were enraged because they felt they were being treated unfairly. Why, they asked, should they have to pay such enormous fractions of their incomes in taxes on the homes that many of them had struggled so hard to buy? What were they paying so much money *for*? And whom was it going *to*? They were convinced that they were paying *more* and getting back *less* than their fair share. If that is a correct interpretation, it certainly places the issue squarely in the domain of equality.

It is true that many home owners on a strained budget have been persuaded that the poor are the cause of all their troubles. "Why," they ask, "should I pay my hard-earned money to support people who won't even work?" "Why," they inquire indignantly, "should I pay someone else's hospital bills? I still owe my own doctor." They are, as we shall see, quite misguided, and their view is distorted, but we cannot deny that the feeling that emerges reflects a belief that rules about equality and fairness are being violated.

Then listen to the answers to their questions: "Why should anybody be able to *buy* necessary medical care? Why should health—even life—be put up for auction?" and "If a person can't work and has no money, what should happen? Should we let him *starve*?" That's another way of appealing to principles of equality.

Looking into the near future, we see national issues beginning to be analyzed in terms of conflicting definitions of equality. What should we do if there is a long-term gasoline shortage? One answer is to impose the rule of the free market: let everyone be free to buy as much gasoline as he can afford, allowing rising prices to balance supply and demand. The other answer, drawing on a different conception of equality, is formal rationing: gasoline is provided to each driver in accordance with his need.

The latent conflicts and ambiguities in our views about equality have struck many observers of American life from Tocqueville to the compiler of a joke book published in 1896. Appropriately, the observation on equality that I found was an ethnic joke. As there are Italian and Polish jokes today, with a fixed form, there was an equivalent form then, called the Irish Bull, which was a joke illustrating the inferior capacity for logic of the slow-witted Irishman, the "thick Mick" of that generation's ethnic mythology. A rally is being addressed by an eloquent and passionate egalitarian, whose peroration begins with the cry "One man is as good as another!" To which the Irishman in the audience, leaping to his feet and applauding wildly, shouts back, "Sure, and a great deal better!"

That may be as good a summation as any of the great American equality dilemma.

The source of the dilemma, the mystery of equality, can be traced back more than two centuries to the time of our nation's birth and the startling words of Jefferson's "self-evident" truth: all men are created equal. The words are in many ways like a promissory note on which the date and the amount of payment are omitted. What the devil did Jefferson mean by that? And did Hancock and the other cosigners of the note—did they all agree on what it meant? Was it clear to them then? It certainly is puzzling and ambiguous to us today and many minds have, over the centuries, struggled to construe the mysterious words of the powerful talismanic phrase and have come to vastly different conclusions. If we are to understand our dilemma today, we must begin with those three words: men, created, equal. What are we to make of them?

Men, but not women? In 1776, probably not. We have, however, progressed somewhat, and, formally at least, we here use the term "men" to denote species rather than gender. Winking for the moment at eighteenth-century sexism, we can agree that "men" equals "persons," but where does that get us? Men, but not animals? Although wise dolphins and chimps that can chat with us have struck glancing blows at our self-esteem, we remain fairly certain that we are superior to other animals. Men as opposed to what, then? Are there *nonmen*? Our history gives clues, such as the Dred Scott decision, which ruled that slaves are a form of living property, and this must remind us that the author of the phrase himself owned slaves. So it would seem that, at least at times, and in the view of some, there exist men who are not men. Another of our foundation documents seems to confirm such an assumption. The arithmetic of Article I, Section 2, of the Constitution is unequivocal: the equation of political power is that three "free men" are equal to five of "all other persons"—that is, black slaves. And many, probably most, read this to mean that blacks are, at best, 60 percent human and thus not really men. The question whether some persons are less *human* than others, or whether they can be declared to be so, was presumably decided in the negative a century ago. We now agree that a person's humanity cannot be forfeited, but the barbarous idea that it can remains unspoken in the minds of many.

We come next to "created." Why created? Why not just men *are* equal? The next phrase—"that they are endowed by their Creator with certain unalienable rights"—suggests the answer. Persons are seen as existing within a larger framework—encompassing other creatures, other forms of life, and the vast realm of what we think of as nonliving—that has a Creator. As His creatures we are equal in the *form* of our creation, as members of the human species. Whatever is universally entailed in being human—in this instance the reference is to certain rights—holds equally true for all humans. All human beings share those rights equally. This theme of the universal and natural rights of man formed a dominant strain in the political philosophy of the eighteenth century, and we can, I believe, safely construe that the Founding Fathers were referring to equal *rights*, not dependent on law but deriving from one's status as a human being, which were then spelled out as including "life, liberty and the pursuit of happiness." It is not, then, the idea that all men are created equal that is mysterious or ambiguous, nor, in a general sense, is it unclear that the words were intended to mean that all human beings share equally in the specified rights. The equality dilemma arises when we move from the abstract to the concrete, when we begin to define the meaning of these rights. This is where the disputes and disagreements begin.

What is disputed? The right to life seems fairly simple and straightforward: no one should kill me or you; we are equally entitled to live. But if it were indeed that simple, why even bother to make the point? If we think about it for a while, the idea that all human beings have the right to life is a profound and weighty claim. For example, if you and I have really and truly been endowed by our Creator with an unalienable *right* to life, does it not follow necessarily and logically that we have a *right* to the means of sustaining life? If this assertion does not include the associated right of all to food, shelter, clothing, and other necessities, then it carries very little meaning at all. If the idea of a right is to have concrete significance, it must be possible to exercise that right. Therefore, the right to means of exercising it is linked with it and is itself a right. No one will quarrel with you if you keep it general and say, "Everyone has the right to life." Who could argue with that? But try saying, "Everyone has the right to all that is necessary to sustain life," and someone will start disagreeing with you. That is the basis of dispute number one.

Dispute number two arises when we start digging into the right to liberty. There is broad agreement on the equation of liberty with maximum freedom to think and do what one wishes—up to the point of harming others. But calling liberty freedom is just interchanging synonyms. Freedom—or liberty—certainly implies more than some detached and floating right to *do* something. If we all share equally in the right to liberty, we must be free from arbitrary and unreasonable compulsion and coercion. No one may dictate my religious or political opinions, no one may enslave me (just as important, I may not enslave myself). It would seem, furthermore, that this right suggests that everyone has the right to participate in the political process, since a rule cannot be applied to persons who were completely excluded from the process of making the rule.

The right to freedom also necessarily includes the means to execute that right. If I have no income and no resources whatever and am then offered a job at two dollars an hour, am I really free not to take it? Or does such a situation imply some compulsion to work? Am I free to be a Jew or a "radical" only if I am willing to forgo privileges that are granted to Christians and "moderates"? The right to liberty, then, is also not as simple as it might at first seem. Its meaning must encompass the fact that one person's existence is inextricably bound up with that of many others who could—but may not—coerce him or her and whom he or she could—but may not— coerce; moreover, in order to be guaranteed protection against coercion, one must possess certain means of resistance that are also guaranteed. Thus we see there is a necessary conjoining of the right to life and the right to liberty, since a person is not free if he is subject to coercion because he is deprived of the means of sustaining life.

We come, finally, to the "pursuit of happiness," the interpretation of which is the most obvious source of disagreement. According to the modern consensus, this phrase clearly means that every individual has the right to pursue his or her own particular desires and visions, which tend, of course, to be quite different for each person. In other words, in the current dialogue about equality, this particular issue tends to be defined as the individual's own pursuit of *private* happiness. (There are other plausible interpretations that stress *public* happiness, but this line of analysis has received little attention in modern times.[1]) The source of conflict here is manifest: it might very well happen that one individual can successfully pursue his own dream of happiness only if he may critically diminish the means available to others to sustain life or if he may in some measure coerce others. If pursuing happiness is taken to mean primarily achieving command over resources—and it is frequently given that primary meaning—then it involves an immediate clash of interests between the individual pursuers and those who must have a certain stock of resources if they are to preserve their own rights to life and liberty. The latter's right of access to resources limits somewhat the former's efforts to obtain resources in order to insure his own happiness.

It should not surprise us, then, that the clause "all men are created equal" can be interpreted in quite different ways. Today, I would like to suggest, there are two major lines of interpretation: one, which I will call the "Fair Play" perspective, stresses the individual's right to pursue happiness and obtain resources; the other, which I will call the "Fair Shares" viewpoint, emphasizes the right of access to resources as a necessary condition for equal rights to life, liberty, and happiness.

Almost from the beginning, and most apparently during the past century or so, the Fair Play viewpoint has been dominant in America. This way of looking at the problem of equality stresses that each person should be equally free from all but the most minimal necessary interference with his right to "pursue happiness." It is frequently stressed that all are equally free to *pursue*, but have no guarantee of *attaining*, happiness. The right to obtain and keep property is often subsumed under this larger right, although in writing the Declaration Jefferson consciously altered Locke's triad of life, liberty, and property. The main outward sign of this condition of equality is the absence of encumbrances on the individual—encumbrances deriving from status at birth, from family position, from skin color, sex, age, and the like. Given significant differences of interests, of talents, and of personalities, it is assumed that individuals will be variably successful in their pursuits and that society will consequently propel to its surface what Jefferson called a "natural aristocracy of talent," men who because of their skills, intellect, judgment, character, will assume the leading positions in society that had formerly been occupied by the hereditary aristocracy—that is, by men who had simply been born into positions of wealth and power. In contemporary discussions, the emphasis on the individual's unencumbered pursuit of his own goals is summed up in the phrase "equality of opportunity." Given at least an approximation of this particular version of equality, Jefferson's principle of a natural aristocracy—spoken of most commonly today as the idea of "meritocracy"—will insure that the ablest, most meritorious, ambitious, hardworking, and talented individuals will acquire the most, achieve the most, and become the leaders of society. The relative inequality that this implies is seen not only as tolerable, but as fair and just. Any effort to achieve what proponents of Fair Play refer to as "equality of results" is seen as unjust, artificial, and incompatible with the more basic principle of equal opportunity.

The Fair Shares perspective, as compared with the Fair Play idea, concerns itself much more with equality of rights and of access, particularly the implicit rights to a reasonable share of society's resources, sufficient to sustain life at a decent standard of humanity and to preserve liberty and freedom from compulsion. Rather than focusing on the individual's pursuit of his own happiness, the advocate of Fair Shares is more committed to the principle that all members of the society obtain a reasonable portion of the goods that society produces. From his vantage point, the overzealous pursuit of private goals on the part of some individuals might even have to be bridled. From this it follows, too, that the proponent of Fair Shares has a different view of what constitutes fairness and justice, namely, an appropriate distribution throughout society of sufficient means for sustaining life and preserving liberty.

So the equality dilemma is built in to everyday life and thought in America; it comes with the territory. Rights, equality of rights—or at least interpretations of them—clash. The conflict between Fair Play and Fair Shares is real, deep, and serious, and it cannot be easily resolved. Some calculus of priorities must be established. Rules must be agreed upon. It is possible to imagine an almost endless number of such rules:

- Fair Shares until everyone has enough; Fair Play for the surplus

- Fair Shares in winter; Fair Play in summer
- Fair Play until the end of a specified "round," then "divvy up"
Fair Shares, and start Fair Play all over again (like a series of Monopoly games)
- Fair Shares for white men; Fair Play for blacks and women
- Fair Play all the way, except that no one may actually be allowed to starve to death.

The last rule is, I would argue, a perhaps bitter parody of the prevailing one in the United States. Equality of opportunity and the principle of meritocracy are the clearly dominant interpretation of "all men are created equal," mitigated by the principle (usually defined as charity rather than equality) that the weak, the helpless, the deficient will be more or less guaranteed a sufficient share to meet their minimal requirements for sustaining life.

II FAIR PLAY AND UNEQUAL SHARES

The Fair Play concept is dominant in America partly because it puts forth two most compelling ideas: the time-honored principle of distributive justice and the cherished image of America as the land of opportunity. At least since Aristotle, the principle that rewards should accrue to each person in proportion of his worth or merit has seemed to many persons one that warrants intuitive acceptance. The more meritorious person—merit being some combination of ability and constructive effort—*deserves* a greater reward. From this perspective it is perfectly consistent to suppose that *unequal* shares could well be *fair* shares; moreover, within such a framework, it is very unlikely indeed that equal shares could be fair shares, since individuals are not equally meritorious.

The picture of America as the land of opportunity is also very appealing. The idea of a completely open society, where each person is entirely free to advance in his or her particular fashion, to become whatever he or she is inherently capable of becoming, with the sky the limit, is a universally inspiring one. This is a picture that makes most Americans proud.

But is it an accurate picture? Are these two connected ideas—unlimited opportunity and differential rewards fairly distributed according to differences in individual merit—congruent with the facts of life? The answer, of course, is yes and no. Yes, we see some vague congruence here and there—some evidence of upward mobility, some kinds of inequalities that can appear to be justifiable. But looking at the larger picture, we must answer with an unequivocal "No!" The fairness of unequal shares and the reality of equal opportunity are wishes and dreams, resting on a mushy, floating, purely imaginary foundation. Let us look first at the question of unequal shares.

Fair Players and Fair Sharers disagree about the meaning, but not about the fact, of unequal shares and of the significant degree of inequality of wealth and income and of everything that goes along with wealth and income—general life conditions, health, education, power, access to services and to cultural and recreational amenities, and so forth. Fair Sharers say that this fact is the very *essence* of inequality, while Fair Players define the inequalities of condition that Fair Sharers decry as obvious and necessary *consequences* of equality of opportunity. Fair Players argue, furthermore, that such inequalities are for the most part roughly proportional to inequalities of merit.

It is possible to cite facts that appear consistent with the Fair Play argument. One can look at the average income of persons who do different kinds of work, for example. In 1976 the median earnings for men in several occupational groups were as follows:

Self-employed physicians and dentists	$37,117
Managers in manufacturing industries	$20,496
Machine operators	$11,688
Health-service workers	$ 8,632 [2]

To most persons, it does not seem unreasonable, given differences in responsibility and requirements with respect to knowledge and skill, that a man with a management job in a factory should get about twice as much as a machine operator in the same factory. The gap between the physician and the service worker—say, a nurse's aide—is a good deal harder to swallow. When we assert that one group of persons is, on the average, four or five times more meritorious than another group, we are at the very outer margins of credibility. But, in this case, the apologist for unequal shares will ask us to consider that the physician spent ten or fifteen hard years in education and training before he even began his career, and therefore has to make up for years of lost income. We are inclined to nod sympathetically and shrug it off.

There are also some patterns of ownership that are reasonably consistent with the Fair Play paradigm. In the distribution of such items as automobiles, televisions, appliances, even homes, there are significant inequalities, but they are not extreme. And if the Fair Player is willing to concede that many inequities remain to be rectified—and most Fair Players are quite willing, even eager, to do so—these inequalities can, perhaps, be swallowed.

It is only when we begin to look at larger aspects of wealth and income—aspects that lie beyond our personal vision—that the extreme and, I believe, gross inequalities of condition that prevail in America become evident. Let us begin with income. How do we divide up the shares of what we produce annually? In 1977 about one American family in ten had an income of less than $5,000 and about one in ten had an income of $35,000 a year and up ("up" going all the way to some unknown number of millions).[3] It is difficult to see how anyone could view such a dramatic disparity as fair and justified. One struggles to imagine any measure of merit, any sign of membership in a "natural aristocracy," that would manifest itself in nature in such a way that one sizeable group of persons would "have" eight or ten or twenty times more of it—whatever "it" might be—than another sizeable group has.

Income in the United States is concentrated in the hands of a few: one-fifth of the population gets close to half of all the income, and the top 5 percent of this segment get almost one-fifth of it. The bottom three-fifths of the population—that is, the majority of us—receive not much more than one-third of all income. Giving a speech at a banquet, a friend of mine, James Breeden, described the distribution of income in terms of the dinners being served. It was a striking image, which I will try to reproduce here.

Imagine one hundred people at the banquet, seated at six tables. At the far right is a table set with English china and real silver, where five people sit comfortably. Next to them is another table, nicely set but nowhere near as fancy, where fifteen people sit. At each of the four remaining tables twenty people sit—the one on the far left has a stained paper tablecloth and plastic knives and forks. This arrangement is analogous to the spread of income groups—from the richest 5 percent at the right to the poorest 20 percent at the left.

Twenty waiters and waitresses come in, carrying 100 delicious-looking dinners, just enough, one would suppose, for each of the one hundred guests. But, amazingly, four of the waiters bring 20 dinners to the five people at the fancy table on the right. There's hardly room for all the food. (If you go over and look a little closer, you will notice that two of the waiters are obsequiously fussing and trying to arrange 10 dinners in front of just one of those five.) At the next-fanciest table, with the fifteen people, five waiters bring another 25 dinners. The twenty people at the third table get 25 dinners, 15 go to the fourth table, and 10 to the fifth. To the twenty people at the last table (the one with the paper tablecloth) a rude and clumsy waiter brings only 5 dinners. At the top table there are 4 dinners for each person; at the bottom table, four persons for each dinner. That's approximately the way income is distributed in America—fewer than half the people get even one dinner apiece.

As we move from analogy to the reality of living standards, the pertinent questions are: How much do people spend and on what? How do the groups at the different tables, that is, different income groups in America, live? Each year the Bureau of Labor Statistics publishes detailed information on the costs of maintaining three different living standards, which it labels "lower," "intermediate," and "higher"; in less discreet days it used to call the budgets "minimum," "adequate," and "comfortable."[4] The adequate, intermediate budget is generally considered to be an index of a reasonably decent standard of living. It is on this budget, for example, that newspapers focus when they write their annual stories on the BLS budgets.

To give some sense of what is considered an "intermediate" standard of living, let me provide some detail about this budget as it is calculated for a family of four—mother, father, eight-year-old boy, and thirteen-year-old girl. As of the autumn of 1978, for such a family the budget allows $335 a month for housing, which includes rent or mortgage, heat and utilities, household furnishings, and all household operations. It allows $79 a week for groceries, which extends to cleaning supplies, toothpaste, and the like. It allows $123 a month for transportation, including car payments. It allows $130 a month for clothing, clothing care or cleaning, and all personal-care items.

In his book *The Working Class Majority*, Andrew Levison cites further details about this budget from a study made by the UAW:

> A United Auto Workers study shows just how "modest" that budget is: The budget assumes, for example, that a family will own a toaster that will last for thirty-three years, a refrigerator and a range that will each last for seventeen years, a vacuum cleaner that will last for fourteen years, and a television set that will last for ten years. The budget assumes that a family will buy a two-year-old car and keep it for four years, and will pay for a tune-up once a year, a brake realignment every three years, and front-end alignment every four years. . . . The budget assumes that the husband will buy one year-round suit every four years . . . and one topcoat every eight and a half years. . . . It assumes that the husband will take his wife to the movies once every three months and that one of them will go to the movies alone once a year. The average family's two children are each allowed one movie every four weeks. A total of two dollars and fifty-four cents per person per year is allowed for admission to all other events, from football and baseball games to plays or concerts. . . . The budget allows nothing whatever for savings.[5]

This budget, whether labeled intermediate, modest, or adequate, is perhaps more accurately described by those who call it "shabby but respectable." It is equivalent to, at most, one dinner at James Breeden's strange "banquet."

In 1978 the income needed by an urban family of four in order to meet even this modest standard of living was $18,622.[6] This is a national average; for some cities the figure was much higher: in Boston, it was $22,117, in metropolitan New York, $21,587, in San Francisco, $19,427. More than *half* of all Americans lived *below* this standard. As for the "minimum" budget (which, by contrast with the "intermediate" budget, allows only $62 rather than $79 for groceries, $174 rather than $335 for housing, $67 rather than

$123 for transportation, and $93 rather than $130 for clothing and personal care), the national average cost for an urban family in 1978 was $11,546. Three families out of ten could not afford even *that* standard, and one family in ten had an income below $5,000, which is *less than half enough* to meet minimum standards.

These dramatically *unequal* shares are—it seems to me—clearly *unfair* shares. Twenty million people are desperately poor, an additional forty million don't get enough income to meet the minimal requirements for a decent life, the great majority are just scraping by, a small minority are at least temporarily comfortable, and a tiny handful of persons live at levels of affluence and luxury that most persons cannot even imagine.

The myth that America's income is symmetrically distributed—an outstanding few at the top getting a lot, an inadequate few at the bottom living in poverty, and the rest clustered around the middle—could hardly be more false. The grotesquely lopsided distribution of our yearly production of goods and services is well illustrated by Paul Samuelson's famous image:

> A glance at the income distribution in the United States shows how pointed is the income pyramid and how broad its base. "There's always room at the top" is certainly true; this is so because it is hard to get there, not easy. If we make an income pyramid out of a child's blocks, with each layer portraying $1000 of income, the peak would be far higher than the Eiffel Tower, but almost all of us would be within a yard of the ground.[7]

When we move from income to wealth—from what you *get* to what you *own*—the degree of concentration makes the income distribution look almost fair by comparison. About one out of every four Americans owns *nothing*. Nothing! In fact, many of them *owe* more than they have. Their "wealth" is actually negative. The persons in the next quarter own about 5 percent of all personal assets. In other words, half of us own 5 percent, the other half own 95 percent. But it gets worse as you go up the scale. Those in the top 6 percent own half of all the wealth. Those in the top 1 percent own one-fourth of all the wealth. Those in the top ½ percent own one-fifth of all the wealth.[8] That's one-half of 1 percent—about one million persons, or roughly 300,000 families.

And even this fantastic picture doesn't tell the whole story, because "assets" include homes, cars, savings accounts, cash value of life insurance policies—the kinds of assets that the very rich don't bother with very much. The very rich put their wealth into the ownership of things that produce more wealth—corporate stocks and bonds, mortgages, notes, and the like. Two-thirds of their wealth is in this form and the top 1 percent owns 60 percent of all that valuable paper.[9] The rest of it is owned by only an additional 10 percent, which means that nine people out of ten own none of it—

and, if they're like me, they probably have never seen a real stock certificate in their lives

America, we are sometimes told, is a nation of capitalists, and it is true that an appreciable minority of its citizens have a bank account here, a piece of land there, along with a few shares of stock. But quantitative differences become indisputably qualitative as one moves from the ownership of ten shares of General Motors to the ownership of ten thousand. There are capitalists, and then there are capitalists.

There is an old Jewish joke about a young man who, on becoming successful and quite well-to-do, bought himself a huge motorboat, a compass and sextant, and a complete yachting uniform, and rushed to take his aging parents for a cruise. Preening in front of them and seeking their admiration, he pointed to the gold letters on his bright new white cap. "Look, Ma, I'm a captain!" To which the wise old woman replied, "By you, you're a keptin; by Papa, you're a keptin; by me, you're a keptin; but, Sonny Boy, by a keptin, you're no keptin."

By a capitalist, a plumber with twenty-five shares of IBM is no capitalist.

Another way of grasping the extreme concentration of wealth in our society is to try to imagine what the ordinary person would have if that wealth were evenly distributed rather than clumped and clotted together in huge piles. Assuming that all the personal wealth was divided equally among all the people in the nation, we would find that every one of us, man, woman, and child, would *own* free and clear almost $22,000 worth of goods: $7,500 worth of real estate, $3,500 in cash, and about $5,000 worth of stocks and bonds. For a family of four that would add up to almost $90,000 in assets, including $30,000 equity in a house, about $14,000 in the bank, and about $20,000 worth of stocks and bonds. That much wealth would also bring in an extra $3,000 or $4,000 a year in income.[10]

If you have any doubts about the reality of grossly unequal shares, compare the utopian situation of that imaginary "average" family with your own actual situation. For most of us, the former goes beyond our most optimistic fantasies of competing and achieving and getting ahead. Actually only about ten million persons in the country own as much as that, and, as I suggested before, the majority of us have an *average* of less than $5,000 per family, including whatever equity we have in a home, our car and other tangible assets, and perhaps $500 in the bank.

Still another way of thinking about this is to remark that the fortunate few at the top, and their children, are more or less guaranteed an opulent standard of living because of what they own, while the majority of American families are no more than four months' pay away from complete destitution.

All of this, of course, takes place in the wealthiest society the world has ever known. If we extended our horizons further and began to compare the handful of developed, industrial nations with the scores of underdeveloped, not to say "overexploited," nations, we would find inequalities that are even more glaring and appalling.

III THE VULNERABLE MAJORITY

But perhaps I am making too much of a fuss about huge differences in wealth and income, going on too much and being too literal about presumed correspondence between merit and reward. A less inflexible definition could perhaps accommodate the notion of one person's being ten or twenty or fifty times more meritorious than another. Some concepts are perfectly robust even if they are somewhat difficult to measure precisely. Who can say with confidence whether Elizabeth Taylor is eleven times prettier than your cousin Hannah or only four times prettier? How many times greater a novelist is Herman Melville than Harold Robbins? Seven times better? Sixty times better?

Stripped down to its essentials, the rule of equal opportunity and Fair Play requires only that the best man win. It doesn't necessarily specify the margin of victory, merely the absence of unfair barriers. The practical test of equal opportunity is *social mobility*—do talented and hardworking persons, whatever their backgrounds, actually succeed in rising to higher social and economic positions?

The answer to that, of course, is that they do. Remaining barriers of discrimination notwithstanding, it is plain that many persons climb up the social and economic ladder and reach much higher rungs than those their parents attained and than those from which they started. Fair Players prize these fortunate levitations as the ultimate justification of their own perspective and as phenomena that must be protected against any erosion caused by excessive emphasis upon Fair Shares.

It is necessary, then, to look seriously at the question of mobility. Among the questions to be asked are the following:

• How much mobility can we observe? No matter how rigidly hierarchical it might be, every society permits some mobility. How much movement up and down the scale is there in ours?

• How far do the mobile persons move?

• Is mobility evident across the whole social and economic range? Do the very poor stay poor, or do they, too, have an equal chance to rise? Are the very rich likely to slide *down* the ladder very often?

Given our great trove of rags-to-riches mythology, our creed that any child (well, any man-child) can grow up to be president—if not of General Motors, at least of the United States—we clearly assume that our society is an extraordinarily open one. And everyone knows, or has a friend who knows, a millionaire or someone on the way to that envied position. the patient, plodding peddler who transformed his enterprise into a great department store; the eccentric tinkerer in his garage whose sudden insight produced the great invention that everyone had been saving his pennies to buy.

At lesser levels of grandeur, we all know about the son of the illiterate cobbler who is now a wealthy neurosurgeon, the daughter of impoverished immigrants who sits in a professorial chair at Vassar or Smith—or even Princeton. In America social mobility is an unquestioned fact.

But how many sons of illiterate cobblers become physicians, on the one hand, and how many become, at best, literate cobblers? And how many settle for a job on the assembly line or in the sanitation department? And all of those daughters of impoverished immigrants—how many went on to get Ph.D.'s and become professors? Very few. A somewhat larger number may have gone to college and gotten a job teaching sixth grade. But many just finished high school and went to work for an insurance company for a while, until they married the sons of other impoverished immigrants, most of them also tugging at their bootstraps without much result.

About all of these facts there can be little dispute. For most people, there is essentially no social mobility —for them, life consists of rags to rags and riches to riches. Moreover, for the relatively small minority who do rise significantly in the social hierarchy, the *distance* of ascent is relatively short. Such a person may start life operating a drill press and eventually become a foreman or even move into the white-collar world by becoming a payroll clerk or perhaps an accountant. Or he may learn from his father to be a cobbler, save his money, and open a little cobbler shop of his own. He hardly ever starts up a shoe factory. It is the son of the owner of the shoe factory who gets to do that. So there is mobility—it is rather common, but also rather modest, with only an occasional dramatic rise from rags to riches.[11]

To provide some specific numbers, it has been calculated that for a young man born into a family in which the father does unskilled, low-wage manual work, the odds against his rising merely to the point of his becoming a nonmanual white-collar worker are at least three or four to one; the odds against his rising to the highest level and joining the wealthy upper class are almost incalculable. For the son of a middle-level white-collar worker, the odds against his rising to a higher-level professional or managerial occupation are two or three to one. On the other hand, the odds are better than fifty to one that the son of a father with such a high-level occupation will not descend the ladder to a position as an unskilled or semiskilled manual worker. Upward mobility is very limited and usually involves moving only one or two levels up the hierarchy.

In recent decades, there has been an illusion of greater upward mobility because of the changes in the *kinds* of jobs available; unskilled manual work is becoming rarer, white-collar work commoner. As a nation, too, we have been increasing in overall affluence, and our general standard of living has been rising from generation to generation.

Our patterns of consumption have changed, and so have our life-styles. The refrigerators, the washing machines, and the automobiles that once were reserved for the well-to-do are now found in almost every home. Once only the quality folk could afford a horse and buggy; now five out of six families in town have some kind of car. Once only the elite graduated from high school, and there really were some illiterate cobblers and many illiterate ditchdiggers. Now over 80 percent of our young people graduate from high school, and almost half of them go on to some further education.[12] Are these facts a telling argument in favor of equality as Fair Play? I think not, for two reasons.

First, when what used to be luxuries become common possessions, they are, in fact, essential. It is difficult to do without them.

Second, although everyone's standard of living has risen, the inequality of shares of the overall resources has not changed greatly. The very rich still own most of what is useful to own, and still get an enormous chunk of the annual national product. To return to the Breeden banquet analogy, the dinners being served now may be prime ribs and Yorkshire pudding instead of corned beef and cabbage, but the waiters still bring most of the plates to the tables on the right, very few to the one with the paper tablecloth.

Finally, we have to look carefully to see that, for all our social mobility, the very rich almost all stay at the top and welcome only a select handful to their ranks. The rich of one generation are almost all children of the rich of the previous generation, partly because more than half of significant wealth is inherited,[13] partly because all the other prerogatives of the wealthy are sufficient to assure a comfortable future for Rockefeller and Du Pont toddlers. It may well take more energy, ingenuity, persistence, and single-mindedness for a rich youngster to achieve poverty than for a poor one to gain wealth.

The dark side of the social-mobility machine is that it is, so to speak, a reciprocating engine—when some parts go up, others must come down. Downward mobility is an experience set aside almost exclusively for the nonrich, and it is grossly destructive of the quality of life.

The majority of American families are constantly vulnerable to economic disaster—to downward mobility to the point where they lack sufficient income to meet their most basic needs—food, shelter, clothing, heat, and medical care. Included in this vulnerable majority, who have at least an even chance of spending some portion of their lives in economic distress, are perhaps three out of four Americans.

This does not accord with the common view of poverty. We have been given to understand that "the poor" form a fairly permanent group in our society and that those who are above the poverty line are safe and perhaps even on their way up. This thought is comforting but false. A number of small studies have raised serious questions about this static picture; recently we have received massive evidence from one of the most comprehensive social and economic investigations ever mounted. This study, under the direction of James Morgan, has traced the life trajectories of five thousand American families over a period, to date, of eight years, concentrating on the nature of and possible explanations for economic progress or the lack of it.[14]

Five Thousand American Families indicates that over a period of eight years, although only one in ten families is poor during *every one* of the eight years, over one-third of American families are poor for *at least one* of those eight years.

From the Michigan study, the census data, and other sources, we can readily estimate that a few are permanently protected against poverty because they *own things*—property, stocks, bonds—that provide them with income sufficient to meet their needs whether or not they work or have any other source of income. Another small minority of Americans own only *rights*—virtual job tenure, a guaranteed pension—but these rights also give effective protection against poverty. At the bottom of the pyramid, there are a few who might be called permanently poor. Between these extremes come persons whose income is primarily or wholly dependent on salaries or wages. This is the core of the vulnerable majority—not poor now, but in jeopardy. In any given year one family out of six in that vulnerable majority will suffer income deficit, will go through a year of poverty. Over a five-year period nearly half of them will be poor for at least one year. If we project this over ten or fifteen years, we find that well over half will be poor for at least one year. On adding this group to the permanently poor, we arrive at the startling fact that a *substantial majority* of American families will experience poverty at some point during a relatively short span of time.

Several elements in our socioeconomic structure help account for income deficiency. Let us consider, for example, those who are more or less permanently poor. Why do they stay mired in poverty? The answer in most cases is simple: they remain poor because it has been deliberately *decided* that they should remain poor. They are, for the most part, dependent on what we impersonally call transfer payments—mostly Social Security, some private pensions, some welfare. To put it as simply as possible, these transfer payments are not enough to live on, not enough to meet basic needs. Countrywide, public assistance payments provide income that is only 75 percent of what is required to pay for sufficient food, adequate shelter, clothing, and fuel; the percentage decreases as the size of the family increases. For very large families, welfare provides only half of what is needed to live on.[15] The poverty of the permanently poor is thus easily explained by the fact that the income assistance that we provide them is simply too small.

For the vulnerables, however, economic hills and valleys are created by the job situation. Economic status, progress, and deficit are determined by what social scientists call "family composition and participation in the labor force." In plain English that means they depend on the number of mouths to be fed and on the number of people working—that is, on how many children there are, on whether both wife and husband are working, and so forth. But this, of course, is only synonymous with the natural ebb and flow in the life of almost any family. It should not be an economic catastrophe, after all, when people get married and have children—and, incidentally, families have just about as many children as they plan to have, because family planning has become quite effective at all economic levels and among all racial, ethnic, and religious groups. So, children are born and they grow up, sometimes work awhile, and then leave home. One parent, usually the mother, is tied to the home during some periods, free to work during others. A family member finds a job, loses a job, gets sick or injured, sometimes dies tragically young. All of these events are the landmarks in the life of a family, most of them are common enough, and some are inevitable sources of joy or sorrow. Yet these ordinary occurrences have a drastic impact on families, because they lead to great changes in one or both sides of the ratio of income and needs. In most cases they are direct causes of most of the economic progress or distress that a family experiences.

The haunting paradox here is that the welfare of individual families fluctuates drastically as a result of events whose incidence in the overall population hardly fluctuates at all. The *rates* of birth, marriage, divorce, disabling illness, industrial injuries, highway accidents, and even death itself are all highly predictable. For a given number of families, we can thus predict how many of these events will occur. And we know what their effects will be, for good or ill. But for individual families, they are either perfectly natural events or ones that cannot be controlled.

IV   FIVE FAMILIES

So far I have advanced in general terms the principle that the economic status of the great majority of us is, even in the best of times, precarious—that we are vulnerable to many external forces over which we have little or no control and which push us now up the economic ladder, now down. Let me now try to illustrate this general argument with vignettes from the lives of five different families.

The first family belongs to a type that is becoming more and more common these days. Frank was a man of forty-five who had established himself as an independent consultant to small businesses interested in computerizing their accounting procedures. Elaine, his wife and his junior by ten years, having worked for several years in an office, worked about half time in Frank's firm. It was the second marriage for both of them—and a very happy one. Elaine had two children from her first marriage, a girl aged eleven and a boy aged nine. Frank had two sons from his first marriage; one was twenty-four and a graduate student on the West Coast; the other was seventeen and a junior in high school. Shortly after their marriage they bought a house that Elaine had fallen in love with, even though it cost more than they could really afford. The business was producing an income of almost $30,000 a year for them, but the house cost $110,000. It took all of their savings as well as a loan against Frank's insurance policy to put together the down payment, and the monthly installment for mortgage and taxes was over $1,000. Frank reasoned that the house itself was a good investment, which was bound to appreciate in value, and that their income would increase quickly, since his business was going so well. He was right. Two years later their income had risen to $42,000. They began to talk, half jokingly, half seriously, about whether they should buy a swimming pool or take a trip to Europe. They had joined a country club, and Frank often went golfing there with his customers. One day Elaine got a call from the golf pro telling her that Frank had had a heart attack on the golf course. By the time she got to the hospital, he was dead.

A few weeks later Elaine and her lawyer sat down to consider her financial situation. She had almost $5,000 in savings, $35,000 from Frank's insurance, and an expensive house with an $80,000 mortgage. Elaine thought Frank's business might be worth quite a bit, but the assets of the business, as the lawyer explained, were really intangible—they were in Frank's head and died with him. When she added up everything, Elaine found she had about $70,000, which the lawyer invested for her and from which she began to receive a bit over $500 a month in interest and dividends. As a widow with three children she was entitled to survivors' benefits from Social Security until the children reached the age of eighteen (or twenty-one if they were in school, as Frank's younger son was); this brought her income up to a little more than $1,000 a month. After mourning for more than a year she got a good job with another data-processing company, and life resumed. The economic level of the family had fallen to less than half of what it had been, but compared with most families they were still quite well off.

The second family lived in a manner considerably less grand. Mike and Judy, both thirty-one, and their two children, aged seven and five, lived in a two-family house that they owned. Mike had worked for the same company for twelve years, a firm that manufactured electronic equipment for missiles;

as he had accumulated seniority, he had gradually worked up to a skilled job that paid good wages—almost nine dollars an hour—and overtime work was frequently available and he usually took advantage of it. Judy was an excellent mother and housewife, thrifty and efficient, and the couple had managed to save several thousand dollars. They had a wide circle of friends, drawn mostly from among neighbors, relatives, and Mike's buddies at work. They had had some rough periods—once Mike had been laid off for three months when the company had failed to win an important contract; another time he had been out of work for a while because of illness—but they had weathered the crises, and they now felt fairly secure. They had what most people would consider a reasonably happy middle-class life. But the marriage suddenly went to pieces—there was another woman—and Mike first left home and then the state. After Mike moved to another state, his child support payments became more and more irregular, and Judy soon found herself in a financial hole. She had to sell the house and to live off the proceeds of the sale, while she looked desperately for a job that was flexible enough to give her time to take care of her two little children. She couldn't find one; nor could she find a day-care institution for the children that she could afford. Before long she confronted the fact that she had no choice but to apply for welfare. She was eligible for Aid to Families with Dependent Children—although it meant going through an awful lot of paperwork because of Mike's defaulted payments—and she began to receive a check for $133.75, twice a month. She took advantage of food stamps; she was also eligible for subsidized housing, but the waiting lists for all the available apartments were years long, and she had to settle for a small, three-room apartment that cost her $140 in rent and endless hours of battling mice and cockroaches. It was lucky, of course, that she didn't live in a state like Georgia or South Carolina or Mississippi, where the check she received twice a month would have been less than $40, but unfortunate that she wasn't in a state like Connecticut or Massachusetts or New York, where it might have been $175 or more.

Judy cried a great deal at night when she thought about the food she had to feed her children and the clothes they had to wear. The children talked a great deal, longingly, of their old house and their old way of life, but she tried not to think about these things. Like most welfare mothers, she resolved that somehow, and as soon as possible, she would get off welfare.

The story of the third family is a happy one all the way—a story of newlyweds, high school sweethearts who had married the summer after their graduation. Charlie and Carol were very happy with each other, and their life together went smoothly. Charlie's uncle was a foreman in a local factory and got Charlie a job as a beginning machine operator. Carol had learned shorthand, typing, and bookkeeping in high school, and she, too, went to work full time. They felt absolutely wealthy. Not yet twenty-one, they were already earning over $17,000 a year between them, and they really enjoyed it. They were careful enough to save $300 a month, right off the tops of their checks; the rest they spent as it came in, Charlie said he wanted Carol to have nothing but the best. Everything went right for them. Carol was a good stenographer, and the vice-president of her company asked her to be his private secretary, which meant a good raise. Charlie, too, got regular raises, and when, after a period of turmoil during which union organizers came in (for a long time Charlie and his uncle didn't speak to each other because of their disagreements about the union) and the men in the plant voted for unionization, the new contract brought Charlie an immediate raise of eighty-five cents an hour.

A fourth example, Mrs. Hancock, looked forward to her sixty-second birthday as few women her age do. She was exhausted, and she wanted to retire. She could think of herself as no more than the remnant of a family. She had been a widow for some time, and her children and grandchildren all lived more than a thousand miles away. Life had been hard for her during the fifteen years since the children had grown up and left. She had been able to work most of the time, but for longer than a year she had had to struggle with cancer. She had won, thank God—it had been seven years since they had said she was cured, and it looked as though they had been right. It had cost her every dollar she had, once her medical insurance had been used up, but it was worth it. Still, she was tired, rarely felt really well, and didn't think she could work any more, although she wasn't sure how she would manage to live on Social Security. So she began the life of a "senior citizen," trying to live from the third day of one month to the third of the next on $312. She became well acquainted with television and kept track of when movies were shown, and she got used to watching movies on the little screen instead of in a theater. When she was sixty-six, she had the stroke and was forced to leave her home and go into a nursing home. The woman in the office got the Social Security check, out of which Mrs. Hancock was allowed $35 a month for personal needs. Medicaid paid the difference between the amount of the check and the full cost of the nursing home. Her children managed to visit more frequently, and she usually saw at least one of them, often accompanied by the grandchildren, every five or six months. She had her television at the nursing home, but since the stroke she had a great deal of trouble following the plots of movies, and she tended to watch game shows on which attractive young people won large amounts of money.

Like Mrs. Hancock, Tom and Alice suffered serious economic setbacks as a result of illness. Tom was only in his mid-twenties when he developed a serious illness. For several days Alice thought she read the omens of tragedy in the faces of the doctors. It happened only seven months after the happiest day in their lives, the day little Deborah was born. Unlike Mrs. Hancock, they had very little in the way of resources, no more than a few thousand dollars in the bank. When Tom's medical bills started coming in—his insurance coverage was fair, but did not begin to cover all the costs—the savings account melted away within weeks. Not only were the bills piling up, but because Tom wasn't working there was no income. Alice got a little work now and then from a company that furnished temporary office help, but she couldn't leave little Deborah for Tom to take care of, even after he had come home, and no one else was able to take over the household for her. They borrowed as much as they dared from both sets of parents and from Tom's brother, but ultimately Tom had to sell his car, and Alice some of the fine jewelry Tom had bought her when they were first married. Luckily, Tom's company gave him his job back, and he began to earn what under ordinary circumstances would have been very good wages. But paying the doctors and hospitals, the overdue rent and utility bills, and paying back the money they had borrowed took almost three years, and they were able to do it in that span of time only because they made up their minds to live at the very edge of subsistence. Mrs. Hancock's illness cost her her bank account; Tom's cost him and Alice several years of poverty.

These five stories illustrate the dynamics of economic progress and decline as they exist for the overwhelming majority of persons. Frank and Elaine came closest to making the American dream come true. They nearly got rich. But they weren't genuinely rich, because they didn't really *own* anything that produced riches. Frank's business was just Frank working for himself. It entailed no investment of capital, no machinery, no workers. He and his wife owned a very expensive house but no stocks, bonds, mortgages, or trust funds. When he died, the illusion of getting rich died with him.

Even getting as close as they did to leaping into the ranks of the wealthy depended on fortuitous events in their lives. Frank, having majored in mathematics, seized the chance to enter a rapidly expanding sector of the economy, for which he could take no credit and which carried him with it. Very few of his fraternity brothers, though apparently just as smart and sociable and energetic as Frank, were as successful as he; that was particularly true of the two who had majored in English and history and even of the three who had gone on to become lawyers. His situation was also helped immensely by Elaine's working in the business, for it made them essentially a two-income family, which has by far the best chance of being economically comfortable.

The same was true of Charlie and Carol. They were able to live well because they were both working. Charlie was also fortunate in that he had an uncle who was able to use his influence in getting him a decent job. And, of course, the dramatic improvement in their economic condition owed much to the unionization of the plant. Typically, union members earn about 20 percent more than nonunion members who do the same kind of work.

The story of Tom and Alice brings out the great negative economic impact of what is perhaps the greatest positive experience human beings can have—becoming parents. A new baby brings indescribable joy. Economically speaking, though, it means another mouth to feed, and its arrival usually makes it extremely difficult if not impossible for a working wife to continue in her job. Tom and Alice found their income suddenly reduced, and when Tom got sick and couldn't work, they became genuinely poor and stayed poor for years, as they tried to make a comeback.

Mike and Judy's divorcing is another common occurrence that is economically devastating, as is Frank's death. Judy's life on welfare, which lasted for over three years, was one of the most grinding and degrading poverty. Elaine was far more fortunate, not only because Frank left her relatively well off financially and because her children were old enough that she could work, but also because, as a widow with children, she was eligible for Social Security, while Judy, as a deserted wife with children (a situation functionally identical), was eligible only for Aid to Families with Dependent Children.

Like everyone who lives long enough, Mrs. Hancock finally had to retire, and thereafter, despite Social Security, she barely had enough to live on, although she was technically above the "poverty line."

These potentially devastating events—the birth of a child, illness, divorce, death, retirement—are all common, and some of them are universal. We know almost precisely how many million children will be born next year, how many serious illnesses will occur, how many marriages will break up, how many men in their forties will die, and how many people will retire. For the most part, however, we don't know whom the events will affect. So, what are, in the population as a whole, predictable occurrences are, in the life of a given family, unexpected misfortunes or strokes of luck that might or might not happen to any one of us and that, when they do occur, affect our economic welfare profoundly. And these events, along with ones that we can't predict or influence, account for almost all the variability in the economic fortunes of most of us. Our own individual characteristics, our plans, our efforts, and our attempts to follow the rules of the American dream have very little influence on whether we do well or poorly in life. Diligence or laziness, intelligence or stupidity, thriftiness or extravagance, ambition or inertia—these personal traits, often defined, in various combinations, as "merit," account for very little of what happens. In real life the myths of Fair Play and of the great race of life seldom make an appearance.

This, then, is the fundamental reality of social mobility: the great mass of people bobbing in a sea of economic insecurity, some sinking, some barely staying afloat, some swimming strongly for a little while, until they hit the next towering wave.

In the real world only small numbers of us ever leap across the barrier that separates the vulnerable majority from the relatively secure minority.

Yet these successful leapers—our economic Evel Knievels, so to speak— continue to fascinate and encourage us. We have been taught that they are fascinating and encouraging. But endless vain efforts to decipher the hidden secrets of the few who "make it" only obscure the devastating truth that most Americans spend their lives hauling themselves up and slipping down a rung or two of the very short ladder that has been set aside for the use of the vulnerable majority, like a jungle gym to amuse children in a playground.

V WHY NOT FAIR SHARES?

I have been trying to show, in a preliminary way, that the beliefs and assumptions associated with the Fair Play rendering of equality are quite inconsistent with the facts of life as we know them, although its principles are paraded as a version—in fact, the correct version—of equality and are widely accepted as quite plausible, indeed obvious. To the extent that there is any competition between Fair Players and Fair Sharers for the mind of the public, the former usually win hands down. Yet, as we have seen, the Fair Play idea appears to condone and often to endorse conditions of inequality that are blatant and, I would say, quite indefensible. Such equal opportunities for advancing in life as do exist are darkly overshadowed by the many head starts and advantages provided to the families of wealth and privilege. As for the workings out of the solemnly revered principles of meritocracy, they are—like many objects of reverence—invisible to most persons and rarely discernible in the lives of the vulnerable majority of us. Barely two centuries after its most persuasive formulation, the Fair Play concept of equality has shriveled to little more than the assertion that a few thousand individuals are fully licensed to gather and retain wealth at the cost of the wasteful, shameful, and fraudulent impoverishment of many millions. I will be arguing that equality as Fair Play is, in fact, a semantic fraud and that a more genuine and believable version of equality is more accurately described by the rule of Fair Shares, insisting on the equality of the rights of all to life and liberty and to the resources that are directly implied by those rights. Yet this definition of equality suffers from a bad name; often denounced vituperatively, it is, at best, patted on the head as a nice utopian idea that is simply not practical or realistic.

Why is this so? Why does the average American recoil from the idea of Fair Shares as from some kind of monstrous and unjust proposal that is repellent and un-American? The reasons are not simple, of course, and I will be spending many pages attempting to contribute something to the unraveling of them. But they begin, I think, with the fact that the idea of equality as

Fair Shares has had the misfortune of being defined to a large extent by its opponents, who have been remarkably successful in lampooning it as the recipe for a ridiculous, bizarre, and inhuman world. In current writing and rhetoric, the advocates of Fair Play like to set forth the artificial choice between "equality of opportunity and equality of results." They present this stark dichotomy as though the contrasted terms were mutually exclusive, as though it were an either/or proposition. Logically, of course, the terms are not at all contradictory; more important, defining the issue in this oversimplified fashion obscures and dismisses most of the relevant questions.

Let me illustrate. As we have seen, Fair Play advocates are partial to the metaphor of the footrace. A fair race, they say, and almost everyone would agree, is one in which all the runners begin together at the starting line, in which no handicaps or advantages are allowed, and in which the winners arrive at the finish line before the losers, thus factually demonstrating that they are the fastest runners and deserve the prizes they claim. This, it is said, epitomizes justice. Those who construct this image of "equal opportunity" then go on to criticize what they call "equality of results," using the same metaphor, as a strange and unnatural race so arranged that it somehow ends with all the runners crossing the finish line in a dead heat—an outcome that can be achieved only by giving the slower runners a head start or some other unfair advantage and burdening the faster runners with heavy weights or some other unfair handicap. Such a race, they say, would be manifestly unjust. And so it would be, and ridiculous, as well. One wonders who would propose such a contest and to what purpose. Advocates of Fair Shares equality certainly would not.

A number of obvious questions can be raised about the footrace metaphor that tend to uncover some of the underlying assumptions.

We can begin by asking, In what way is life like a footrace? To carry prominently in one's mind the idea that life is like a race with winners and losers is to perceive life most of the time only as a mammoth competition among millions of individuals, in which the best competitors—however one might define "best"—get the most spoils. This image has an obvious appeal to many, particularly those who find themselves in possession of the most resources. But how many people *feel* that they've been in a race? How many ordinary people have any significant sense of having spent their lives in a fair competition with other entrants in this great race, including such entrants as the president of the local bank, the fellow who owns the Cadillac dealership, and the boss who owns the firm where they work? How many feel, moreover, that they lost fair and square and should therefore be good sports about it? Moving to another kind of race as a basis for analogy, just as it is true that only a few special thoroughbreds ever even get entered in a horse race, only a few persons ever experience anything like that mythical footrace. Most of us, like most horses, spend our lives in ordinary, everyday

work. The stereotypes who fit the metaphor—the biology majors, for example, who cheat and spite each other in order to get a place in medical school,
the new M.B.A.'s who sprint off their marks into the maze of the executive
suite—these are familiar to most people only at second hand. The working
lives of most persons are nothing like a race. If one walked down the aisles
of a factory, the length of an assembly line, the sections of a department
store, the rows of desks in an insurance company, how in the world would
one go about distinguishing the fast winners from the slow losers? The answer is that this is not an issue. It is simply assumed that they are all losers.
In the legendary race of life, most of us are not even participants. We never
even get to the starting gate, let alone the finish line. As they say at the race
track, we are nonstarters. We were scratched at birth.

So, to most people, life doesn't look or feel like a race at all. But, for the
sake of the argument, let's grant the Fair Players their most precious analogy
and raise a few subordinate questions. For example, how do we define advantages and handicaps? If everyone gets a fair start, why do those with
black skin or female reproductive organs rarely arrive in the winner's circle?
What, moreover, are the relative advantages we would like to eliminate? Is
being born rich one of them? In order to insure a fair scramble for the
goodies of life, would the Fair Players advocate that everyone begin with no
resources, no wealth, or at least with equal resources? I, for one, have never
heard rhapsodies about the footrace analogy carried to that point, have you?

What is the equivalent, in real life, of being able to run fast? We easily
define who *can* run the fastest in a race by observing who *does* run the
fastest. It would seem logical, then, that in life we decide who *can* acquire
the most by observing who *does* acquire the most. If we carry out the analogy, we see that running fast is analogous to being acquisitive, which may
not be as flattering as being "best." It all boils down to this: just as the
winners of the race can claim to be the fastest, so the very rich can claim to
be the most acquisitive. Who would dispute their claim? Most of us assume
that simple truth; it really doesn't need the fancy masquerade costume provided by far-fetched comparisons to track-and-field events.

We now come to the heart of the matter: where did the prizes come from?
In the legendary race, they are waiting on a table at the finish line, provided
by someone outside the race—the committee, the sponsor, God—who
knows? In real life, the "prizes" are laboriously produced by the runners
themselves and by the great bulk of us who are nonstarters. Did we know we
were working so hard to make prizes for the winners to take home? If we
did, it was damned sporting of us. If we did not, where did the rule come
from? I don't know about you, but I never agreed to make prizes for rich
people to take home. Nobody even asked me.

This characterization of what the Fair Players persist in labeling "equal
opportunity" suggests pretty strongly that opportunity is nothing more than

the guarantee of a well-groomed playing field on which individuals can compete for wealth. Surely equal opportunity is not that barren an idea; it has a much richer store of connotations. We are also concerned, I think, with equal opportunities for obtaining knowledge, health, and culture, and for achieving self-development, social integration, and political participation. Does equal opportunity, to pose another crucial question, always dictate individual competition and unequal outcomes, winners and losers? Following this model, would we insist that we can be absolutely certain that we have equal opportunity to obtain knowledge when we can be satisfactorily assured that only a few are learned and most are ignorant? And if we seek to reduce ignorance, will we be accused of demanding "equality of results" and imperiling the cherished rule of "equal opportunity"? It's really an odd way of looking at life and our relationships with other human beings.

"Equal results" is a term that I, for one, would be hard put to define; it seems almost meaningless and is, as far as I can tell, just a straw man invented by antiegalitarian Fair Players. What I have read and heard gives me the impression that most of those who are concerned about achieving greater equality think more generally about what we might call equal rights of *access*, both to the material necessities of life and to the nonmaterial—spiritual, if you will—elements of human existence. It is true that there is a significant distinction to be made—between an actual equal *right* of access to the goods and amenities mentioned above and an equal "opportunity" to *obtain* access. A Fair Shares egalitarian would hold that all persons have a *right* to a reasonable share of material necessities, a right to do constructive work, and a right of unhindered access to education, to gratifying social memberships, to participation in the life and decisions of the community, and to all the major amenities of society. This principle doesn't lend itself to the calculation of "equal results," and it certainly doesn't imply a demand for uniformity of resources. No one in his right mind would entertain some cockeyed scheme in which everyone went to school for precisely thirteen years; consumed each year 19,800 grams of protein and 820,000 calories; read four works of fiction and six of nonfiction; attended two concerts, one opera, and four basketball games, and voted in 54 percent of the elections.

The caricature of "equal results" conceals trepidation about the possibility that some will be discontented with the present distribution of resources and will desire a redistribution. (It is interesting to note, in passing, that this uneasiness is dependent on the *direction* of redistribution: when it moves goods from ordinary people to the wealthy it is praised as a healthy outcome of "equal opportunity.") Unfortunately, many persons who are upset about the present state of inequality tend to talk vaguely about the need "to redistribute income" or even "to redistribute wealth." When such ideas are tossed out without consideration of the fact that they will then be discussed within the framework of Fair Play, we have a surefire prescription for disaster.

From that viewpoint, which is, after all, the dominant one in America, such ideas appear both extremely impracticable and not particularly desirable. For example, are we to take redistribution of income to mean that every individual will somehow receive the same compensation, no matter what work he or she does or whether he works at all? And would we try to redistribute wealth by giving every person, say, a share of stock in GM, Exxon, IBM, and the local paper-bag factory? Hardly. Fair Players can make mincemeat of such silly ideas, and they love to pretend that that's what Fair Share egalitarians are proposing. I don't think many of us have strong objections to inequality of monetary income as such. A modest range, even as much as three or four to one, would, I suspect, be tolerable to almost everybody. (And one would suppose that, given some time for adjustment and perhaps some counseling and training in homemaking and budgeting skills, those who now get a lot more could learn to scrape by on something like eight or nine hundred dollars a week.) The current range in annual incomes—from perhaps $3,000 to some unknown number of *millions*—is, however, excessive and intolerable, impossible to justify rationally, and plain inhuman. The problem of wealth is more fundamental. Most of the evils of inequality derive from the reality that a few thousand families control almost all the necessities and amenities of life, indeed the very conditions of life. The rest of us, some 200 million, have to pay tribute to them if we want even a slight illusion of life, liberty, and the pursuit of happiness. But the solution to this problem is certainly not simply the fragmentation of ownership into tiny units of individual property. This naive solution has been well criticized by serious proponents of equality, perhaps most gracefully by R. H. Tawney:

> It is not the division of the nation's income into eleven million fragments, to be distributed, without further ado, like cake as a school treat, among its eleven million families. It is on the contrary, the pooling of its surplus resources by means of taxation, and use of the funds thus obtained to make accessible to all, irrespective of their income, occupation, or social position, the conditions of civilization which, in the absence of such measures, can only be enjoyed by the rich. . . .
>
> It can generalize, by collective action, advantages associated in the past with ownership of property. . . . It can secure that, in addition to the payments made to them for their labour, its citizens enjoy a social income, which is provided from the surplus remaining after the necessary cost of production and expansion have been met, and is available on equal terms for all its members. . . .
>
> The contribution to culture of the reading-room of the British Museum is not to be calculated by dividing the annual cost of maintaining it by the number of ticket-holders. If each of the hundred thousand men who landed in France in 1914 had been presented with the one-hundred-thousandth part of the cost of the first expeditionary force, and instructed to spend it, in the manner he

thought best, in making the world safe for democracy, it is possible that the arrangement might have been welcomed by keepers of *estaminets*, but it is improbable that the German advance would have stopped at the Marne. . . .

Such a policy is open to more than one criticism, but it is obvious that its effects are not to be ascertained by the most assiduous working of sums in long division.[16]

The central problem of inequality in America—the concentration of wealth and power in the hands of a tiny minority—cannot, then, be solved, as Tawney makes clear, by any schemes that rest on the process of long division. We need, rather, to accustom ourselves to a different method of holding resources, namely, holding them in common, to be *shared* amongst us all—not divided up and parceled out, but shared. That is the basic principle of Fair Shares, and it is not at all foreign to our daily experience. To cite a banal example, we share the air we breathe, although some breathe in penthouses or sparsely settled suburbs and others in crowded slums. In a similar fashion, we share such resources as public parks and beaches, although, again, we cannot overlook the gross contrast between the size of vast private waterfront holdings and the tiny outlets to the oceans that are available to the public. No one in command of his senses would go to a public beach, count the number of people there, and suggest subdividing the beach into thirty-two-by-twenty-six-foot lots, one for each person. Such division would not only be unnecessary, it would ruin our enjoyment. If I were assigned to Lot No. 123, instead of enjoying the sun and going for a swim, I might sit and watch that sneaky little kid with the tin shovel to make sure he did not extend his sand castle onto my beach. So, we don't divide up the beach; we own it in common; it's *public*; and we just plain *share* it.

We use this mode of owning and sharing all the time and never give it a second thought. We share public schools, streets, libraries, sewers, and other public property and services, and we even think of them as being "free" (many libraries even have the word in their names). Nor do we need the "There's no such thing as a free lunch" folks reminding us that they're not really free; everyone is quite aware that taxes support them. We don't feel any need to divide up all the books in the library among all the citizens. And there's no sensible way of looking at the use of libraries in terms of "equal opportunity" as opposed to "equal results." Looking at the public library as a tiny example of what Fair Shares equality is all about, we note that it satisfies the principle of equal access if no one is *excluded* from the library on the irrelevant grounds of not owning enough or of having spent twelve years in school learning how not to read. And "equal results" is clearly quite meaningless. Some will withdraw many books; some, only a few; some will be so unwise as to never even use the facility.

The *idea* of sharing, then, which is the basic idea of equality, and the *practice* of sharing, which is the basic methodology of Fair Shares equality, are obviously quite familiar and acceptable to the American people in many areas of life. There are many institutions, activities, and services that the great majority believe should be located in the public sector, collectively owned and paid for, and equally accessible to everyone. We run into trouble when we start proposing the same system of ownership for the resources that the wealthy have corralled for themselves. It is then that the servants of the wealthy, the propagandists of Fair Play, get out their megaphones and yell at everybody that it's time to line up for the hundred-yard dash.

One can think of many similes and metaphors for life other than the footrace. Life is like a collection of craftsmen working together to construct a sturdy and beautiful building. Or, a bit more fancifully, it is like an orchestra—imagine a hundred members of a symphony orchestra racing to see who can finish first! When we experience a moving performance of the *Eroica*, how do we judge who the winners are? Is it the second violins, the horns, the conductor, Beethoven, the audience? Does it not make sense to say that, in this context, there are no losers, that all may be considered winners?

Most of the good things of life have either been provided free by God (nature, if you prefer) or have been produced by the combined efforts of many persons, sometimes of many generations. As all share in the making, so all should share in the use and the enjoyment. This may help convey a bit of what the Fair Shares idea of equality is all about.

VI   SOME HARD QUESTIONS

The equal-opportunity–equal-results dispute is, as we have seen, artificial, trivial, and for the most part irrelevant. There are, however, other arguments upholding the Fair Play perspective and challenging the Fair Shares viewpoint that are more serious and more logical. Some are minor but striking. For example, whatever else one might say about it, is it not true that the Fair Play rule does somehow work? The United States is certainly far from being a closed society; many persons do seize opportunities, do raise themselves up, and do "get ahead," often to an amazing extent. But it is really neither surprising nor persuasive that the prevailing rules do produce winners, even spectacular ones. It is, in fact, necessary if the claims of equal opportunity and meritocracy are to have any credibility at all. The problem of maintaining this credibility is not unlike that faced by the bookie who takes daily bets on the numbers (or by the more respectable state lotteries); occasional and highly visible big winners are indispensable if one wishes to encourage the suckers to continue contributing their daily dollars and quarters to the cause.

The weightier arguments against Fair Shares equality get at the very heart of our ideas of justice and of human nature. Consider four of the most common and difficult of these objections:

• If there is an outstanding characteristic of mankind as a species, it is its spectacular *inequality*—the extraordinary diversity, the range of striking differences in every conceivable dimension. Does not nature teach us, by example, that equality is altogether unnatural?

• The idea that all men are literally equal is not only unnatural and absurd on the face of it, but actually dangerous. Can any society function effectively if it fails to take steps to identify the most able, to recruit them into the crucial positions in society, and to reward them appropriately? Is not equality, then, the enemy of social efficiency?

• It is an almost instinctive principle of fairness that rewards should be proportional to effort and contribution. If this principle of distributive justice is violated—and the idea of fully equal rights of access to resources does appear to violate it—human enterprise will languish, for who will strive to be better or best if the best remain undifferentiated from the worst? Is not equality incompatible with the laws of human motivation and incentive?

• To take the idea of equality literally would be to blur hopelessly the differences between, say, Beverly Sills and my Aunt Molly, who can scarcely squeak her way through an approximation of a full octave; between Einstein and the math teacher at your local junior-high school; between Pasteur and Marcus Welby, M.D. Would not equality overwhelm excellence?

Let me identify my own position early by answering these questions as straightforwardly as possible. To each of the four questions, my answer is "No." I believe that Fair Shares equality is natural and just and that it allows for both excellence and efficiency. Let me elaborate:

• That human beings differ from one another in most characteristics is obviously true, and, with respect to many of these traits, there exists general agreement that some persons are superior, some inferior. Some are stronger, smarter, faster, more talented, sweeter-tempered, funnier, taller, more pious, prettier, or more creative than others. But the crucial questions are these: First, do superiorities and inferiorities cluster together in some way? That is, are those who are stronger also smarter, and are those who are funnier also prettier? Second, what is the logical connection between superiority or inferiority in such respects and the broader issues of unequal life conditions and equal rights? If I am stronger than you, shall I live and you die? Clearly not, for it is agreed that we both have the right to life. If I am blacker than you, shall I be a slave and you be free? That was not clear for a long time, but we finally settled it in the negative at great cost some years ago. But let us go on. If I am taller than you, do you have to obey me? If I can make people laugh louder and longer than you can, does that entitle me to a steak bigger than yours? If I can sing more sweetly than you, should I run the factory and you run the drill press? Obviously not, everyone would agree. But what of other relationships? If I am stronger than you, must you obey me? If I am smarter than you, should I get the larger steak? If I am more energetic than you, do I get to run the factory? If so, why? And how much smarter or more energetic do I have to be to get, for example, one hundred times more income than you do? I, for one, see no logic and no morality that dictate some inevitable correlation between differences in personal characteristics and inequalities in wealth and power, in living conditions, respect, life chances, or access to cultural amenities.

• The argument based on social efficiency is perhaps the most widely cited and accepted argument against any kind of equality other than that of opportunity. While it is superficially plausible, there is in fact no demonstration—and perhaps no way of demonstrating—that the most able, virtuous, and intelligent members of society are in fact occupying the leading roles in it. To adduce one obvious example, are we to say that Nixon, Agnew, Haldeman, Mitchell, Ehrlichman, and company attained the top positions of political leadership in America because they were the outstanding statesmen available in our land? Or because they were morally superior? Or perhaps because they had the greatest political talents? What is the correlation between their abilities and characters and their achievements? In fact, the richest and most powerful persons in America are not more able or virtuous, in any demonstrable way, than are the rest of us. Furthermore, how are we to determine the positions that are crucial to an efficient society and that must therefore be made highly rewarding, in order to attract the best suited individuals? A tax lawyer who advises wealthy clients how to minimize their contributions to the United States Treasury receives great rewards, for example. Is his social role a crucial one? Does he insure a more efficient society? And how does a millionaire movie star meet this test? I will be arguing that we have no measure of any characteristics that might make up so vague a notion as "ability" that isn't patently nonsensical. These days the favorite ability meter is the IQ test, which is a very frail instrument that taps a limited set of abilities, and (to reveal what many may consider a trade secret) there is little relationship between high IQ and occupancy of crucial social positions. Finally, what are we to take as our standard of an "efficient" society? Economists are about the only ones who use the term with any kind of precision, and in their sense efficiency is essentially a matter of producing, with as little waste and friction as possible, a large quantity of commodities that can be sold for a decent profit. Using that standard, we must conclude that America reached its peak under the presidency of Calvin Coolidge and that the societies of ancient Athens and of Renaissance Florence were hopelessly inefficient.

• As for the necessity for some correlation between reward and merit in order to sustain a sense of justice and a degree of motivation, it is an unassailable argument until one comes to the problem of defining "merit." As used by the Fair Players, it resists rational examination. What is it? How can we recognize or quantify it? A major Fair Play polemicist, Daniel Bell, has summed up the social-efficiency and meritocracy argument in an elegant and persuasive epigram: "A society that does not have its best men at the head of its leading institutions is a sociological and moral absurdity."[17] This seems incontestable until we try to think of some way of spotting the "best men" apart from looking for them at the head of "leading institutions." If—as I shall argue—the proposition that the possession of superior merit, talent, and ability leads to success, material rewards, and high position can be demonstrated only by citing high position, material reward, and success as the best measures of ability, talent, and merit, then it is hardly superior to such maxims as "Possession is nine points of the law," "Might makes right," or even, God help us, "Finders keepers, losers weepers."

• The question about the threat to excellence raises the problem of the relationship between inequalities of personal characteristics and motivation. Here the issue is, What does it take to make a Beverly Sills sing or an Einstein think? How much in the way of rewards and privileges? In particular, does it take great wealth and the obedience and obeisance of all of us with lesser talents? I don't believe that Sills or Einstein or Pasteur or most men or women endowed with a particular kind of excellence would answer in the affirmative. The caricature of an egalitarian society implicit in this question conjures up a situation in which any tone-deaf croaker could claim the right to sing the lead in *Don Giovanni* and in which medical research laboratories would be staffed by untrained nincompoops. My own belief is that artistic, scientific, and technical talents and creativity would flourish more readily in a more egalitarian society, where they would be subject neither to suppression because of material want nor to corruption through great material rewards.

These are only brief and simple answers to these four difficult questions. In succeeding chapters, I will be dealing with them and some of their corollaries much more fully and with the kind of detail and documentation they deserve. But, for now, let me ask the reader to suppose that I have succeeded in showing that the Fair Play objections are not sound and, furthermore, that the kind of social equality I tried to sketch in the previous section is not only feasible, but is obviously in the best interests of the overwhelming majority of Americans. What is holding us back? Why not genuine equality, Fair Shares, without the hypocritical cover-up of Fair Play rhetoric? Why can we not admit that the principle of meritocracy and equal opportunity is not a variant definition of equality but its precise opposite?

Why can we not come out and say that it is wrong that the rich have fifty or a hundred times more of everything than the rest of us do, because there is and can be no standard or measure of merit, talent, skill, or knowledge that demonstrates that the average rich person is fifty or a hundred times greater—in any way—than we are? Why can we not confront the truth that effort and ability rarely get any reward, that the rich stay rich and the rest of us shove and shuffle back and forth, bewitched into thinking that in pushing each other around we are struggling for success?

Equality of opportunity is, inevitably, a pathway to inequality, and Fair Play is not a rule for achieving equality, but rather an excuse for inequality. These ideas are a fraud, a simulation, and a counterfeit, and the circulation of this Counterfeit Equality steals from us our rights and our human claims to Fair Shares—counterfeiting is, after all, a subdivision of theft.

So, the underlying questions become: How have we been persuaded to sign away our right to Fair Shares? To whom have we assigned our shares? By what authority? With what instrument? Who sealed the deed and where is it registered?

These mysteries constitute the subject matter of the following pages. I will attempt to analyze and expose the underlying belief systems whose spell leads us to accept Counterfeit Equality as the genuine article. I will also try to describe some of the mechanisms that maintain and prop up Counterfeit Equality. Finally, I will try to derive some principles of action that might lead us in the direction of Fair Shares.

2

Knowing What's Good for You

BELIEF AND EQUALITY

I SUNRISE THEORIES

In trying to understand why the Fair Play idea has such a firm grip on the minds and hearts of Americans and why Fair Shares is such an unpopular notion, we first confront the striking anomaly that so few of us get upset about the enormous inequalities in the ownership and the distribution of resources. The very rich, those who exercise so much control over the rest of us, constitute at the most 1 or 2 percent of the population. What I have called the vulnerable majority includes, by the most conservative calculation, at least 70 percent of us. The facts are no secret. The rich not only make little effort to conceal how much more they have than we do; they often go to some pains to display their affluence. Why are those of us without wealth so complacent and uncomplaining? Most Americans have very little—some so little they can barely stay alive—while a few have so much that they can scarcely count their wealth accurately and are able only to make a rough estimate of their incomes. Everyone accepts the situation as normal and reasonable. Except for an occasional paranoid millionaire, everyone assumes that the poor would likely starve to death before they would dream of plundering the rich in order to stay alive.

That the have-nots in our society are so cooperative is not unusual. Most other societies have also been characterized, in one way or another, by great inequalities, and yet its impoverished members have usually accepted their lot. A number of writers have given us some insight into this state of affairs, which, considered coolly, must be judged to be in some sense irrational. In his recent book, *Injustice: The Social Bases of Obedience and Revolt*,[1] Barrington Moore, Jr., has shown that one of the main conditions that determine the response to what might objectively be viewed as injustice—that is, whether the great majority are accepting and remain obedient or, rarely, revolt against their condition—has to do with the perception of whether or not accepted norms are being violated. There is a prevailing interpretation of the specific terms of the "social contract" that is implicitly in force in a given society. These terms, these "rules of the game," have usually secured a considerable legitimacy, deriving from custom and tradition. If the objective injustices seem to be consistent with those rules, there is a tendency to accept the situation. Only in the rarer cases, when injustice is viewed as springing from the flouting of traditional rules, is rebellion or revolt at all likely.

Students of ideology offer complementary insights. The Marxist approach, for example, sees ideas and concepts as arising from the actual reality of the world around us.[2] A specific element of its explication of ideology is the idea of *false consciousness*, which may be defined, in a highly oversimplified way, as a belief system that reflects, not reality as it actually is, but the illusions that provide a justification for the interests of a particular class that has gained a dominant position in society. The dissemination of false consciousness throughout all layers of society tends to support the position of those at the top, or, in Marx and Engels's trenchant formulation, "The ruling ideas of each age have ever been the ideas of its ruling class."[3]

Writing at a later time and from a more psychological point of view, Karl Mannheim noted, "There is implicit in the word 'ideology' the insight that in certain situations the collective unconscious of certain groups obscures the real condition of society both to itself and to others and thereby stabilizes it."[4] Mannheim's definition of ideology thus has four components: it is (1) a set of ideas or beliefs (2) that have an "unconscious" basis, (3) that are distorted by the interests of a particular group, and (4) that serve the interests of that group in maintaining the status quo.

The maintenance of a particular system of inequality, then, is to a large extent dependent on the prevailing belief system. The accumulated traditions that define the rules of the game, the ruling ideas of the ruling classes, the distortion of reality to serve the interests of the group benefiting from the status quo—these are powerful props justifying the way things are, even when the way things are might from some points of view seem quite unjust and include glaring inequalities. Such a prevailing system of beliefs tends to be a theory of immutability. Things are because they are. Imperfect society is imperfect human nature writ large. That's the way God made the world, so what are we to do? We can describe social phenomena, but we can't really do anything about them. I refer to these as "sunrise theories," because they are very much like the belief that the sun came up each morning, traveled across the sky, and set, and then repeated the process the next day—like it or not. The sun never stopped because of human, and rarely because of divine, intervention.

The assumptions of such a belief system, it must be emphasized, are held at a very deep, almost unconscious, level. If thought about at all, they are considered to be obvious realities rather than hypotheses or premises. Although usually unverifiable, if not demonstrably erroneous, they are not regarded as subject to verification or requiring proof.

The kinds of belief systems that are ideological in nature must be distinguished from simple opinions or evanescent attitudes about political or social issues. An ideological belief is one that is strongly, though almost unconsciously, motivated and that is, in turn, strongly motivating. If one doubts the motivating power of belief, one needs only to consider some of the human events—from superstitious practices to religious wars—that are, in fact, the result of putting belief into action.

What does one have to *believe* to be motivated, on the one hand, to achieve equality, or, on the other, to accept inequality, even if it's the direct cause of one's own misery and starvation? Beliefs of this power, I would argue, must be felt to be *facts*, must have the quality of unquestioning certainty. that's the way things are; that's the way human beings are; that's the way God created the world.

It is inadequate to say that the Saint Sebastian who welcomed the arrows of martyrdom was of the opinion that God existed, that he calculated that the odds of heaven's existence were a good deal greater than fifty-fifty, or that he held a religious attitude about Christianity and martyrdom. He would have been rightly outraged to hear that he was accepting death voluntarily for the sake of attitudes, sentiments, or opinions—he was dying for his *faith* and his *beliefs*, and he *knew* for certain that Jesus would soon be welcoming him into heaven.

Such lack of questioning, such calm certainty, is a primary characteristic of the type of belief system or ideology I am discussing. As Louis Wirth put it in his introduction to *Ideology and Utopia*, "The most important thing, therefore, that we can know about a man is what he takes for granted, and the most elemental and important facts about a society are those that are seldom debated and generally regarded as settled."[5] One tends to take for granted the prevailing explanation of why things are the way they are in the same sense that one takes for granted that tomorrow morning the sun will rise.

In every society characterized by great inequality, a few people were on the top and many on the bottom, and there was a "sunrise theory" to explain why this was necessarily so, why the very nature of humanity was such that it could be no other way. In every case, a few members of the higher class had the land or the gold or the other important resources, they were looked up to and usually bowed down to, and what they said went, while the more numerous members of the lower class were poor, took care of all the bowing down and looking up to, and did what they were told.

Each of these arrangements had its own explanation, widely accepted as obvious, which did not at all stress the realities of inequality—the harsh lives of those on the the the bottom, the opulent lives of those on the top—but which, rather, demonstrated why this particular arrangement was inevitable and, usually, why it was both just and indispensable. In one case it may have stressed the inherently servile nature of the enslaved groups. In another, it may have carefully demonstrated that kings ruled by divine right and that "nobility" and "baseness" were matters of blood—when a noble lady and a noble gentleman conceived a child, they produced a noble heir; when a peasant man and woman coupled, they bred a peasant baby. This seemed no more remarkable than the observation that when a lady goose and a gentleman goose got together, what ultimately crawled out of the egg was a goose rather than a duck. That was the way it went, and a noble could no more be blamed for having blue blood than a peasant could be for having red.

Prior to modern times most such apologies for inequality were relatively simple, widely agreed to, and accepted as a fairly obvious fact of life. The "sunrise theory" that we have to contend with in the United States in the late twentieth century differs from most earlier ones in that it does not *directly* justify inequality, but rather goes through complicated maneuvers in attempting to define inequality as a different version of equality, a counterfeit version.

II WHAT'S A LIBERAL, WHO'S A CONSERVATIVE?

Most efforts to understand the relationship between belief systems and attitudes toward equality have dealt with the dimensions of liberal-conservative or radical-reactionary. These labels and dimensions are defined primarily in terms of manifest attitudes and opinions, usually about such issues as government programs to help the disabled or impoverished, economic distribution, and the like. For example, presented with the question "Should every family be guaranteed a minimum standard of living?" some people will say yes, others no. And the former will usually agree that "employees should have the right to organize and bargain for wages," while the latter will tend to disagree. Putting a number of such questions together, social scientists have constructed scales to measure the extent to which a person may be defined as "liberal," "conservative," "radical," "moderate," and so on.[6]

Although data from research using these scales do, in fact, give us some glimpse into the ideological problems of inequality, there are a number of shortcomings, paradoxical findings, and conceptual contradictions suggesting that the manipulation of labels like "liberal" and "conservative" is not really very helpful in analyzing these ideological problems. Before suggesting a different framework for analysis, let me briefly review some of the advantages and shortcomings of the liberal-conservative dimension.

First, despite the shortcomings, we find that these scales do relate rather well to one's position within the inequality structure. The weight of the evidence shows quite clearly that those who benefit most from America's inequality structure—that is, the most highly educated, the wealthiest, those with the best jobs—usually answer these kinds of questions in a way that earns them the label "conservative." They tend to be against guaranteed minimum incomes, national health insurance, labor rights, and similar measures. Those who have little education and money and who work with their hands take the opposite position, on the whole, and wind up with the label "liberal" or "radical."[7] These are the general patterns, now verified by a large number of well-done studies by social scientists. At that level, they are consistent with an interest-group theory of political attitudes or of a social-class analysis.

Knowing this, however, does not carry us very far. In theorizing about inequality, we find it difficult to move beyond these facts, because the *specifics* of the data tend to be very particular, bound to a definite time period, and they do not, of course, have the character that we attributed to genuinely ideological beliefs. To know that most working-class people have what we call "liberal" political attitudes only makes their acquiescence to the Fair Play ideology more puzzling. Free and Cantril[8] did a study that sheds a bit more light on the question. They divided their scale items into one group that they called measures of the "operational level" of liberalism-conservatism (items proposing that the government should try to do away with poverty, that we should have a national health-insurance program, and so on) and another group that they believed were measures of what they called the "ideological level" (e.g., "We should rely more on individual initiative and ability and not so much on governmental welfare programs" and "The government has gone too far in regulating business and interfering with the free-enterprise system"). They found that while an overwhelmingly high proportion of working people were, predictably, "liberal" at the operational level, a somewhat smaller, but still very substantial, majority of middle-class people also earned that label. At the ideological level, the great majority of both groups were conservative.

It would seem, then, that a typical blue-collar worker, for example, despite his desire for improved social security systems, national health insurance, strong government-protected unions, and, if not a guaranteed income, at least a guaranteed job, remains convinced that a capitalist system emphasizing individual initiative, a free competitive market, and the principles of equal opportunity and meritocracy is good and just and moral. (Free and Cantril did, to be sure, find a substantial minority who were "liberal" on both levels—they tended to be blue-collar workers—as well as a smaller minority—situated predominantly at the upper levels of the ladder of inequality—who were conservative at the "operational" as well as the "ideological" levels.)

The Free and Cantril study, then, confirms the fact that, at what is presumably a "deeper" level, there is among all groups a widespread belief in the rhetoric of equal opportunity and free enterprise, perhaps justifying the Marxian claim that the ruling ideas of a society are the ideas of its ruling class. This is, however, only a clearer *definition* of the problem that I posed at the beginning of this chapter; it does not help us very much to explain why the great majority who suffer from the real inequality of America's social structure still believe in the sunrise theory of Counterfeit Equality.

An additional problem in trying to think about equality in terms of liberals and conservatives is that the concepts have been broadened far beyond what has been defined as "economic liberalism" to include such issues as civil liberties and ethical and moral values. Who is the "real" liberal? The man who is an enthusiastic supporter of civil liberties but who is grimly set against the idea of permitting a union shop in his factory, or the worker in that factory who is ready to strike for a union shop but who will tell you that a doctor who performs an abortion is a murderer? The terms are too loose and complex to provide a ready answer. What are we talking about when we say someone is a radical or a liberal? In one sense, we focus on political and economic issues—the establishment of a minimum wage, graduated taxation, control of large corporations, and the like. In another, we are talking about issues that are not at all in the realm of economic inequalities— "patriotism," abortion, legalization of pornography or marijuana, and fundamentalist or modern religious beliefs. In other words, there are *several* dimensions of attitudes or opinions that are called "liberal" as opposed to "conservative" but that pertain to very different things, and they are not very closely related.

It seems clear that the liberal-conservative dimension is too ambiguous to help us very much in trying to answer the question I have raised in this chapter. Most important, it is not an ideological dimension, in the sense, for example, that Mannheim used the term. Liberal or conservative positions do not really constitute fundamental belief systems; they are often unrelated and rather lightly held attitudes or opinions. The latter are quite conscious and can readily be argued about and disputed. Since they are not unquestioned or taken for granted, they lack the indispensable characteristic of ideological beliefs.

III THE FAIR PLAYER'S CREED

If the liberal-conservative (or radical-reactionary) dimension does not provide a sufficiently sharp tool for dissecting out the basic ideological belief system that is the underpinning of the Fair Play ideology, what other instruments are available? I would suggest that we turn back to some of the fundamental issues that have always recurred in discussions and disputes about the nature of mankind and society. These basic questions—"Are human beings good or evil?", "What is man's relationship to God?" and a half-dozen or so others—provide a framework for identifying the major components of any belief system. Which of such issues, we may ask, are prominent in the works and arguments of the exponents of equal opportunity and meritocracy? (I will try to show that three are particularly relevant to the question of equality.) What are some of the axioms and assumptions that appear to be held in common? What, using Wirth's criterion, does the Fair Player take for granted? How does he view the fundamental characteristics of human nature? What is his vision of how God made the world?

In order to identify these issues—and the assumptions held about them by the Fair Play proponents—I propose that we examine some of the words of the proponents themselves. We can begin with Irving Kristol. He is a leading figure among the writers and politicians who have come to be known as "neoconservatives"; he has, in fact, been called their "godfather." Members of this group have been very active and vocal in defining and defending what I have called the Fair Play viewpoint, and Kristol's seminal article "About Equality"[9] gives an excellent summary of their arguments and rhetoric.

As a disciple of the Aristotelian scholar Leo Strauss, Kristol appropriately refers, early in his argument, to Aristotle's well-known discussion of the principle of distributive justice: "A just and legitimate society, according to Aristotle, is one in which inequalities—of property, or station, or power— are generally perceived by the citizenry as necessary for the common good."[10] Kristol then goes on to expound the "bell-shaped fallacy," which he calls the "natural tyranny of the bell-shaped curve," in a manner that neatly summarizes this article of the Fair Play faith. He also summons the spirits of the Founding Fathers, which appears to be an obligatory component of any essay extolling this perspective:

The founding fathers of modern bourgeois society (John Locke, say, or Thomas Jefferson) all assumed that biological inequalities among men—inequalities in intelligence, talent, abilities of all kinds—were not extreme, and therefore did not justify a society of hereditary privilege (of "two races," as it were). This assumption we now know to be true, demonstrably true, as a matter of fact. Human talents and abilities, as measured, do distribute themselves along a bell-shaped curve, with most people clustered around the middle, and with much smaller percentages at the lower and higher ends. That men are "created equal" is not a myth or a mere ideology—unless, of course, one interprets that phrase literally, which would be patently absurd and was never the bourgeois intention. Moreover, it is a demonstrable fact that in all modern, bourgeois societies, the distribution of income is also along a bell-shaped curve, indicating that in such an "open" society the inequalities that do emerge are not inconsistent with the bourgeois notions of equality.[11]

I cannot restrain myself from making a few, perhaps premature, comments on this last passage. First, as any economist will tell you, it is not only *not* demonstrably *true* that income is distributed along a bell-shaped curve, it is demonstrably *false*. (I call to your mind the famous quotation from Samuelson cited in Chapter One.) This is an excellent example of what Mannheim referred to as "distortion of reality." Second, note the ease with which Mr. Kristol slides back and forth between "equality" and "inequality." That men are created equal is not a myth, he says, unless one takes the statement literally (that is, unless one has been let in on the secret that, to the initiate, "created equal" really means "created unequal"). Later we discover that emerging *inequalities* are not inconsistent with *equality*. Mannheim refers to this as the "collective unconscious" obscuring reality to *itself*.

Another frequent entrant in the polemical combat is Paul Seabury, whose influential essay "The Idea of Merit" directly confronts the conflict between what I have been terming Fair Shares and Fair Play.[12] Following the custom of the group, Seabury prefers to talk about "equality of opportunity" and "equality of results." It is important to note, here, that many, perhaps most, of the advocates of Fair Play are quite aware that America has not achieved the ideal state posited by Fair Play theory. Seabury discusses many of its ambiguities and imperfections, and goes on to say,

> Yet none of these special arguments against the practice of merit and equal opportunity denies the principle. This is not, however, the case with the principle of equality of results which does thrust at the heart of the principle of equal opportunity and merit.[13]

He prophesies even worse consequences:

> . . . those who value equality of results over equal opportunity, and over the principle that all men should be judged and treated according to their individual

merits, are attempting to lead us into a new era of discrimination on the basis of race, creed or color.[14]

Later he not only defends the idea of merit and the feasibility of measuring it, but again raises the specter that defection from the principles of Fair Play is a grave danger to us all:

> For a complex society like our own, after all, depends on the skills of the individuals composing it. . . . We can hardly argue that there are no such things as skill or competence or that there is no way of measuring them. But there are those among us who do make this argument . . . and its spreading influence may well constitute the single greatest threat to the quality of our lives today.[15]

Finally, I will quote some passages from Daniel Bell's lucid and persuasive essay "On Meritocracy and Equality."[16] Bell's exposition of the Fair Play perspective is, in my judgment, the most rational and the most humane, primarily, I think, because he is concerned not simply with meritocracy but with *just* meritocracy. (I am inclined to believe that if push came to shove and Professor Bell had to choose between "just" and "meritocracy," he would mournfully but unhesitatingly pick the former.) Like most of the others, Bell hauls up the Founding Fathers fairly early in the game:

> Among the Founding Fathers, the idea of virtue and of election by ability (if no longer by grace) predominated . . . in the very use of a Lockean language there was an implicit commitment to a hierarchy—the hierarchy of intellect. Since thought was prized, it was assumed that some men "thought" better than others, were more able, more intelligent—and so formed the natural aristocracy.[17]

He then tackles some of the basic conflicts inherent in the problem of defining equality:

> What is at stake today is the redefinition of equality. A principle which was the weapon for changing a vast social system, the principle of equality of opportunity, is now seen as leading to a new hierarchy, and the current demand . . . requires the reduction of all inequality or the creation of *equality of result*—in income, status, and power—for all men in society. This issue is the central value problem of the post-industrial society.
>
> The principle of equality of opportunity derives from a fundamental tenet of classical liberalism: that the individual . . . is the basic unit of society and that the purpose of societal arrangements is to allow the individual to fulfill his own purposes . . . . It was assumed that individuals will differ—in their natural endowments, in their energy, drive, and motivation, in their conception of what is desirable—and that the institutions of society should establish procedures for regulating fairly the competition and exchanges necessary to fulfill these diverse desires and competences.[18]

It is not insignificant that Bell identifies the Fair Play set of ideas as a rather direct continuation of the ideas of classic liberalism:

> The liberal theory of society was framed by the twin axes of individualism and rationality. The unencumbered individual would seek to realize his own satisfactions on the basis of his work—he was to be rewarded for effort, pluck and risk—and the exchange of products with others was calculated by each so as to maximize his own satisfactions. . . . Today we have come to the end of classic liberalism. It is not individual satisfaction which is the measure of social good, but redress for the disadvantaged . . . inevitably, the disadvantaged are identifiable largely in group terms, and the principle of equity is linked with the principle of quota representation.
>
> The claim for group rights stands in formal contradiction to the principle of individualism, with its emphasis on achievement and universalism.[19]

In a final section, outlining the principles of what he calls a "just meritocracy," he first characterizes negatively the drive for equality and then makes the case for meritocracy as a guarantee of a better quality of life:

> What the populists resent is not power . . . but authority—the authority represented in the superior competence of individuals.[20]
>
> The quality of life in any society is determined, in considerable measure, by the quality of its leadership. A society that does not have its best men at the head of its leading institutions is a sociological and moral absurdity.[21]

These examples are, I think, sufficiently representative of the Fair Play perspective that there is no need to belabor the matter with additional, repetitive quotations. From them we can readily infer the dominant themes that make up the basic Fair Play ideology. The first is the extreme emphasis on the primacy of the individual:

> —the individual is the basic unit of society
> —to allow the individual to fulfill his own purposes
> —the unencumbered individual
> —individual satisfaction

Of course, the central place of individualism in America's value system has been noted frequently and consistently,[22] but in these passages we can see the details of the assumptions about individualism in more specific detail. The Fair Player views human life as—almost exclusively—the behavior of discrete individuals seeking their own individual ends and believes that, ideally, a good society leaves the individual as unfettered as possible in this search. Collectivities, racial or ethnic or any other kinds of groupings, are seen as being, in a sense, less "real" than the individual and as having less legitimate a place in discourse about human affairs. One clear principle of the Fair Play ideology, then, is the primacy of the individual.

A second principle that emerges quite vividly is that individuals differ significantly from one another, that some are better than or superior to others and can be identified as such:

- individuals will differ in their natural endowments
—the superior competence of individuals
—best men

It can be seen, then, that to Fair Players it ranks as an obvious truth that what life "really is," is the working out of these individual differences; they furthermore take for granted that the individuals who demonstrate superior competence will occupy the preeminent positions in society and receive the most rewards.

The first two principles of this belief system, to repeat, are the extreme emphasis on the primacy of the individual and the great significance of differences among individuals. The third has to do with the *source* of these differences. We read about:

—skills of the individual
—energy, drive, and motivation
—relation between achievement and intelligence
—talent and ambition

The emphasis falls on differences in qualities of mind, motivation, character, and the like—differences that may be thought of as being somehow "inside" the person and that, even if acquired rather than innate, have been internalized so that the individual, so to speak, carries them around with him. Fair Players emphasize these internal causes of behavior and behavioral differences, paying little or no attention to, for example, social or environmental factors—external causes—such as racial and sexual prejudice, income, family background, and stressful or beneficent life events.

These three assumptions constitute the core of the Fair Play belief system. When he turns his mind to matters of human behavior, the Fair Player focuses on the nature and the working out of *internal, individual differences.* There are other subsidiary themes, such as achievement and competition, but I think they can readily be derived from the primary triad.

As I suggested before, these three conclusions about the nature of human behavior are implicit answers to questions that have for thousands of years preoccupied and puzzled philosophers, psychologists, and others concerned about human beings and their nature. One can render the questions explicit:

1. Is human behavior to be understood principally or predominantly as the discrete actions of individuals? Or is it more accurate and useful to think

of human behavior as social and collective and of human life as the life of the family, of the community, of the nation?[23]

2. Are we to think of people as very similar to one another, their common characteristics as a species far more relevant than the minor variations one can observe? Or are we to suppose that each person is quite different, perhaps even unique, one of a kind, endowed with a set of characteristics, strengths, defects, and needs that is unmatched by that of any other person?[24]

3. Is human behavior to be traced more accurately to a source "inside the skin" from which it ultimately originates? Or is it largely contingent on the characteristics of the external environment? Is behavior better explained and understood as the consequence of internal psychological, temperamental, and constitutional factors or as a response to the situations within which it occurs?[25]

That these questions have remained so consistently prominent (at least in the history of Western thought) testifies to their significance; that they have never been settled perhaps suggests that they are not answerable in any definitive way. Of course, human beings are both individuals and parts of larger social entities; all human beings are very similar in most respects, but one can find differences among them that can be judged important; and behavior can logically be understood only as the interaction between internal factors and the external environment, the situation and circumstances in which it occurs.

Nonetheless, it is apparent that most persons lean one way or another on these questions and that a substantial number take positions rather near to the extreme points of these three dimensions. The answers can be argued about forever because they cannot be settled in any finally convincing way. A given person's answer to the three questions is almost surely a reflection of values, of unquestioned assumptions and beliefs that are taken for granted and are *experienced* as the perception of facts, of *reality*. One person *perceives* unique individuals acting on the basis of internal factors; another confronts the same physical data and does not question his own perception of a collectivity of similar persons behaving in response to their environmental situations.

We have here, I would argue, the ingredients of a type of analysis (not only about equality, but about other issues that are usually defined as political or technical or even moral) that is more productive than the liberal-conservative continuum. We have three dimensions that provide at least a partial framework for identifying an ideological position or belief system:

- individual versus collective
- different versus similar
- internal versus external

We can then formulate opposing positions—the individual-different-internal as against the collective-similar-external, with a range of actual or potential positions between the extremes—defining belief systems that are enormously powerful in conditioning other, more specific, beliefs. Let me give, first, a relatively simple and concrete example—one's stance on problems of illness and health.

Confronting what might appear to be the same problem or set of facts, one person tends to see illness as something that happens to individuals, that occurs inside the person because of conditions, such as the presence of microbes or the uncontrolled growth of cells, that render him different (deviant, abnormal, disordered). The person who takes the opposite position typically perceives illnesses as occurring in certain numbers within some population—the community, the state—to persons who are essentially like other people and who are being affected by some external, environmental source, such as a mosquito-breeding swamp or a carcinogenic industrial chemical. The first observer, on reflecting about illness, thinks first of becoming, or paying for, a physician; the second will focus on joining, or collectively paying for, an effective public health enterprise.

Let me now try to make the final connection between belief and the issue of equality and inequality. In order to persuade the great majority of people to accept and maintain the Fair Play system of inequality, it is essential to establish, as a foundation, the belief system that emphasizes the individual, the different, and the internal. Similarly, it is only from a position emphasizing the collective, the similar, and the external that one can prefer or perhaps even envision the kinds of social and economic arrangements that I have sketched out as those of Fair Shares equality. (Let me emphasize that I am here asserting only that such a belief system is necessary; I am not—at least not yet—saying that it is sufficient.)

The ideas that some persons are worth more than others because they can perform certain tasks and functions better than others can and that there should be as little interference as possible with the individual's seeking and attaining various forms of property form the bases of the two key explanations of, and moral justifications for, our present system of inequality. These ideas would be neither rational nor ethical if they did not rest on the three basic assumptions I have been discussing.

In order to justify our system of inequality, it is necessary to regard human activity primarily as the behavior of individuals, to see specific persons occupying specific roles that are quite separable from those occupied by other specific persons. The folklore of free-enterprise capitalism is filled with just such myths of individual achievement—Edison inventing the light bulb, Ford developing the assembly line, and so forth. These are seen as independent actions of particularly remarkable individuals, who thereby merited great rewards. The very idea of such great, individual rewards is predicated on the belief in such separable, individual accomplishments.

Similarly, only when we emphasize the differences among human beings does our continual ranking of them as better or worse appear defensible. Those ranked as higher or better must be perceived as having significantly greater abilities or more valued characteristics. It would be difficult, indeed, if all persons were thought of as being pretty much the same, to construct plausible arguments for valuing some at a rate of thirty dollars a day and others at a rate of three hundred, let alone three thousand. It seems unlikely that, say, their productivity would vary by such multiples.

Finally, inequality can be justified within the American ethical consensus only with respect to certain kinds of differences. A remarkable capacity to plan successful bank robberies, for example, or such extraordinary physical strength as to enable one to impose one's will on others, or differences due to external circumstances on which one has had little or no influence—inherited wealth or severe disability resulting from an automobile accident—none of these differences are deemed valid grounds on which to justify inequality. The American emphasis has been on the ability, the intuition, the character, and the willpower of the lone individual, which he carries around with him as a part of his inner self. These internal differences provide the basis for justifying inequality in terms of the Fair Play ideology of Counterfeit Equality.

This ideological tripod sustains our entire social structure of inequality. We have been led to believe that the high and the mighty are individuals who are very different from others in that they possess these superior internal characteristics; conversely, we are told, the internal characteristics of those who rank low are inferior.

IV   ROBINSON CRUSOE'S CHILD: ALONE AND TOGETHER

In the preceding section, I spoke of "individual versus collective," "different versus similar," and "internal versus external," in order to convey the either/or quality of these three dimensions as *ideological* dimensions, implying that the opposing terms were experienced as mutually exclusive positions. As we try to understand how these positions are felt as components of a belief system, we do indeed have to grasp this quality. On a general level, everyone will, of course, agree that collectivities are made up of individuals and that individuals are always part of collectivities—and will similarly agree on the other two dimensions. Despite this acknowledgment of some kind of duality, however, the average person will nevertheless be inclined to set aside the reality of groups, communities, and the like as simply a given or as part of the background—that is, as true but not particularly significant. The significant reality, the crucial one, they feel, is the individual; it is the individual who is the *human* being.

In trying to comprehend the certainty of this primary belief in only *one* end of the continuum, we must at the same time step back and try to understand more fully (less ideologically, if you will) the relationship between the individual and the collectivity. This is particularly true as we attempt to develop an empathetic understanding of the minority view, the perspective that is largely obscured by the Fair Play ideology—in this case, the belief that the collectivity is more significant and a more basic reality than is the individual.

Let us begin this process by trying to imagine the individual *apart* from any collectivity, any human group. It is probably intuitively apparent to most persons that to become a human being, a child must be raised among other human beings. In other words, we must learn social aspects of behavior—how to speak the language, how to dress and eat acceptably, how to give and to receive, how to work, and so forth—from others. What is not so intuitively evident is that the same requirements hold true for *all* human characteristics and behavior, including those that are not so obviously social as customs, manners, and language. Composing music, inventing technologies, writing poetry—these are usually conceived of as much more intensely individual and personal activities. But these human endeavors, although apparently quite individual in nature, could occur only in the context of a human community; they are completely dependent on membership in a social entity.

Consider for a moment the myths about single individuals who are cut off from the company of others. The most enduringly fascinating one is that of Robinson Crusoe. Anyone who begins to read his story becomes caught up in his situation and enchanted by his actions, which are directed toward recreating the elements of his own civilization—the calendar, agriculture, animal husbandry, hunting, transforming nature's givens into useful objects. Defoe would not have strained our imaginations if he had had Crusoe writing a poem or composing music and inventing an instrument to play it on.

But imagine a change in the Crusoe story. Suppose that Friday had been a woman, that she and Crusoe had a child, and that when the child was very young they went to sea to catch fish and never returned. That would be about as close as we could get to a single human being, just mature enough to survive, living out his life completely as an individual. What would Robinson Crusoe's child be like?

We can scarcely say for sure; but we can speculate.

Rather than expanding his command of language, he would probably forget how to speak—because he would have no other human being to converse with. He might remember snatches of songs, but he would have no real conception of music. He would not invent zero or the calculus, nor would he write anything resembling *Hamlet* or *La Traviata*. Rather than designing new technologies, he would, at best, learn to reproduce the artifacts left by his parents; at worst, he would use them until they broke or decayed. He would not invent the steam engine or the assembly line or the laws of property and inheritance.

Achievements of this kind are properly attributed to civilizations, to societies, to collectivities of humans. Each of them is meaningful only in relation to other persons and could be contrived only by a group of persons.

Most important, Robinson Crusoe's child would never know who or what he was—whether human or animal, mortal or immortal, good or bad. Whatever self-consciousness he had when he was left cast away as a lone individual would either be fixed forever or fade away. The most extremely individual human being we can imagine would thus not even know that he *was* an individual human being. Because of this extreme of *individualism* his *individuality* would be completely irrelevant.

A sense of individuality, that is, a conscious awareness of being a separate person, is possible only within a collective of other persons. All individual actions are similarly dependent on such membership—we must learn all human activity within a human context, in a social setting, in contact with an organized collectivity of others.

Probably no one would accept as credible the idea that Robinson Crusoe's child could have composed *La Traviata*. Yet many persons believe that Verdi did so in essentially the same way—alone and independently of his world and his society, relying solely upon his own individual creative gift. So too, no one would expect the Crusoe child to contrive all by himself to produce a thousand Model T's a day on an assembly line; yet we have all been told, and some of us even believe, that Henry Ford did just that.

A moment's consideration should suggest that the "individual" achievements of Verdi and of Ford were but tiny increments to an already existing body of knowledge, technique, and work, built up by tens or hundreds of thousands of persons; that the individual "creators" were assisted in their achievements in their own lifetimes by the work of dozens or hundreds or thousands of fellowmen; and that the achievements themselves were a reflection and an expression of the social fabric within which they occurred.

On the other hand, it has happened over and over again that two contemporaries have made the same discoveries or inventions almost simultaneously and in complete ignorance of the other's work: Darwin and Wallace with natural selection, Newton and Leibniz in the case of the calculus, and the still unresolved dispute about the invention of the motion-picture camera are examples that come to mind. Merton and Barber have identified scores of scientific discoveries made by as many as three, four, even nine, different investigators, all working independently.[26] More recently, we have had the example of the terrifying competition of Allied and Axis scientists, during World War II, racing each other to "invent" the atomic bomb. It was invented, but no individual holds the patent. Future history books will never be able to give us a name and a date, comparable to "James Watt invented the steam engine in 1769"—which, of course, he didn't do.

Yet we are told—again and again—that it is the *individual* who "achieves." One of the most striking phenomena of our bicentennial year was the profusion of institutional advertisements by the great corporations, praising the individual enterprise and individual achievement of everyone from Columbus to Thomas Edison and Babe Ruth. The message was clear: Our greatness as a nation derives from our emphasis on and recognition of the singular importance of the individual as the basic source of all progress and accomplishment. Not only do we exalt and venerate the individual, but in a complementary fashion we neglect and demean the collectivity.

These values are the underpinnings for a favorite American myth that provides the plot for many Western movies. The hero, the lone cowboy, appears, Messiah-like, as the good and able *individual*, who saves the *community*, which has collectively been unable to summon the intelligence, the bravery, and the will to save itself from the *bad individual*—the cattle baron, the corrupt official, the land-grabbing railroad man.

Individualism is also a constant theme in the most cherished, if least read, of America's literary classics: Emerson on self-reliance, Thoreau's self-righteously anarchic noncomformity; Whitman singing of himself.

How might we understand the relationship between the individual and the collectivity in a different, perhaps more useful and productive, way?

At the simplest arithmetical level the terms "collectivity" and "group of individuals" are identical; a quartet is the same as four persons. But common experience and the very nature of language tell us that collectivities have qualities and characteristics above and beyond those of the units that they include. Perceptual studies, for example, show that four dots are not always the same. Arranged as ••• they may simply seem to be four dots. Arranged as :: they look like a square; as ••• like a diamond.

At the level of language, too, quartet means far more than four persons; it suggests that the four persons do something together cooperatively, usually playing music.

So, one may say that human life exists at the level of the collectivity in a very real sense, no less real than life at the level of the individual. Families act *as* families, for example, in numerous incidents and are perceived as doing so. Towns, neighborhoods, and states have characteristics that cannot sensibly be judged as simply the sum of the characteristics of their citizens. The phenomena of individuals and collectivities, then, are neither mutually exclusive nor identical. They are, however, *simultaneous*.

With respect to *human* life, one cannot logically separate the two levels in reality, or even in the imagination. One may conceive of a single tree, growing alone in the middle of a meadow, with no other tree in sight. It is still a tree and will behave like a tree. One can even imagine a dog that never sees another dog after leaving its mother, growing up and living in some remote place with its master. It will very clearly be a dog. But one cannot imagine a single human being. Even with young Crusoe, it was necessary to hypothesize some relatively long period of residence with, and dependence on, other humans. Beyond that, it is almost beyond our imagination to conjure up a scenario involving him as a lone individual human. Certainly few would disagree that if we met him, it would be on little more than biological grounds that we would classify him as a human being.

Within these limitations, we see some persons more or less favoring an individualistic perspective, others a collectivistic perspective. I have labeled these as "ideological" perspectives in the sense that they conform to Mannheim's defining characteristics of ideology.

The relationship between one's ideological position on the individual-collective dimension and that on the Fair Play–Fair Shares dimension is linked by the association between reward and merit. But when one departs from a conception of human activities, achievements, and productions as simply the sum of the activities of so many individuals, one begins to have great trouble in justifying the bestowal of *individual* rewards for *individual* "merit." If my own individual actions can account for only a portion of the outcome, the product, or the achievement, the remainder being accounted for by a larger social organization, the functioning of a collectivity of which I am a part, then how do I sort out in any simple fashion how much of that outcome is to be credited to me or how much of the product is "mine"?

Let me try to give a highly oversimplified hypothetical example. Suppose that twenty men who manufacture eggbeaters can produce, when working together in some cooperative formation, two hundred of them a day. Suppose, furthermore, that if each man makes eggbeaters all by himself, he can make only five a day—a total of one hundred produced by twenty individuals. We account for the hundred additional eggbeaters produced cooperatively as a function of the collectivity that exists as a real entity when the twenty men are working together rather than as individuals. To whom do those extra hundred eggbeaters "belong"?

Before leaping to an immediate conclusion by the process of long division, consider a few further factors: (1) some additional number of persons—presumably former members of the eggbeater-making collectivity—together invented and designed the components of the overall procedure by which a team produces twice as many eggbeaters as an equivalent number of individuals; (2) the physical material from which the eggbeaters were fabricated existed before anybody even thought of eggbeaters—having been created by God or, if you prefer, gradually produced by nature; and (3) the value of an eggbeater depends in no small measure on the existence of eggs and of the complicated processes by which eggs ultimately arrive in the refrigerator of somebody who is planning to make a soufflé.

One could go on citing factors that are, broadly speaking, social—tied to the collectivities that exist in time as well as space—in order to make the argument that only a small fraction of the value and usefulness of the eggbeaters can logically be attributed to the traits and actions of the individuals or that the total amount of the "reward" (the income from selling the beaters) proportional to individual merit is really quite small.

When we consider the vastly more complicated processes of the real world—the production of automobiles, inventions, novels, and other things—it becomes more difficult to discern the role of a single individual as decisive or even as much more important than that of another.

In the absence of such a capacity to define vastly greater merits in particular individuals, it is very hard to justify their receiving vastly different rewards.

V   OF ARTICHOKES AND ANTELOPES: DIFFERENTIATING
THE SIMILAR

The boxes in which Girl Scout cookies come this year feature two pictures, on opposite sides. One shows a group of eight or ten Girl Scouts, a mixture of racial and ethnic types, engaged in a group activity, and bears the title "We have a lot in common." The other is a tight close-up of the face of one of the girls and is entitled "I'm not like anyone else." This is, I think, an excellent pictorial summation of the issue of similarity and differences and of the nature of the relationship between the two concepts.

In attempting to underline the ideological significance of these concepts, I presented the issue as similarity *versus* difference because it is the emphasis on one or the other of these as opposing terms that leads to the kinds of unthinking assumptions that underlie extreme positions on the Fair Play–Fair Shares dimensions (and, as I have suggested, on other moral, political, and social issues).

When we use one of the words "similar" or "different," we rely on the fact that the seeming opposites depend on each other to supply part of the meaning, that neither conveys any information without implicit reference to the other. Groups of things are *similar*, are in the same category, because we can systematically *differentiate* them from things in other categories. And it is only meaningful to say that one thing is *different* from another if the two things are in other significant ways *similar*.

Consider the following pair of statements: "That rock is at least five times bigger than that rabbit" and "Most rabbits are bigger than most squirrels." Or consider another pair: "The World Trade Center is taller than the Empire State Building" and "An antelope is taller than an artichoke." Which of the members of these pairs seem like sensible, moderately significant statements? For example, if you were strolling through the park and a man came up to you breathlessly and announced, "That rock over there must be at least five times bigger than that rabbit!" what would you do? You might call a cop or say, "Excuse me, I'm late for a lunch date," or you might just sidle away, muttering, "Yeah, yeah; sure is." You certainly wouldn't expect to engage the person in a sensible, significant communication. The one about rabbits and squirrels, though lacking much in the way of news value, is at least not off the wall.

The statement regarding the two buildings seems reasonable, if not exciting; but why would anyone compare an antelope and an artichoke? The comparison is so trivial as to approach the suburbs of lunacy or nonsense. That a rabbit is different from a rock is also true but trivial. One feels no way of getting a handle on it, no way of knowing where to begin to think about it, because in noting differences we must begin with an assumption that there are similarities. In the absence of very significant similarities, a great number of differences are perceptible, by definition, and focusing on any one or two of those differences doesn't forward our understanding to any important degree. Before we can begin to have the feeling that a rabbit's being different from a rock, an antelope's from an artichoke, makes any difference, we must also sense that there exist some considerable similarities. And since we can't observe any similarities between rocks and rabbits or between antelopes and artichokes that make any sense to us, the question of various differences between them does not seem relevant. In fact, to mention such differences seems downright silly.

Rabbits and squirrels, on the other hand, are alike in many respects and very similar in others; we can find a number of reasonable categories that fit both: small, mammalian, furry, pesky but cute, and suitable for stardom in Walt Disney movies. We can also find a host of similarities between the two big office buildings. The notation of difference with any degree of emphasis thus implies—indeed, absolutely requires—the existence of many similarities, before any *information* can be conveyed by the mention of differences. If someone knows absolutely nothing about rabbits and squirrels, telling him that one is bigger than the other gives him no information. Check it out. If I tell you, right now, that a gurb is larger than a tranleg, what do you know that you didn't know before I began the sentence? However, if I have never seen a rabbit but already know that a squirrel is a cute, small, furry mammal and if someone tells me that a rabbit is something like a squirrel except that it's a little bigger and has long ears and a short tail, then I will certainly be able to distinguish at a glance a rabbit from a mouse. At least.

An ideological emphasis on difference, however, will tend to deny the very similarities that make difference at all significant. The characteristic American way of thinking, based on the dominant American belief system, tilts heavily in this direction. We are primarily interested in differences, particularly in those between individual persons, and we sometimes seem almost obsessed with discovering differences, no matter how trivial or uninformative they might really be. This preoccupation reaches remarkable extremes.

Take, as an illustration, the dimension of size. One can say, fairly, that a man seven feet tall and weighing three hundred pounds is vastly *different* from a man four feet tall and weighing eighty pounds. This makes sense to us and is worth pointing out, in a way that the difference between rabbits and rocks is not. If we saw the big man and the little man side by side, we would be struck by the contrast. Why? On a scale ranging from, say, the size of a microbe to that of a whale, the differences in size between the two men is relatively trivial. Our ability to focus on the difference in size of the four-foot man and the seven-foot man is based on our implicit acknowledgment of their essential similarity in almost all other respects. It is the fact that they are extremely similar *as men* that enables us to focus on the relatively minor differences in height and weight.

What I am trying to get at is the inseparability, with respect to meaning, of similarity and difference, their necessary connection with one another—a connection of which most Americans have very little sense. We are so encouraged to preoccupy ourselves with separating ourselves from one another on the basis of small differences that we overlook the unifying force of the enormous number of things that we have in common.

The sermons on difference are often preached on the text that each individual is unique and supremely important. In practice, of course, the paradoxical result is a separation into a few who are important and the great majority who are unimportant and a grinding away and blurring of all the fine, subtle gradations of differences that are the real basis of individuality and of the richness that arises from the unification of individuality with general similarity. Just like the Girl Scouts on the cookie boxes.

There appear to be some interesting relationships between these first two dimensions, and there is some evidence that an emphasis on middle-range collectivities has a tendency to stimulate emphasis on intergroup rather than interpersonal differences.[27] For example, during a great crisis, such as a war perceived as just, we tend to shift our emphasis somewhat from the individual to our common membership in the same nation. I remember having been made aware of this phenomenon very acutely during World War II.

You might have talked funny and eaten strange food because you came from Alabama, and I might have done so because I came from Boston; but we wore the same uniform, slept side by side in identical beds, learned to behave as interchangeable units in close-order drill, and when we went to the mess hall, we had the same food slapped on our identical tin trays, and we ate it together and probably voiced very similar complaints.

But the increased emphasis on *our* similarities was accompanied by an ominous attention to *their* differences. *They* were "sneaky Japs" and "blood-thirsty Krauts." They were so vastly different as to be essentially nonhuman, so much so that we felt no qualms about mounting the fire raids on Tokyo and Dresden and had no compunction about dropping the atom bombs on Hiroshima and Nagasaki. We made the judgment that fascism was such an intolerable evil on the face of the earth that war and killing were justified and necessary. But, in order to carry out this judgment, it was psychologically necessary for us to blind ourselves to the fact that the Japanese people, the German people, and the Italian people were not significantly different from us, that we all shared a common humanity.

This moral dilemma—which has led some persons to embrace the principle of absolute pacifism—was dramatically rendered by Ernest Hemingway in *For Whom the Bell Tolls,* which is set during the Spanish Civil War. He describes a fight between a band of republican guerrillas and a troop of fascist cavalry. One of the guerrillas, Francisco, an old and sweet man, is firing a machine gun at the Franco soldiers and as his bullets hit and kill them he weeps. He continues to fire, tears streaming down his cheeks, knowing that as he is killing his enemy he is also killing his brother. He believes that to kill a fellow human being is evil under any circumstances, but that one must sometimes accept the guilt caused by one evil in order to overcome a greater evil.

One is reminded of a Jewish legend associated with Passover. One of the ceremonies during the Seder is the dipping out of one's glass a drop of wine as each of the ten plagues visited upon the Egyptians is named. One explanation of this tradition is that, as a full cup symbolizes joy, so we diminish the wine in our cup to symbolize sorrow for the suffering of the Egyptians. A legend that goes with this holds that when the Egyptian army was trapped and the waters of the parted sea closed over them, the angels watching from above rejoiced. But God rebuked them, saying, "Are these, too, not My creatures, the work of My hands?"

Sadly, our perception of similarity seldom rises to such heights, to the recognition that all humans are the children of God, "the work of His hands." We tend almost always to stop at a lower point—the nation, the race, the neighborhood, the family. At this level, we may see considerable similarity, but all others are different. And we almost always go further. Consciously or not, we immediately weight difference with value and with questions of superiority and inferiority. As Americans, we see ourselves not merely as different in some ways from Russians, but as *better* than them; as men, better than women; as Protestants, better than Catholics or Jews; and so forth.

The direct relationship between inequality and similarity versus difference is contained in the idea that differences between persons account for, and justify, the material conditions of inequality. Some are smarter, thriftier, more industrious, more favored by God, more virtuous, more ingenious, or more energetic. Those are the ones—those who are most different—who rise to the top as naturally as cream rises to the top of the milk bottle.

Conversely, the assumption that most persons are essentially alike, with minor differences that are often very interesting, leads to the feeling that no one is so special, so dramatically different, or so obviously superior that he or she should have vastly more than the rest of us and, with it, the right to run our lives.

VI   DRIVING TRUCKS MERITORIOUSLY: INSIDE AND OUT

The third leg in the ideological tripod of inequality is the notion of internal versus external. Again, we must step back and acknowledge that human behavior and its consequences cannot be fully explained either by internal characteristics or by environmental, situational factors. Both must be taken into account, since behavior always reflects some kind of interaction between the two realms. Moreover, it is apparent to most persons that phenomena that are initially purely external are somehow or other taken inside the individual person—are internalized or "introjected"—and ultimately function more powerfully as internal determinants. This is most apparent to those who study child development and socialization; at birth language is absent from the behavior of a child, but within a few years his native tongue becomes an intimate, deeply incorporated aspect of his internal apparatus. Particular values and customs of a specific culture follow the same pathway, moving from outside to inside. Nevertheless, the relative emphasis that one places on internal or external determinants of human behavior and experience has extremely important, indeed crucial, effects on one's view of the world in general and on one's opinions in matters of equality in particular.

When the Fair Player argues with the Fair Sharer, some central questions sooner or later arise: In what way are individuals supposed to be different from one another that can validly lead to a judgment that one is superior to the other? Different on what dimension? Superior in what way? It's one thing to say that superior individuals naturally and necessarily take charge of human affairs, make the significant decisions, provide the significant inputs, and, of course, reap the bulk of the rewards. It's quite another to specify the nature of the differences we are talking about.

One way of categorizing differences among persons is to specify whether they are internal or external. Among the former would be constitutional or genetic variations, temperament and character, and special aptitudes, talents, and intellectual gifts. Among the latter would be luck, fate, predestination or election, the spatial relationship of planets, environmental events or conditions, and the circumstance of being born into a rich or a poor family. Thus we find theories of differences among people that emphasize the internal—their chromosomes, their nobility of descent, or their superior morality or intelligence—and theories that attend to the external—to their astrological sign, the climatic conditions in which they live, or their position with respect to control of material resources.

In medieval times the question of equality could be boiled down to a simple issue: Are members of the higher orders so well off because they were born noble (the internal explanation) or because they were born rich (the external)? In our time essentially the same question is asked in somewhat different terms. Did those who are well off reach their lofty positions as a consequence of internal characteristics—ability and merit—or as a consequence of external events—access to wealth by birth or recruitment? To justify inequality, one must make the case for ability and merit.

Before going on to discuss the arguments for or against this case, I must raise a point of logic. Why are certain internal differences specified as relevant and others as of no consequence? Ability, motivation, character—these and related qualities have been identified as rightfully leading to greater rewards and higher positions in life. Why these and not others that one might think of? For example, in a highly competitive, individualistic society organized around the central question of gains or losses in the marketplace, one might easily imagine that we would encounter straightforward, bald assertions about the desirability and social usefulness of such valuable internal traits as avarice, duplicity, selfishness, and ruthless disregard of the welfare of others. It would certainly seem logical to expect that these character traits would at least be allotted some substantial significance in explaining individual differential success in acquiring wealth and position. The opposite characteristics—lack of acquisitiveness, honesty, altruism, and empathy with others—would presumably lead to lack of success, if not outright poverty.

As we know, the early classical economists made the specific case that the society at large—or at least its material economic conditions—would best be served if each individual single-mindedly pursued his own self-interest. Through the magical workings of the "invisible hand" of the marketplace, productivity, efficiency, and wealth would increase rapidly. The feverish interaction of individuals competing selfishly, it was said, would paradoxically increase the well-being of everyone, winners and losers alike. Thus, individual self-interest, pursued as vigorously as possible, was the source of the energy that made the economy whir. The more vigorously self-interest was

followed, the healthier the economy would be. Modern mainstream economists still base their theories squarely on the assumption that all human
motivation is unitary and that it can be defined as the individual pursuit of
self-interest.

But what has happened to single-minded self-interest as a major ingredient in the theory of Fair Play meritocracy? Can you imagine Daniel Bell's
saying that a society wouldn't make sense unless its leading institutions were
headed by its most avaricious and ruthless men? It is unthinkable, because
the apologists for Fair Play are genuinely making a *moral* case for inequalities of outcome, contending they are completely congruent with principles
of justice. (Recall that Bell is advocating a *just* meritocracy.) One has a bit of
difficulty, in erecting a persuasive moral case on a foundation constructed of
a series of deadly sins—particularly when they would be valued more highly
than a parallel series of capital virtues. Given such a problem—a problem in
rhetoric, more than in anything else—two processes are required to get oneself safely within the borders of justice and morality. First, vices must be
transformed into virtues, and virtues into vices. This, as we shall see, is a
relatively simple matter, involving some changes in words. Second, the underlying economic process must be redefined so as to deemphasize the raw
and savage image of merciless, individualistic competition. The standard
remedy for this difficulty is to call on some wise men to invent a new theory.

The changing of words to solve the virtue-vice problem is a developmental
process: avarice must become drive and ambition and ultimately renamed
something like "need for achievement"; ruthlessness can first be euphemized
as single-mindedness and then transformed into perseverance; duplicity can
charitably be altered to shrewdness and foresight and then scientifically labeled "intelligence" or "talent." On the other side of the balance, honesty is
gradually changed into naiveté, which is not far removed from stupidity;
lack of avarice, when looked at from a different perspective, can emerge as
something like lack of interest, and it is not a long journey from lack of
interest to laziness. Presto chango! One has transformed vices into virtues
and virtues into vices, and the rhetorical problem is solved; the discussion
can now be begun since all the internal qualities and characteristics have
been set into their proper light.

It is never difficult to find wise men to discover new realities that lead to
a new theory. In this case the most influential ones were Kingsley Davis and
Wilbert Moore, who produced the "functionalist theory of social stratification."[28] This argument, which plays down active individualistic competition,
emphasizes a more passive process by which society (presumably using its
other "invisible hand") maximizes its own efficiency by selecting and assign-
ing individuals to the positions in society in which they would be the most
useful and do the most good. It is argued that social efficiency *requires* that
greater material rewards and higher levels of prestige be attached to the

most important and technically difficult positions, in order to induce the most able members of society to take on these challenging tasks. The argument that those with the greatest ability and willingness to exercise that ability fully deserve larger shares of the available resources and have a primary claim to positions of power and prestige lies at the core of the Fair Play argument of meritocracy—the conception that a society should be led and ruled by its most able and hardworking members. By this logic, a just society is one in which rewards and social position are perfectly correlated with the combined product of effort and ability—that is, personal merit—in which no advantage stems from birth or family status and no disadvantage results from personal characteristics such as sex or color or religious or sexual preferences, and which allows the least possible distortion of this correlation by corruption, favoritism, discrimination, nepotism, and other methods of achieving reward and position without merit. This general position is the most carefully worked out, and most widely accepted, substitute for actual equality, as Sanka is the most accepted substitute for coffee, and with a similar rationale. Equality of opportunity containing the beneficial ingredient of meritocracy is, so to speak, genuine equality less all those irritating ingredients that cause heartburn, a sour stomach, and that harsh bitter taste. And, of course, once you accept the substitute for the real thing, you will sleep more restfully.

Two questions arise: First, do the best men and women really rise to the tops of the heaps that are important to us? Is it true that the smartest and most diligent of businessmen ascend straight and sure to the presidencies of General Motors and Exxon and IBM? Are the professors who sit in the most distinguished chairs at Harvard and Yale and Chicago and Stanford really the most able and learned scholars in our land? Are our state houses and the White House and the United States Capitol populated by the wisest, most resourceful, and most far-sighted statesmen of our times?

In thinking about that, it is of some interest to note that it is the rich, not the poor, who argue most passionately that the acquisition of wealth is evidence of great ability and character. It is the governor and the senator, not the frustrated voter, who assert most vigorously that political power accrues to the wisest, most noble, and most patriotic. It is the comfortably established professor, not the struggling instructor, who is prepared to prove logically that tenure, promotion, and high salary are justly allocated to the most erudite, insightful, and brainy scholars.

The second question goes a long way toward making the first one moot: How do you tell? How would you know a meritocracy if you saw one? How do you distinguish the meritorious from the rest of us? Bell's assertion that a sensible society insures that its best men head its leading institutions is plausible and convincing. The basic problem, however, is often completely overlooked; it is assumed that the mere fact that an individual is at the head of a "leading institution" is sufficient proof that he is one of our "best men." The obvious tautology is ignored and the crucial question never asked. How does one find out just who a society's "best men" really are?

The constant use of the metaphors of the playing field or the footrace suggests that we have available something equivalent to a moral or intellectual stopwatch that can measure precisely who the best is. When the meritocrats talk about their assumptions regarding the unequal distribution of merit among mankind, they are, of course, speaking about characteristics far more complex than fleetness of foot or eye-hand coordination. Sometimes the qualities they mention are moral virtues or personality traits—persistence, diligence, capacity for hard work; at other times they are intellectual gifts or talents—foresight, good judgment about money matters, ingenuity, inventiveness, keen insight. Lately a consensus appears to be developing that intelligence is the principal index of ability or merit—more narrowly, the talk is about one's score on an intelligence test, one's IQ. Those with high IQs become justly rich and powerful and famous; those with a low IQ become, or more probably remain, poor and feckless. Bell's phrase "the best men" is generally interpreted as "the men with the highest IQs."

In the next chapter I will try to demonstrate that this touching faith in IQ tests is sadly misplaced. IQ tests—and all their descendants and relatives: personnel placement tests, Scholastic Aptitude Tests, and the like—measure something much more trivial and specialized than the quality most people have in mind when they use the word "intelligence." They certainly don't come close to measuring anything as broad as talent or ability or merit. Much of the current debate about such tests focuses on two issues that are basically irrelevant to the issue of equality. The more dramatic of these is whether or not "intelligence"—that is, the capacity to do well on IQ tests— is attributable to heredity or to environment. The answer is that, of course, intelligence is inherited; the physical basis of all human processes and behavior is necessarily based on one's genes. When certain genes are missing or abnormal, one person may be unable to learn to talk or add or walk; another may not be able to metabolize food properly and may evince symptoms of particular illness. Furthermore, the potential contained in the genes can unfold and manifest itself only in a particular environment. The productivity of corn, for example, is highly heritable. But take two batches of genetically identical corn and plant them in two different fields, one fertile, the other arid, and you will obviously get different results: the corn in the fertile field will be taller and more fruitful. Does heredity account for this height and fruitfulness? Of course. Does environment account for it? Of course.

The second dispute concerns the ways of making the inadequate existing tests better or fairer. How can we eliminate racial, ethnic, regional, and sexual biases? How can we control the advantages persons from upper-middle-class families seem to have? This dispute is a minor technical argument about the *method* of measuring individual internal qualities. Both sides of the dispute implicitly acknowledge that it is important to do so, in order to improve the efficiency of the meritocratic process.

But the issues of the heritability of intelligence and the best way to measure that quality become minor matters as soon as we recognize the basic fact that ability meters of all kinds, notably IQ tests, do *not* single out those persons who are going to be most successful and highly rewarded in their vocations. If we control for other factors, especially for social class and years of education, we find that the most successful (as indicated by such factors as earnings or occupational status) have IQs that are only a few points higher than are those of the least successful. This matter, too, I will discuss in more detail in the next chapter.

Finally, as we saw in Chapter One, a number of *external* factors have an enormous effect on one's economic status. Social mobility is quite restricted, and the relative economic position of the family one is born into is a far better predictor of one's own economic status than is the most complex array of internal traits and abilities. Whether or not the firm one works in is unionized makes a difference of 20 to 30 percent in the size of the paychecks of workers doing identical jobs. The stories of the five families in Chapter One demonstrated concretely that stability in the seas of economic life largely depends on routine events (birth, death, illness) and on unpredictable occurrences (separation or divorce, accidents, working steadily as against being periodically laid off). In addition, many differences in economic well-being and progress are dependent on simple environmental and situational facts, such as the part of the country and the sector of the economy one works in. Let me give a couple of concrete examples using established minimum union wages, beginners' wage rates, for two different occupations in diverse cities.[29] In 1975 newspaper printers in New York had a minimum union wage of $9.04 an hour, while those in Chicago got only $8.02; however, beginning truck drivers in Chicago earned $7.15 an hour, those in New York $6.53. In Philadelphia the starting wages for both occupations were almost the same ($7.04 for printers and $7.00 for truck drivers). Now, is there anyone who would expect us to believe that, by some strange twist of fate (or maybe heredity), internal differences coalesce differently in different occupations in different cities? Who would not laugh aloud at the assertion that Chicago truck drivers are more skilled and energetic than New York truck drivers, but that New York printers are more talented and ambitious than their brother union members in Chicago, while in the City of Brotherly Love the two occupational groups are equally meritorious? The most devout adherent of the Fair Play faith could not be expected to believe such an explanation. There must exist *external* reasons for these kinds of differences. Nothing else would be logical. I will also explore this issue more fully in the next chapter.

This completes the Fair Play ideology. Rewards are based on *individual* merit; individuals *differ* in merit; merit is a complex of worthy *internal* characteristics. Justice is served, according to this paradigm, when these internal individual differences correspond to the individual rewards received. External differences do not justify differential rewards. The person with a gun in his hand has an unfair advantage in competing for the wallet in his adversary's pocket. The person who happens upon a wallet full of hundred-dollar bills is not justly enriched by this lucky find; he should return it to its owner. The person who is locked out of particular competition because of color or sex or religion may justly cry "Foul" and claim that the rules of Fair Play have been broken. Only the morally and socially valued internal characteristics by which we differentiate individuals justify the ultimate inequalities of condition that those individuals experience.

This is the way the Fair Play believer thinks; this is how he perceives the workings of the social world. This, too, is the basis of his moral and pragmatic objections to the vision of Fair Shares. From these assumptions his objections to the justice and feasibility of Fair Shares arise, the kinds of objections that I briefly surveyed in Chapter One. In the next chapter, I will try to show how these objections are, in fact, based on assumptions of internal individual differences and how, furthermore, the real world shows those assumptions to be false and the consequent objections to Fair Shares to be groundless.

3

Some Hard Answers

THE CASE FOR FAIR SHARES

I You Don't Know What a Moiety Is?

The Fair Play theory rests in very large measure on the ancient principle that individual rewards should be proportionate to individual merits. Put in this abstract way, the principle elicits agreement from the overwhelming majority, although, as I tried to suggest, it is based on a series of very dubious assumptions. Sometimes Fair Players talk about "merit," sometimes about "talent" or "ability," sometimes about "character" or "thinking better." But when we try to pin down these nebulous characteristics, when we ask "What the hell *is* this trait that's supposed to be so important?" we get vague and ambiguous answers.

How are we supposed to recognize merit when we see it? How does it reveal itself? How do we go about measuring it? In recent years the meritocracy addicts have seized on intelligence as the best single index of what they are referring to. Individuals differ in respect to this internal trait called "intelligence," and those who have more of it and apply themselves diligently are the meritorious ones who get the big rewards. This provides a particularly useful answer to what merit is all about, because intelligence, it is said, reveals itself clearly in an individual's performance on an intelligence test (plausible assertion), which produces specific numbers by which individuals can be differentiated (useful, that). The IQ that emerges from the intelligence test is the superduper meritometer. You can hardly be accused of being vague and ambiguous when you are able to assert that this individual is precisely two IQ points more meritorious than that one. This is not only admirable precision, it sounds downright scientific!

It sounds very good if you don't know anything about IQ tests. I happen to know a lot about IQ tests and it's happy I am to pass on my knowledge to you. As a practicing clinical psychologist for over twenty years, I administered IQ tests to about three thousand individuals. Even after one has given the tests to only a few dozen persons—if one has given some thought and attention to what one was doing—one must already view the claim that these tests accurately measure some kind of broad inborn, intellectual capacity as simply preposterous. One reason that people speak so glibly and inanely of IQ and intelligence testing is that they literally don't know what they're talking about; that is, they don't know what intelligence tests are like, how they're given, how they're constructed, and how they're scored and interpreted. Permit me to share a bit of inside information about these matters as a way of suggesting just how feeble an instrument we are talking about, just how narrow a range of responses is grandly labeled "intelligence," not to say "merit."

I will draw most of my examples from the original adult intelligence scale constructed by David Wechsler,[1] the test with which I have had the most experience. It should be noted, however, that almost all individually administered intelligence tests are similar to one another and are clearly direct descendants of the first widely used American intelligence test, the Stanford-Binet,[2] adapted in 1916 by Stanford psychologist Louis Terman from the French instrument produced by Alfred Binet and T. H. Simon.[3] The core of the Wechsler, and of all the others, is a test of vocabulary, of the knowledge of word meanings. Words are arranged presumably in order of difficulty; actually, they are ordered according to their commonness or rarity—an easy word is a common word that almost everybody has heard and knows the meaning of; a hard word is one that virtually no one ever heard and very few have even read. It is assumed—don't ask me why—that the larger the number of rare words you can define, the smarter you are. The list starts off with words like "apple," "donkey," and "fur" and ends up with words like "chattel," "amanuensis," "moiety," and "traduce."

Now, think a little bit about this process as a way of testing innate, inborn intelligence. Is one person really born *with* the capacity to learn words like "chattel" and "moiety," and another *without* it? Furthermore, is the actual knowledge of these words merely the result of inborn braininess? What conceivable way is there of answering that question with any finality? Several things must be fairly obvious when we think about vocabulary as an index of innate intelligence. The first is that one is not, of course, born with a ready-made vocabulary; word meanings are learned. If one wishes, then, for some obscure reason, to define intelligence as the ability to learn the meaning of words, one has to say that the testing of that ability has to be limited to what has *already* been learned—one is testing actual acquired knowledge rather than some generalized capacity to obtain knowledge. And there is clearly a huge gap between some presumed innate ability of that sort and its actualization. I imagine, for example, that you or I could learn to speak, say, Russian, but what conceivable measure could there be for calculating our *innate* ability to learn the meaning of Russian words, particularly of *rare* ones?

That leads to a second important point. Even if you allow yourself to be saddled with a measure of *actualized* ability as an index of *potential* ability, how do you go about choosing samples for that measure? Why "moiety" as an index of extraordinary mental capacity, why "amanuensis," why "traduce"? True, they are rare, so rare that I doubt whether one out of a thousand readers of this book has ever spoken them aloud and more than one in a hundred has heard them from another person's mouth. They are, almost exclusively, words found in books, and you have to have read an awful lot of books that are self-consciously "literary," or ones that are thought of as "classics," in order to have a large number of such rare items in your vocabulary. A lot of writers who are considered pretty good don't play that game. I imagine you could comb through the collected works of, say, Ernest Hemingway, Saul Bellow, and Robert Lowell and not find a single "moiety" or "amanuensis" in the pile.

At this level of the vocabulary test, then, it seems much more plausible to say that you are measuring whether or not a person had a particular kind of education, whether he liked to read, or was pushed into reading, certain kinds of books, and, very likely, whether he has some kind of particular interest in and fondness for words themselves. But is this enough to assert that he is extraordinarily "intelligent"? To me, it doesn't follow. Certainly there is no ground whatsoever for saying that *not* knowing these words is an indication of *lack* of intelligence. There are dozens of reasons why you may not know what "traduce" means, only one of which is that you lack the intelligence to learn it.

What about some of the other sections of IQ tests? Again, one finds that most of them measure past learning, often with the same bias in favor of those who had a rather literary middle- or upper-class education. For example, some of the most difficult questions in the information subtest (said to be a measure of what the testee has learned about the world around him) are "Who wrote *Faust*?" "What is a *habeas corpus*?" and "What is the Apocrypha?" Now, really, is there anyone who is ready to accept that you're a very smart fellow if you know who wrote *Faust* and even smarter if you know what the Apocrypha is? But this is precisely how you build up a high IQ.

The comprehension (or "common sense") test is also very interesting in the kind of questions used, because they reflect a very clear set of values emphasizing conformity, knowledge of urban middle-class mores, and the general tendency to be a good little boy or girl. Witness the following selection: "Why should we keep away from bad company?" "Why should we save money?" "Why are laws necessary?" and "Why does land in the city cost more than land in the country?" (Why, indeed?) If you know that you should avoid the influence of bad folks, that you should save your money for a rainy day, and that laws are needed to "put people in their place," you're right—and on your way to a high IQ. But if you say that bad company gets you into trouble, that you save for yourself or your own interests, and that laws are "to make people obey—they make me obey," then you're wrong—and won't come close to heading a leading institution.

This may give some flavor of what an individually administered IQ test is like and what one has to do or not do in order to score high and be labeled as very bright. You have to have the kind of background that has exposed you to a lot of fancy words and a lot of relatively esoteric information—knowing and having something to say about Faust-type myths is one thing, but what's so brilliant about simply remembering the name of the author of a particular one? (Who wrote *Exodus*? Who wrote "A stitch in time saves nine"?) Finally, you have to be pretty well acquainted with the mainstream values of our society.

Let me try to suggest even more concretely how ludicrous it is to make judgments about intelligence and ability from these tests. Let's suppose that you and I are taking the six tests of the verbal scale of the Wechsler test. On three of the tests (which I haven't discussed), we do exactly the same, but you can define a few more words than I can (you define three of those rare words that escape me); you remember three more pieces of information than I do (for example, I say that Christopher Marlowe wrote *Faust* and get zero, you say Goethe and get full marks); and you give the right, and I the wrong, answers to three of the comprehension questions (such as the ones about bad company, saving money, and the necessity of laws). How much difference is that going to make in our "verbal IQs"? About twelve points! If the tester certifies that I have an IQ of, say, 109, he'll declare that yours is a lofty 121. In other words, on the basis of these few differences in our relative performance, I will be labeled as a person of average intelligence, and you as one of superior intelligence. (An IQ of 109 is in the average range, which is 90–110, while fewer than 10 percent of all people score as high as 120.) Add to this the facts that persons giving the test frequently make scoring errors (and just as frequently conscientiously disagree about how to score the same response) and that subjects' performances are seriously affected by their moods, their levels of anxiety or depression, their alertness or sleepiness, whether or not they like or trust the examiner, whether he acts pleasant toward them, and a host of other factors, and it becomes easy to see that IQ tests are really very unreliable instruments. It shouldn't surprise us at all that the same person will fairly often score 100 in January and 120 in June. Nor should it be surprising that one's previous education has an appreciable effect on one's IQ. And there is nothing remarkable about the fact that, if you spend a few sessions teaching kids *how to take tests* (not, of course, coaching them or exposing them to the tests themselves), you can increase their IQs by fifteen or even twenty points rather regularly.[4]

It should not be necessary to interrupt the flow of my argument at this point to clarify my own personal position, but I know from previous experience that it is. Briefly, then, I am *in favor* of everyone's having as large a vocabulary and store of information as he can acquire, and I believe that it's a good thing for more young people to know who wrote *Faust* and *Hamlet* (preferably as a result of having read these works). And, as a curmudgeon, I yield to none of my academic colleagues in the extent of my exasperation at the fact that students pursuing a liberal education read, write, spell, and reason poorly and are shockingly ignorant of the history of the Western world.

If I have allowed a note of sarcasm to slip into my description of the content of IQ tests, it is because I find ridiculous the idea of judging a person's *intelligence* by the vocabulary and information he possesses. From such items one *can* judge—and all too often deplore—that person's *education*. Being smart and being well educated are two different, though not mutually exclusive, conditions. In my judgment, it's a good thing to be educated, and it's a good thing to be smart, but learning word meanings and disembodied pieces of general information neither makes you nor marks you smart. My criticisms, then, pertain not to learning but to IQ tests, which, I have been trying to show, are not the miraculous scientific intruments for measuring merit that they are claimed to be.

All of my critical remarks—and I could make many more[5]—have to do with individually administered tests, where there is at least an opportunity of establishing rapport with the subject, of trying to create an atmosphere in which he'll be willing to try his best and be comfortable enough to do so. But only a small fraction of IQs derive from such tests; most are the results of performances on *written* tests, administered to *groups* of persons by relatively untrained persons like teachers or personnel officers; the defects described above are thus magnified manyfold.

Still, it is said that, despite all the objections, IQ tests do, in fact, *work*. They might be measuring something a lot narrower than the characteristics most people have in mind when they use the word "intelligence"; they might be badly biased by the personal and educational background of persons being tested; they might be heavily influenced by nonintellectual traits like working quickly and always trying to do as well as possible on a given task;

but, nevertheless, they have been used for decades on millions of people in schools and other institutions, and they work—they select the best men and women and the worst, they predict related kinds of behavior, and that makes them very meaningful. In other words, they are what test makers call "valid." In particular, they mark at a relatively young age those who will succeed in life, enter important occupations, make a lot of money, and, indeed, head our "leading institutions." That is what the IQ test publishers insist on, what most teachers and school administrators believe, and what a lot of psychologists say.

All of them are just wrong.

At first glance, though, they seem to be absolutely correct. Those who occupy the highest rungs of the ladder—as measured by the income or the prestige accorded to their occupations or by other signs of social rank—do indeed have higher IQs.[6] Consider IQ and income: The top fifth in income (over $30,000, in 1978) has an average IQ of about 109; the bottom fifth (below $10,000) has an average IQ of about 93. Only about one out of three of the high-earning group has a below-average IQ (less than 100), while two-thirds of the bottom group score below the midpoint. Although these average scores—93 and 109—are both well within the so-called normal range of 90 to 110, and although they are only averages (there are plenty of persons with high IQs and low income and many others with low IQs and high incomes), the overall pattern, nevertheless, does seem to support the Fair Play thesis that, by and large, the most meritorious (the high IQs) receive the most reward. How could this be explained otherwise?

Let me begin with an analogy that shows a similar pattern. Tall people, on the average, wear larger shoes than do short people. Those over six feet would have an average shoe size of, say, 10½; those under five feet six inches an average size of, say, 8½. Does shoe size *cause* height? (Analogous question: does high IQ cause high income?) Of course not, we say immediately, *shoe* size is only a sign of *foot* size. (As they say, IQ is a sign of something they call "intelligence.") All right, then, does foot size cause height? (Does "intelligence" cause high income?) Obviously not. It is a corollary or an accompaniment to height, but foot size has no greater influence on height than has shoe size. (Only the brassiest con man would attempt to sell a short man big shoes with the argument that they would make him grow taller.)

I will try to show that, in a very similar fashion, a high IQ goes along with higher income in a general way, but that it has no *causal* effect. In order to understand why this is so, we have to introduce two additional items of information—the extent of one's education and the economic status of one's family. Children from well-to-do families tend to get higher scores on various kinds of intelligence and aptitude tests (for example, the mean family income in 1974 for students scoring in the 750–800 range on the Scholastic

Aptitude Test was $24,124; for those in the 550–600 range, it was $19,481; for those in the 450–500 range, $18,122; and for those in the 200–250 range, $8,639).[7] Those children go further in school, very frequently through college. They then get better jobs and earn higher incomes. The careers of children from low-income families present the opposite face of the same coin. So, there is no question that test scores, the economic status of one's family, the number of years of one's education, and one's own income are all related. The problem comes in sorting out what causes what. This is particularly difficult because the facts seem to lend themselves so naturally to the Fair Play fairy stories.

Let's start by looking at the apparent effect of education on income. In 1972 adult males twenty-five and over with a college degree had an average income of $16,200; those with only a high school diploma earned $10,400.[8] It would appear that education pays off financially. But it is not at all clear that it is education as learning or improving skills that accounts for the effect. Note that it is years of schooling, not grades, that count—it's how long you stay in school, not how well you do there. The result, curiously enough, is that a college graduate with a C− average will usually do much better in regard to job and income than will his roommate who dropped out after his junior year with an A− average. With a few exceptions (such as the need for higher grades to get into medical school), it appears to be the *diploma* rather than the *education* that does the trick. How does IQ fit into this picture? If we take two groups with exactly the same IQs and find that those in the first group graduate from college, while the education of those in the second stops after they finish high school, we discover essentially the same income differences that prevail in the overall population.[9] (Remember that the two groups have the *same* IQ.) Of the first group, more than half would be making more than $30,000 a year; of the second, fewer than one in five would be making that much.[10] In other words, a college diploma all by itself gives a person over two and one-half times the chance of earning a high income as does a high school diploma. Put as simply as possible, the more years you stay in school, the more income you are likely to earn—no matter what your IQ is!

But, the Fair Players would say to all this, you're not being fair; you're diddling with the data. After all, it's the young people with high IQs who graduate from college; so, when you take college graduation into account, you're also taking IQ into account. Maybe so. Again, at first glance, it might look that way. For example, a 1972 study by the Department of Health, Education, and Welfare found that when a population of young people is divided into four ability groups, among those in the top group (roughly equivalent to an SAT score above 575) four out of five go on to higher education, while among the bottom group (approximately those with SAT scores below 425) only about three in ten go on.[11] The Fair Play apologists would argue that the effect of IQ (merit) on income (reward) is worked out through the intermediate meritocratic institution of education, as Fair Play theory would naturally predict. Bright kids get more education, find better jobs, and earn more money. Right? Wrong.

This is where the economic status of one's family comes into the picture. The same study shows that of children from families earning less than $8,000 a year, about one in six was attending a four-year college; of those from families earning more than $18,000 a year, about one in two was attending college.[12] This information can be combined with the well-known findings of Project Talent regarding the combined effect of ability and economic status.[13] Briefly, this study found that, at four different ability levels, those in the top quarter economically were from two to five times more likely to go to college than those from the bottom quarter. For example, among youngsters in the bottom quarter of the population in ability (approximately, IQ below 90), about one out of four from the well-to-do families went to college anyway, as compared to a tiny handful of those from the poorest group who did so. Even among those in the highest ability group (IQ over 110), the richer kids were twice as likely to go to college—over 80 percent as against about 40 percent. Again, we see that "intelligence" plays a very minor role in this imaginary merit-reward scenario.

The basic facts can be boiled down in a couple of different ways. Bowles and Gintis have calculated what the effect of pure IQ, so to speak, on income would be, if IQ were the only force at work—that is, if the effect of one's family background and one's education were removed. They estimated the probabilities that persons from various IQ groups will be in the top 20 percent of income recipients. Obviously, the overall chance for everybody is 20 percent. Those with IQs of 120 or higher would have about a 21 percent chance; those with IQs of 80 or lower would have about a 19 percent chance.[14] A difference of forty IQ points would improve your chance of earning a high income by 2 percent. This can be put another way: given two groups, one relatively poor, one relatively well off, both with exactly the same educational level, we would find that the poor kids with IQs over 120 would earn just about as much as the rich kids with IQs below 80. In other words, if you're a youngster from a poor family who doesn't go to college, with a high IQ and a quarter you can buy a Hershey bar anywhere in the country.

Where does all this leave the meritocracy theory? With regard to IQ as a measure of merit, certainly, the theory is left high and dry. It simply doesn't hold in real life. A young person's earnings can be predicted best by knowing, first, his or her family's economic status and, second, the amount of education obtained, that is, the number of years he or she was able to stay in school (which is also highly dependent on one's family's income). If you also know the youngster's IQ, it will improve your prediction of his or her income so little as to be hardly noticeable.

The only possible way that a Fair Play advocate can retain his faith in the idea that IQ is of any significance with respect to rewards and income is to take the ultimate hard-line position, which maintains that the children of the rich really are more talented, smarter, and more meritorious than are those of the poor. Such a state of affairs could be explained logically only by claiming that these various signs of "merit" are, in fact, hereditary—that rich kids inherit "merit" in much the same way that young barons and dukes in the Middle Ages inherited "nobility." Then we would be engaged in a completely different dispute, which would, I think, divert us from the points I am trying to make here. That controversy has been well analyzed and argued elsewhere by others.[15]

At this point, I will say only that if the Fair Play argument has to include some assertion about hereditary intelligence, it has moved quite a distance from the image of everyone's lining up together at the starting line and enjoying an equal opportunity to win the race.

II   VIRTUE IS ITS OWN REWARD, ALAS

Before the current love affair with IQ tests, definitions and conceptions of who were the best, the most meritorious, or the most able were somewhat broader. Joseph Schumpeter, for example, attributed much of the vigorous explosion in productivity that accompanied the capitalistic system of production, and the consequent industrial revolution in the nineteenth century, to the fact that the early pioneer entrepreneurs were what he called "supernormal," but he did not mean simply that these men had high IQs.[16] He had a broader sense of superiority in mind, as did most others who perceived relationships between wealth and extraordinary personal characteristics. These traits, though definitely internal in nature, go beyond narrow intellectual abilities and include elements of character, temperament, and personality.

What are the aspects of character and temperament that are supposed to account for success, achievement, and the occupation of positions at the head of leading institutions? One necessary characteristic that seems to receive a lot of attention is a *desire* to achieve, to get ahead, to be successful—drive, ambition, motivation. Another is perseverance, stamina, or a capacity to persist over a long period of time, to keep a distant goal in mind, and to keep pushing toward that goal. A third is the capacity to plan ahead, to conserve one's resources, to be thrifty and economical, and to have good judgment about what one should do next and for the several moves beyond that.

This complex of personality traits is, I would hope, readily recognizable to the reader. We have reached a general consensus in this society that the most successful competitors, in addition to being smart, also possess the personality traits of ambition, planfulness, thrift, and the like. To reinforce this notion, we have also established a mirror image of this stereotype, picturing the unsuccessful, the poor, and the failures in the competition as apathetic, flighty, and unable to think beyond the present moment and its potential for pleasure.

So we must consider the possibility that, even if the equation of IQ with merit is untenable, the general theory that superiority of internal characteristics is an explanation of and justification for inequality could be adequately demonstrated by appealing to the data concerning these items of character and motivation. The idea, then, would be that the ambitious, planful, thrifty, achievement-oriented person would translate these character traits into equivalent actions and that these actions would lead to success.

This particular version of the leading-men theory of meritocracy has now been thoroughly tested in real life, and the sober conclusion has been reached that it is simply not correct. The test was carried out as part of the study of five thousand families that I have referred to.[17] A major part of this mammoth research project was an effort, first, to measure in great detail many of these attitudinal and behavioral characteristics and, second, to see to what extent they were related to economic position and to economic advancement.

The designers of the study carefully assessed a whole series of attitudes, characteristics, and behaviors that fall into this ambition-thrift-planfulness complex.[18] They measured achievement motivation. They had a number of questions to measure what they called "aspiration ambition" and others to measure "personal sense of efficacy," "future orientation," "economizing behavior," "real earning acts," and so forth. The study was a carefully constructed, large-scale, precisely aimed assessment of these ideas, such as had never been approached in the fragmented and often contradictory research that had preceded it. Five thousand families, made up of tens of thousands of individuals, were followed over a period of years (eight years' worth of data have been published at the time I write this), and the economic status and the economic progress or decline of this huge sample were followed in exhaustive detail. The data were subjected to incredibly detailed and complex alternative statistical procedures, so that every drop of possible information was squeezed out.

The results were quite clear. They indicated no relationship between attitudinal, characterological, and behavioral traits and economic position. The traits were distributed in essentially the same proportions among rich and poor. There was, furthermore, no relationship between the presence or absence of these traits and whether one did or did not achieve economic progress; they were distributed in the same proportions among winners and losers. So, although there is undeniable variation among individuals in regard to these traits—some are more ambitious than others, some thriftier—these differences bear no relationship whatever to their economic fates.

The authors of the study, in their report of the results of the first five years of data, write,

> We have not been able to find much evidence that people's attitudes or behavior patterns affect the trends in their well-being . . . (f)or public policy purposes and for arguments about the extent to which we could reduce dependency in our society by changing the behavior and attitudes of dependent members, the findings certainly do not encourage expectations that such change would make much difference.[19]

After the seventh year, they pretty much decided to give up the search for what was apparently not there. No matter how hard they looked, the results were overwhelmingly negative.[20]

Internal individual differences of this type, then, have no appreciable influence on whether or not those who seek their fortune do in fact find it. For every ambitious rich man, there are scores of ambitious men who never made it. For every wealthy family congratulating itself on how well it anticipated the future and constructed well-laid plans, there are dozens of families still wondering why their visions never came true. For every thrifty millionaire, there are a thousand thrifty paupers.

It is the externals that make a difference, most notably the wealth or poverty, the race, and the color of one's family. Beyond that, the expected vicissitudes of life—the lost jobs, the accidents, the illnesses, the early deaths—most clearly impede the struggle for economic progress.

It's certainly a good thing to have a good character, to be strong and upright, prudent and thrifty, and thoughtful of the future. These are all wonderful virtues, but we must learn to enjoy them for their own sake—they will not make us rich.

III   THE STUPIDITY PROBLEM

The Fair Play appeal to *justice*, on the basis of the individual–merit–individual–reward argument, is difficult to hang on to, I believe, in view of the knowledge we have about IQ tests and character traits, as outlined in the preceding two sections. But the same formulation can essentially be turned upside down and an argument made, no longer on the basis of justice, but on the basis of *social efficiency.* Anything like the kind of Fair Shares arrangements that I have suggested would produce, they say, a terribly inefficient society. This is the central proposition of Davis and Moore's functionalist explanation of why inequality is necessary in order for a society of any complexity to function.[21] Their reasoning can briefly be recapitulated: (1) social efficiency requires that the most able persons be recruited to fill the most important positions; (2) to this end, society must attach significantly higher rewards to these positions; and (3) it must join extra rewards to positions that require rare talent and prolonged training, in order to give the talented an incentive to undergo the necessary training. This train of logic is not implausible. Certainly, few would take the stance that, with respect to socially crucial occupations, competence is not desirable. And we are so used to thinking that material rewards and incentives are the most effective way of making happen that which ought to happen that we scarcely notice this element of the argument.

At the risk of seeming a bit repetitious, I would like to point out that we here encounter, once again, the extreme emphasis on the importance of individuals in specific situations and the equally extreme stress on the significance of differences among them—ideas about "talent," "competence," and "ability" are central to this argument, and the detection of individual differences in these qualities becomes a matter of vital concern.

Additional underlying assumptions can readily be derived: first, that the primary human motivation to work is the acquisition of material rewards; second, that persons occupying the most highly rewarded, and therefore presumably most important, positions do, in fact, perform with a high degree of competence; and, third, that a direct correlation can be discovered between the level of rewards attached to a particular position and its social importance (some additional variation being accounted for by the amount of talent or training, or both, required in order to perform its functions). Obviously, no one claims that this theoretically ideal state of affairs actually exists in pure form. But, after granting that there are all kinds of anomalies, imperfections, and distortions in real life, many nevertheless assert that this pattern is followed in some approximate way and, most important, that its working out makes absolutely necessary a definite hierarchical structure.

Let us consider these assumptions one at a time. If we rank positions according to their social importance, will we find that those of greatest social usefulness are indeed granted the highest rewards? The big problem that becomes immediately apparent is how to define "social usefulness." If we confined ourselves to extreme examples, we could probably achieve a high level of consensus. There would be very little dispute, I think, about the proposition that a physician is more socially useful than a burglar, a United States congressman more valuable than a sidewalk pitchman, or a research chemist more important than a bartender. But which of the three "more useful" persons—the doctor, the representative, or the chemist—is *most* useful? Is there a way of ranking them? Could people agree on that ranking?

One way of trying to solve this problem is to ask a large sample of persons to make these very distinctions, to evaluate occupations and positions in relation to one another. Such studies have been done, and a particular study by the National Opinion Research Center, in which ninety occupations were evaluated by a very large sample, is often used as the model for this approach.[22] The resulting rankings seem to approximate what the functionalist theoreticians refer to when they talk about social value. For example, physicians and scientists are among the top ten, bartenders and janitors are among the bottom ten, and electricians and newspaper reporters are among the middle ten. Moreover, there is some gross relationship between the relative ranking of an occupation and the average income of persons in it. This relationship is by no means overwhelmingly obvious, however; nor does it necessarily support the functionalist theory—it is perfectly possible that knowledge about the relative average incomes attached to different occupations could, in fact, influence the evaluations of those occupations. There are many striking exceptions that raise interesting questions. Let me give a few examples.

Physicians (ranked 2nd in the NORC's ninety-occupation scale) and college professors (7th) would seem to be roughly at the same level of social value, and they require about the same amount of education and training, yet physicians, on the average, earn more than twice as much as professors. Similar comparisons can be made for ministers (14th) and dentists (17th), welfare workers (46th) and undertakers (47th), and many other anomalous pairs. On the other hand, we find that architects (15th) have approximately the same average income as policemen (55th).

This kind of information does not seem to fit very neatly into the functionalist view of how the world works. One possible reason for this is that the evaluative scales themselves are not actually judgments of "social value." They are, in fact, more often referred to as measures of "prestige," which may well be an entirely different quality. We might then say, for example, that although architects have higher prestige than policemen, policemen really are judged very useful, as their salary indicates. In addition, two of the three lowest-ranked positions—"garbage collector" and "street sweeper"— are of extremely high social utility. In a modern city the sanitation worker is virtually indispensable, as has been demonstrated on several occasions when such workers felt compelled to go on strike.

There is another problem with the equation of occupational reward with occupational usefulness. In most occupations, there is a tremendous spread in the rewards *within* the occupation itself.[23] If we are able somehow to come to terms with the idea that the social value of physicians in general is more than twice that of professors in general, how do we account for the fact that physicians in different parts of the country have significantly different average incomes?[24] In the East South Central States (Tennessee, Kentucky, Mississippi, and Alabama) physicians earn on the average 25 percent more than do physicians in New England; this would seem to suggest that a physician in Memphis or Louisville is somehow significantly more valuable to society than is his colleague in Boston or New Haven. On the face of it, this seems a bit strange. One would think that New England, with its famous medical schools and treatment centers, would have a supply of unusually skilled doctors and that these would be, almost by definition, quite socially valuable. Yet, when one strains these facts through the functionalist theory, it appears that persons who come from all over the world to Boston to get medical treatment are making a serious error; they apparently should be heading for Natchez or Mobile. There is, of course, a more plausible explanation, namely, that the physician in Birmingham is not, in fact, more socially valuable than his colleague in Providence in any rational sense. He is simply scarcer. In those states where physicians are so much more prosperous, the proportion of doctors to the population is only 60 percent of what it is in New England. It is not that the invisible hand of Tennessee society has parceled out high rewards to its socially valuable physicians; rather, the physician controls a commodity, medical care, that people want and need and he makes them pay handsomely for it.

If this were all that is meant by "social value," it would be easy to make the case. For example, a famous movie star or a great professional athlete is clearly "worth" a million dollars a year to his or her employer when the latter can take the former's talent and performance and sell them as a commodity for two million dollars. But is that all we mean by *social* value? The lawyers who successfully defended the Ford Motor Company against charges of criminal homicide in connection with the deaths resulting from the allegedly negligent placement of gasoline tanks in Pinto cars probably earn ten, twenty, or thirty times what lawyers working as public defenders receive for defending indigent citizens against similar charges of criminal homicide. As I write this the verdict has come in—not guilty. Doubtless, that verdict was worth the million dollars or more that Ford paid for it. A more common example from the same realm is the corporation lawyer who knows the statutes governing taxes, mergers, and so forth and who may use his knowledge and training to insure his corporate employers profits of an extra million dollars or so a year. He is thus "worth" his $200,000 salary and is clearly at least ten times more valuable than a legal services attorney who forestalls an unjust eviction or helps a battered wife escape her husband's attentions. But the question is not vaguely about who is worth what. The specific question is, To *whom* is the corporation lawyer worth $200,000 a year? To society at large? To you and me? Or only to that corporation?

Just as the Memphis doctor earns more because the medical care market in his town is such that he can charge more, so the "value" of the movie star and the highly paid lawyer is contingent on their presumed contributions to the profits of the firms that employ them. When the time comes to negotiate their fees or salaries, their value to society at large is, to say the least, irrelevant.

There is another aspect of geographical variability in incomes that I mentioned briefly in Chapter Two, illustrated by the average salaries of high school teachers, which in 1979 ranged from $11,400 in Arkansas and Mississippi to $18,700 in New York (and a munificent $24,200 in Alaska).[25] One response to this information is to say that salaries are higher everywhere than in Arkansas and Mississippi, or something to that effect. But how do we explain salaries of $18,700 in New York as against $15,500 next door in Connecticut? And $18,300 in California, $18,000 in Washington, but only $15,200 in Oregon, in the middle of the sandwich? Or $18,000 in Michigan but only $14,600 in neighboring Ohio? A common explanation for these kinds of variations is the "cost of living" (which, of course, doesn't explain anything); but, in any case, one can demonstrate that the cost of living does not have much to do with the kind of geographical variation I am referring to. For example, in the city of Houston, wages are in general very low. In October of 1978, for instance, the average city employee in Houston earned $1,223. In Detroit—a city of approximately the same size and level of cost of living—the corresponding city worker got a check in October for $1,688.[26] What price "social value"? Or is there some other possible explanation?

Consider union membership. In Michigan, as of 1976, approximately 33 percent of the work force was unionized; in Texas only 12 percent was.[27] Does that suggest anything? Or, going back to state variations in teachers' salaries, note that in each case the state with the higher unionization rate had the higher teachers' salaries, the average difference in the rates being 25 percent.[28] To me this implies that the *balance of power* between workers and employers differs considerably from one part of the country to another and that in areas where employers have more control they can get away with paying lower salaries and wages. There's nothing complicated about all this, and I would hazard a guess that a mainstream economist would offer the same kinds of explanations that I have offered and would consider the functionalist theory of the iron law of hierarchy to be just as much of a pipe dream as I do.

So much for the high-rewards-for-the-socially-useful argument. It cannot be justified by the facts unless one makes the circular assertion that high rewards are themselves a *measure* of social usefulness. The next assumption requires us to jump over the fence and look at the picture from the other side. Do persons in high positions perform in that "supernormal" way that the theory requires them to? We can begin at the top of one heap—with the

presidency, a position most of us would rank relatively high in social importance. How are we to fit into the theory all those towering statemen who
have been selected for the office, men like Franklin Pierce, James Buchanan,
Ulysses S. Grant, Rutherford Hayes, Warren Harding, Calvin Coolidge? In
these cases, did the machinery for selecting the "best men" go out of whack
for a bit? In the year when an obvious dunce like Harding was elected
president, there must have been literally tens of millions of persons more
qualified than he by any measure. And how are we to explain what happened in 1972, when, in one of the greatest shows of consensus since the
selection of George Washington, we chose a moral imbecile like Richard
Nixon? Over the long run, it would be hard to dispute the judgment that the
average president (and his average defeated opponent) has been a man of
ordinary ability and mediocre character. (In the recent election—won by
Reagan or lost by Carter depending on your viewpoint—the appalling medi-
ocrity of the available major candidates was a matter of great public concern
and discussion.) However one chooses to explain this fact, it seems to me
that the history of the presidency is, by itself, a powerful argument against
the "best men" theory of the functionalists.

This is one example of what is, in truth, a major social problem that exists
in societies that choose to wrap themselves in the mantle of Counterfeit
Equality. I refer to the stupidity problem. Things constantly go wrong in our
daily lives in the midst of a society that is supposed to be so efficient.
Telephones suddenly go dead in our hands or bring us into unwanted contact with a puzzled housewife in Dayton when we try to call our Aunt Sally
in Detroit. Department store computers insist that we have made enormous
purchases and owe them appalling sums, and they will not listen to our
desperate denials. Occasionally, one of us will request an income tax refund
for $108.60 and receive a genuine Treasury check for $108,600,000. One-
page letters in envelopes of standard size and shape are delivered across
town eleven days after we drive down to the post office to mail them. Brilliant engineers design huge networks of completely unobstructed, high-speed
expressways that instantly produce traffic jams a mile or two long, with
automobiles creeping trunk to tail like a parade of tired elephants. If we buy
a brand-new car created by the industrial geniuses of Detroit, the odds are
about even money that it will shortly be recalled to have one or more disas-
trous design errors corrected. It seems like a monthly ritual to read that yet
another foolproof nuclear reactor, like the one at Three Mile Island, has
gone wild and brought matters to the verge of disaster. And each time that
Detroit or Harrisburg or some other city is saved in the nick of time from
complete destruction, it is difficult not to recall the smug and smiling faces
of the designers and shipbuilders that one can see in photographs of the
launching of the unsinkable Titanic. Endless lists of tragic blunders can be
set forth—from the Charge of the Light Brigade to the marketing of thalid-

omide—confidently executed by persons certified beyond question as extremely competent and therefore entirely fit for their positions of social importance.

We can still shudder at the thought of the Vietnamese War, which we fought, as David Halberstam has told us so vividly,[29] under the tutelage of, supposedly, the best and the brightest men of our generation, who carefully, methodically, and confidently drew us step by step into one of the most insane horrors of our history. Every president, from the beginning to the end of that nightmare, was up to his arse in advisers who were outstanding Ivy League professors, brilliant West Point geniuses, and the wisest of elder statesmen. Talk about your best men and leading institutions! These collections of geniuses made one recommendation after another that was totally wrong and incredibly stupid. Year after year, endless streams of military, diplomatic, and political leaders, experts first class, with forests of oak-leaf clusters, flew to Saigon and returned smiling, reassuring us about "light at the end of the tunnel."

Another case, more remote in time but equally illustrative, was the boom and bust of the 1920s that culminated in the stock market crash of 1929 and the Great Depression of the 1930s. There was the same kind of unanimous optimism among the experts. Not only all the leading bankers and brokers, but also all the great economists in the best universities, lacked the vaguest idea of what was really going on and were, as late as 1932, still agreeing with Herbert Hoover's pathetic insistence that prosperity was just around the corner. At the same time, any man on the street could look around any corner and see men in bread lines and know immediately that we were in the midst of the worst economic disaster in our history.

This aspect of the stupidity problem—the plain fact that so many of our leading men are, at best, only marginally more competent than the average person, and, at worst, downright incompetent—is the direct result of our misplaced faith in tests, in the "proving ground of education," and in other formal and informal methods of picking out the "best men." As we have seen, what these selection devices actually do is to pick out the children of the well-to-do, without at the same time measuring very much that has to do with competence. We should not be surprised, then, that most important positions of great "social value" are occupied by children of the well-to-do and that the duties of these positions are so often performed rather ineptly.

Even if we could really find the mythical "most competent persons" in order to fill the "most important" positions, only the smaller portion of the stupidity problem would be solved. The larger part, the major cause of the stupidity problem, is the deliberate waste of intelligence. For purposes of control and tight management, most institutions are organized so that most decisions are made at higher levels, with very little input from lower levels. Persons at these lower levels are, therefore, contributing to the processes of the institutions only a small fraction of their abilities, their ingenuity, their intelligence. At each level, one person thinks and decides for a number of other persons—directly embodying the ideological emphasis on the overriding importance of the individual. In each instance, the probability is quite low that the decider is significantly more able than those for whom he is deciding. More important, the *collective* wisdom and ability of the latter are largely lost. (They are not completely lost, because, in practice, groups of workers usually develop informal methods of circumventing and revising the more stupid instructions and decisions of their supervisors.) This method of organization is, logically, *less* rather than more efficient. It consciously sacrifices efficiency in order to maintain close control of the processes of the organization and the power of those in charge. The myth of the superior competence of those in the higher positions is only a cover story to distract us from the truth.

Finally, we come to the assumption about incentive—that the principal motivation to work is material reward (and accompaniments like social status). To use a commonly cited example, if we want well-qualified persons to go through all the bother of becoming physicians, we must make the material goal at the end of the process quite substantial.

This is a curious theory psychologically, rather like a primitive version of behaviorist learning theory, which holds that behavior is determined by the "reinforcements" (rewards and punishments) that are the consequences of behavior. Probably the most widely known example of this general type of learning theory is that of Pavlov's experiments in which he trained dogs to salivate at the sound of a bell. A hungry dog will salivate when presented with food. If one consistently associates the sound of a bell with the presentation of food, the dog will "learn," or be conditioned, to salivate when the bell is rung without the food. The application of this paradigm in functionalist theory would go something like this: The human being is motivated to enter an occupation in order to gain material reward (the counterpart of the dog food); if we associate material reward with the idea of becoming a physician (ringing the bell), he will learn to want to become one. As the dog associates food with the bell, so the human associates getting rich with becoming a physician and is thereby properly motivated for a medical career.

There are problems with this notion. First of all, we must remember that the hungry dog doesn't salivate when he hears the bell because he likes bells—he probably couldn't care less about bells. He salivates because he likes food, and the bell gives him the notion that food is on the way. If we apply this principle literally, we would have to conclude that persons who become physicians like money a lot but are basically indifferent to the practice of medicine. This may be logical but it doesn't square with experience. Young people who want to become physicians clearly have a specific motive to engage in healing, to practice medicine, although, of course, many of them may *also* be attracted by the associated rewards. If this weren't true, young people wouldn't care whether they became well-off lawyers, well-off business managers, or well-off car salesmen—anything with a big payoff would do fine, thank you. In fact, of course, young people have very definite and specific ideas of what they want to do vocationally, and their ideas are based, not only on the money involved, but also on their interests, on what they find absorbs and engages them, and on what they enjoy.

Within occupations we often find, for example, that many of the "best" medical students will choose to pursue a relatively unrewarding research career rather than to go into practice and make a lot of money. Outstanding law students often turn down offers from prestigious firms to join a legal services agency and practice poverty law. To go back to an example cited in Chapter One, it obviously took *no* material incentive to persuade Einstein to think. He produced his most influential and revolutionary work when he was employed full time as a patent office clerk.

Material rewards *do* seem to be necessary, not to attract people to do "important" jobs, but to get them to do dull and uninteresting ones that make very little use of their abilities. Not that all the so-called important jobs always require much ability, either. A great many highly paid executive and professional jobs are not particularly difficult, and the conditions of work connected with them often demand little effort or product. They are *easy* jobs, and most people would be willing (and able) to do them for half the salary. In his recent book *The Credential Society*, Randall Collins demonstrates very convincingly the reality of these and other facts of hierarchical life and concludes:

> The great majority of all jobs can be learned through practice by almost any literate person. The number of esoteric specialties "requiring" unusually extensive training or skill is very small. . . .
>   We have elaborated a largely superfluous structure of more or less easy jobs, full of administrative makework and featherbedding. . . .[30]

The social efficiency argument sounds plausible, because it resonates so well to the dominant assumptions about internal individual differences. But, when we set aside these assumptions and look at reality, we discover that the facts bear no relationship to this theory. The social-efficiency argument, then, is just another cover story for, and distraction from, the reality that America's economic, social, and political life is dominated by a small minority. It is efficient only in the sense that it preserves the property, power, and privilege of that minority. In any other sense, it is grossly wasteful. And it is shockingly inefficient, to the point of threatening, all too often, the health, safety, and well-being of millions.

The functionalist argument holds, implicitly, that social hierarchy and vast inequalities are necessary to solve a problem, the *imaginary* problem of the stupidity of the ordinary person. The real stupidity problem is to be found, not at the base of the inequality pyramid, but at its apex and, more important, in the nature of the individual-oriented organization of all our institutions. It can be solved only by reclaiming and using the individual and collective talents and wisdom of the vulnerable majority that are now running down the drain unused. And only a society following the principle of Fair Shares, rather than the illusions of Fair Play, can salvage this waste and solve the stupidity problem in America.

IV   MINE, ALL MINE

So far, I have tried to demonstrate that the ideas that cluster around such notions as meritocracy, distributive justice, and social efficiency, which form the core of the ideology of Counterfeit Equality, rest, not on any factual basis, but rather on the unsupported belief in internal individual differences among human beings. The function of this ideology is to justify and prop up the domination that a tiny minority of the very rich exercise over the rest of us. The arguments of the Fair Players, which I tried to refute in the preceding sections, would have us believe that the wealthy, because they are superior individuals, have justifiably enriched themselves and that their continued domination astride the peak of the inequality pyramid is not only fair but is really beneficial to all the rest of us. The social institution that makes this possible is the modern conception of relatively unrestricted private ownership and accumulation of wealth-producing property. To accept this conception of private property, one must believe quite strongly that the individual is supremely important and that the talents of the superior lead naturally and inevitably to the acquisition of wealth. In other words, the constant insistence on the importance of "I" (and the complementary insignificance of "we") is accompanied by a parallel insistence on the *necessity* of "my" and "mine."

If "I" have a great deal and you have nothing, it is simply to restate the obvious to insist that *my* treasures are *mine*, to explain that I got them as a consequence of my superior individual traits and actions and thereby obtained the right to keep them. And, of course, your nothing is yours—that's what you got from your individual efforts.

If I take the trouble to locate a promising plot of land, to buy a drill rig, and to dig for oil, the oil that emerges from the earth is *mine*, and if you want some, you have to get it from me. If the textile mill is *mine*, then its profits are mine; if your hands on the loom are yours, they are worth what they can bring. At this level, relations are between individuals only, and the main issue to be settled is what is mine and what is yours. Historical perspective of any kind is taboo. Broader questions are not even asked: How did the oil get there in the first place? How did you get there? Where are the people who used to be there? Where did you get the money to buy or lease the land and to buy the rigging? None of these questions are deemed relevant; we concern ourselves with the individual in the present.

It was the individual who built the mill, bought the machinery, hired the hands, taught them what to do, and sold the cloth they made. The wealth that accumulates from that process is his and his alone, to do with as he pleases. Similarly, the oil man did it all himself—found the oil, wrested it from the earth, and sold it. The money is his. It *belongs* to him.

Such assumptions about humanity and human nature imply that life is a competition of each individual against all others, and one of the necessary— and, indeed, desirable—consequences is that the most able do well and can say, "Mine, all mine." Others, less able, look at what they have won and see nothing.

But how does it really get to be *yours* or *mine*? What do we mean when we say that he *owns* it or that it *belongs* to him? How do you get to own something? Well, you usually buy it. But how did the fellow you bought it from get to own it? Where did the idea of *owning* come from? Or was it always there, perhaps in the mind of God?

No one really knows, of course. The idea of owning and property emerged in the mists of unrecorded history. One can try to imagine the scene. Some Cro-Magnon innovator, seized with a fit of entrepreneurial passion, took his club and drew a line in the earth and called out, "Okay, you guys! Everything inside this line is mine. It belongs to me. I own it." Now, very likely, this first would-be landowner was a skinny, little, near-sighted Cro-Magnon who couldn't throw a spear straight and was able to drag by the hair only the homeliest girls of the tribe. A couple of his fellow cavemen may have kicked sand in his face, but most of the others probably laughed indulgently, kidding him about his intellectual pretensions, his ways of using big words like "belong" and "own" that nobody else knew the meaning of. "That Herman! A regular walking dictionary!" And they rubbed out Herman's line on the ground. (I am counting on a fair amount of good humor among the Cro-Magnons; another telling of the story might assume more malevolence and end with their rubbing out Herman himself.)

But, as we all know, a good idea never dies, and sooner or later a hefty, well-respected caveman who carried a big club picked up Herman's notion, drew his own line in the earth, and made his claim stick. Others drew their lines, taking possession of the land merely by outlining its boundaries, and then talked about what they owned and what belonged to them. The forcible seizure of what had been until then common property, if property at all, led first to emulation, as others also seized portions of land, and ultimately to the development of ideas and relationships that could be thought to coincide with the new reality. Rather than having men who had the muscle power to seize and men who had not, we had landowners and the landless; instead of loot from the seizure, we had "property," then property laws by the chapter, and finally the revelation that the institution of private property had been ordained by God. These concepts—landowner, property, and property rights—became common currency, unquestioned and unquestionable ideas, as natural and expected as the sunrise or as water flowing downhill, which we take for granted and don't give another thought. And that is the central nature of ideology.

If you do stop and think about it, it's quite remarkable. An individual human being, occupying a blip on the screen of time, has the incredible gall to stand up and say, "*I* own this land; this land is *mine.*" He's talking about an acre or a hundred acres of the *earth*, a piece of the *planet*! And he says it's *his*! Isn't that really an incredible claim to make?

And he doesn't just say he owns the earth, he also says that he owns what comes out of it and what is buried beneath it. The owner of the land lays claim to the grain and the grass that spring up from it and to the cattle that feed on the grain and the grass. He lays claim to the oil and the iron that lie beneath the ground and then to the steel made from the iron and to the automobile made from the steel and to the gasoline made from the oil. He counts as his property the tree that grows on the land and the wood of the tree and the buildings on the land made from the wood. He *owns* those things, he says; they *belong* to him. And we all act as if it were true, so it must be true. But behind all these claims, supporting and upholding them— and our willingness to believe them—is the big club of the hefty Cro-Magnon who made the first claim and dared his fellows to oppose him. The club is smaller and neater now, hanging from the belt of the policeman, but the principle remains the same.

Is it possible that the ideas we have today about ownership and property rights have been so universal in the human mind that it is truly as if they had sprung from the mind of God? By no means. The ancient Jews, for one, had a very different outlook on property and ownership, viewing it as something much more temporary and tentative than we do. Mosaic law with respect to ownership of land (the only significant productive property of the time) is unambiguous:

> And the land shall not be sold in perpetuity; for the land is Mine; for ye are strangers and settlers with Me. And in all the land of your possession ye shall grant a redemption for the land. (Lev. 25:23–24)

The buying and selling of land was based on principles very different from those we know. It was not, in fact, the land itself that changed hands, but rather the right to use the land to cultivate crops. The price of the land was determined by the number of years, and therefore the number of crops, remaining until the next jubilee year, when the land reverted to the family that originally possessed it. Under such a law, buying land is similar to the process we call leasing.

The institution of the jubilee year was a specific mechanism for rectifying the inequities that had accumulated, for simultaneously restoring liberty *and* equality for all:

> And ye shall hallow the fiftieth year, and proclaim liberty throughout the land unto all the inhabitants thereof; it shall be a jubilee unto you; and ye shall return every man unto his possession, and ye shall return every man unto his family. (Lev. 25:10)

There is no doubt that these laws were violated. Prophet after prophet condemned as violations efforts to accumulate wealth unjustly:

> Woe unto them that join house to house, that lay field to field, till there be no place, that they may be placed alone in the midst of the earth! (Isaiah, 5:8)

But that the law was violated and the violation condemned is a demonstration of its existence and applicability. Although the law of jubilee was evaded more and more and ultimately fell into disuse, there can be no doubt that it was adhered to for many generations.

Similarly, the tenure of land in the agrarian feudal ages was hedged all about with restrictions and accompanied by specific obligations that the landowner owed to his tenants. These restrictions and obligations, too, were frequently evaded and violated—perhaps more often than they were honored—but they were unquestionably part of the structure of law and custom until the dawn of the modern era, when the very idea of land began to change and when land began to be equated with capital, as the new commercial classes began to impose their own view of private property as something with which one could do more or less what one pleased.[31]

A bit later, Europeans invented a new method of earning riches, that of "discovery," and they came to America and claimed the land—on the grounds that they had never seen it before—and then went through the arduous labor of possessing by bounding. To most of the Native American tribes, the land was not subject to "ownership" by individuals. Their thinking was expressed eloquently by a Blackfeet chief:

> As long as the sun shines and the waters flow, this land will be here to give life to man and animals. We cannot sell the lives of men and animals; therefore we cannot sell this land. It was put here by the Great Spirit and we cannot sell it because it does not belong to us.[32]

The Europeans' peculiar ideas about individuals' claiming exclusive ownership of specific portions of God's earth seemed strange, at first incomprehensible and then irksomely eccentric. The Indians eventually learned to their
sorrow that it was no eccentricity, but rather a murderous mania.

In modern times, of course, we have the example of socialist countries
where private ownership of any significant amount of property that constitutes "means of production" is prohibited as antisocial and antihuman.

So, the ideas we have in America (and in the majority of the world's
nations) about the private ownership of productive property as a natural and
universal right of mankind, perhaps of divine origin, are by no means universal and must be viewed as an invention of man rather than a decree of
God. Of course, we are completely trained to accept the idea of ownership of
the earth and its products, raw and transformed. It seems not at all strange;
in fact, it is quite difficult to imagine a society without such arrangements. If
someone, some *individual*, didn't own that plot of land, that house, that
factory, that machine, that tower of wheat, how would we function? What
would the rules be? How would we know how to act? Whom would we buy
from and how would we sell?

It is important to acknowledge a significant difference between achieving
ownership simply by taking or claiming property and owning what we tend
to call the "fruits of labor." If I, alone or together with my family, work on
the land and raise crops, or if I make something useful out of natural material, it seems reasonable and fair to claim that the crops or the objects belong
to me or my family, are my property, at least in the sense that I have first
claim on them. Hardly anyone would dispute that. In fact, some of the early
radical workingmen's movements made a Fair Shares claim on those very
grounds. As industrial organization became more complex, however, such
issues became vastly more intricate. It must be clear that in modern society
the social heritage of knowledge and technology and the social organization
of manufacture and exchange account for far more of the productivity of
industry and the value of what is produced than can be accounted for by the
labor of any number of individuals. Hardly any person can now point and
say, "That—that right there—is the fruit of *my* labor." We *can* say, as a
society, as a nation—as a world, really—that what is produced is the fruit of
our labor, the product of the whole society as a collectivity.

Over eighty years ago, Edward Bellamy, in *Equality*, the less widely
known sequel to *Looking Backward*, made very well the point I have been
struggling to formulate. In these utopian novels Julian West, a rich young
man in late-nineteenth-century America, awakens from a hypnotic trance in
the year 2000 into a world of peace and cooperation. His guide to this
utopian vision is Dr. Leete, who explains the system that has replaced that
of private capital:

"The main factor in the production of wealth among civilized men is the social organism, the machinery of associated labor and exchange by which hundreds of millions of individuals provide the demand for one another's product and mutually complement one another's labor. . . . The element in the total industrial product which is due to the social organism is represented by the difference between the value of what one man produces as a worker in connection with the social organization and what he could produce in a condition of isolation. . . . It is estimated, I believe, that the average daily product of a worker in America today is some fifty dollars. The product of the same man working in isolation would probably be highly estimated on the same basis of calculation if put at a quarter of a dollar. Now tell me, Julian, to whom belongs the social organism, this vast machinery of human association, which enhances some two hundredfold the product of every one's labor?"

"Manifestly," I replied, "it can belong to no one in particular, but to nothing less than society collectively. . . ."

"Exactly so. The social organism, with all that it is and all it makes possible, is the indivisible inheritance of all in common. To whom, then, properly belongs that two hundredfold enhancement of the value of every one's labor which is owing to the social organism?"

"Manifestly to society collectively—to the general fund."[33]

A recognition of the reality of the collectivity, a backing away from the exclusive focus on the individual, makes it possible to see the potential of other kinds of relationships between things and human beings than exclusive individual ownership. To go back for a moment to a previous analogy, that of the house built by a dozen different craftsmen, even at this very simple level it must be evident that the collaboration of the dozen men as a team vastly increases the productivity and value of the collective labor invested in constructing the house (without, for the moment, even thinking of the endless additional complexities introduced by questions about the origins of the lumber, the nails, the tools, and the electric and telephone wires and the sewer pipes that will connect the house and its occupants with society). No one man could conceivably build a house with only twelve times the amount of time and effort that twelve men expend in building the same house. Yet we ignore this evident reality. Even the workmen, though their experience makes them aware of it, have no way of thinking and talking about it. So, when the man who bought the land, the lumber, the nails, and the wire comes around at the end and gives them each a check for the "value of their labor"—and then even has the chutzpah to bestow upon himself the title "builder"—no one doubts that he, that individual, now is the rightful owner of that house. It has become his property.

With all of this distortion and overemphasis on individual action, the idea of private property and ownership of pieces of the earth is still pretty much limited to that portion of the earth that is actually land. We cannot readily imagine buying a piece of air or seeking a mortgage on a segment of ocean. The idea of owning the air and the seas seems as incomprehensible to us as the idea of owning his own factory must seem to a Russian (although we are beginning to see a rapidly growing interest in extending the idea of ownership to these elements, particularly as the oceans come to be seen more clearly as a means of production, not only of fish, but of other food, of oil, and perhaps of minerals).

We would have a similar feeling if we watched someone sailing out into the Atlantic and marking out a line of buoys to the north, east, south, and west and then proclaiming to whoever might listen, "These waves are mine. I own this piece of ocean. This water and the fish therein and the plankton and the salt and the seaweed belong to me. The water is mine and the fullness thereof." Hardly anyone would agree with him or honor his claim, no matter how much he might talk about the divine rights of man to own the ocean.

We have to recognize that the right of private individual ownership of property is man-made and constantly dependent on the extent to which those without property believe that the owner can make his claim stick.

One way of making the claim stick is to remove it from the realm of human agreements, to mystify it, to clothe it in myths, of which the most important with respect to the so-called right of private ownership of social product and the things that make this product possible is the myth of the lone "supernormal" individual. It is only by saying—louder and louder, over and over again—"I! I! I!" that we can then get away with saying "my" and "mine."

V   DEFICIENCY, EXCELLENCE, AND EQUALITY

When all else fails, when all the arguments about justice and merited rewards and social efficiency and the divine right to own property are exposed as mythological corollaries to Counterfeit Equality, we reach the argument that might be termed the dullness and grayness prophecy.

It is said that, should we try to live in a world of Fair Shares, we would find it unbearably dull. In an order based on the assumption that human beings are, in all essential respects, remarkably similar to one another, how would we avoid a gray, monotonous, mediocre completely uniform existence? What would we do about the residual differences?

As I tried to suggest briefly in the preceding chapter, there are, of course, real individual differences among us—more limited in number and extent than we are told, but certainly sufficient to provide for a great deal of genuine and interesting variety within an overall context of great similarity. How would these individual differences be dealt with? Does Fair Shares equality lead necessarily to a world in which all wear the same clothes, eat the same food, live in identical houses, watch the same television programs, think the same thoughts?

I think not. These kinds of notions represent a manufactured nightmare, used by antiegalitarians to frighten us and to obscure the issue by high-flown talk of freedom and liberty. The only freedom threatened by economic equality is the freedom of one individual to oppress and exploit another by virtue of his or her specific talent for oppression or exploitation. One can observe no logical connection between the idea of equality and the picture of the extinction of human individuality that one finds in such works as *1984*. It's unlikely that the members of any sizeable society would voluntarily choose such a world; it would have to be imposed. But a society with the means to impose such conditions would possess significant features that would disqualify it from any claim to equality. Who would make all those decisions? Who would design the identical clothes and housing? Who would write the books that everyone would have to read? The control of a vastly disproportionate share of resources by a relatively small group of persons would be, it seems to me, a prerequisite for such a regime. And that, in itself, is one definition of social inequality.

One can imagine a society that would *choose*, whether out of convenience or necessity, certain realms of life within which everyone would behave more or less identically. An example common to almost all societies is the use of the same language and the same units of measurement; not to employ them would be very inconvenient indeed. In the case of scarce necessities, rationing is an obvious solution to the distribution problem that would insure that some would not go without them. But my guess is that such voluntary homogeneity would not be very extensive. And this is so because human beings, though extremely similar, are not identical. Identity means exact likeness; similarity means likeness in *most* significant characteristics. There is no contradiction in saying that humans are very similar in all essential ways, but vary somewhat in others.

This point can perhaps be more readily grasped by shifting into other realms of creation. It has been said that no two snowflakes are identical. Yet, when they start to fall, snowflakes surely do look very much like one another, and no one would have any trouble distinguishing between, say, snowflakes and moth flakes.

Or consider thoroughbred horses. To the average nonhorse, like me, they look remarkably alike. Although I spent an inordinate portion of my younger years watching them, I don't think I could very often pick the horse I bet on out of the field without the signal provided by the colors of the stable silks the jockey was wearing. Yet the whole sport of kings is based on slight differences in how fast these horses can run. But these differences don't actually amount to much—the fleetest race horses run about 10 percent faster than the slowest. In the average race the winner runs only a fraction of a percent faster than the place horse. This fundamental fact about race horses—that they are really very much alike, differences in potential speed being minimal—has led many a man, overconfident of his ability to detect those tiny differences, to the office of the finance company.

So it is with human beings. We probably seem as indistinguishable to race horses as they do to us. And with good reason. The variability among us is not extreme, even in highly valued and very interesting characteristics like intelligence, strength, artistic talent, and athletic ability. But they do exist. So we must confront the question: how can we insist on the primacy of similarity among persons as a proposition necessary to equality, without threatening to violate or erode interesting and valued individual differences?

This question usually concerns the vicissitudes of those who are most different—the "best" and the "worst." What do we do about significant deviance or deficiency? What do we do about significant excellence? Can we have equality and still treat both deficiency and excellence fairly? Let's consider some examples.

A large number of persons who have life-threatening deficiencies in the functioning of their kidneys would die without access to a treatment called dialysis, which consists, in effect, of running their blood through an artificial kidney. Until recently many got such treatment and lived; some did not and died. Those who died were—almost by definition—unequal to those who lived. The signs of position in America's inequality structure, such as income and occupation, show that those who were high in that structure tended to live, while most of those who died were low in the structure.

How would a society emphasizing equality deal with such a situation, deal with this kind of deficiency? Exaggerated caricatures of equal treatment and of mindless obsession with similarity would picture two absurd extremes as alternatives. In one caricature, difference—deficiency, illness, and so on—would not be accorded any legitimacy, would not be treated as real. "In this egalitarian paradise," the health commissar would intone, "everyone is healthy. Kidney failures are not permitted! Go home, repent, and reform."

The burlesque of equality at the other extreme would have it that, since everyone must share equally in all resources, everyone would get an equal share of time on the dialysis machine—good kidneys or bad—and everyone would have to schedule seven minutes a month for his egalitarian dialytic treatment: "Your turn, comrade. Share and share alike!"

A rational and egalitarian solution to the dialysis problem is fairly obvious: everyone whose kidneys could not function without dialysis would have it guaranteed without regard to cost. And, with no revolution, almost without debate, and even without much public knowledge, we have recently chosen to apply that precise, obvious solution by making dialysis a special category covered by Medicare.

Antiegalitarians, however, don't seem to worry all that much about what equality would mean for those who experience deficiencies. Their concerns tend toward self-interest: they worry about what would happen to them and to other "leading men."

One term for the phenomenon that they fear so deeply is "leveling" (leveling down, of course; they can't seem to conceive of leveling up). Excellence would be ignored and allowed to rot unexercised, they imply, and everything would consequently go to hell.

How realistic this terror of equality is depends a good deal on what you think excellence is *for*. Is it a basis for competition and therefore to be *envied* by others or used by the excellent ones for personal gain? Or is it an expression of human potential, manifested as something to be *emulated*? Or, perhaps, simply something to be *consumed*, a commodity like any other?

If excellence is only a commodity, either to be possessed for its value or to be offered for consumption at the highest price the market will bear, then excellence is indeed headed for hard times in a society dominated by norms of equality. If he who worries about the dread fate awaiting excellence is, in fact, simply concerned about his right to personal profit from the exercise of particular talents with which he may have been graced, through no effort on his part, he is right to be concerned. Excellence in preparing television commercials to persuade people to buy electric toothpicks is not very likely to be as remunerative in an egalitarian society as it is in our own. And the relatively small differences in the talents of a big-league star who hits .300 and those of a minor leaguer who bats .280 would not, in all likelihood, be differentially evaluated on the order of a ratio of fifty or a hundred to one. Nor would supreme talent as an artist, an athlete, or an actor be treated as something to be taken to the marketplace and offered as a spectacle, to be consumed by thousands willing to buy high-priced tickets or by millions in front of a television willing to pay the price of watching advertising for a dozen minutes out of every hour.

Another way of looking at excellence is to think of it as representing the attained height of our potential as humans beings, something to be shared, enjoyed, and, if possible, emulated. It represents an achievement of mankind.

Return, for a moment, to the metaphor of the athletic field, so beloved by equal-opportunity fans. When I was young, a question that was always good for a sports columnist with nothing fresher to write about was "Will a man ever run a mile in four minutes?" In other words, is man, as a species, capable of such a feat? The question was not whether Glenn Cunningham, the great miler of the 1930s, would ever do it—although specific runners were of course discussed—but whether *some* human being would ever do it.

Who, right now, without going to an almanac, can recall the name of the man of excellence who finally broke through that barrier? Don't get up—it was Roger Bannister, and he did it in May 1954. Only a month later John Landy broke Bannister's record by over a second. And in August of the same year, the men raced against each other, and both finished in under four minutes (Bannister won).

Today a four-minute mile is a relatively common feat, and the records of Bannister and Landy are almost forgotten. This does not detract from their excellence any more than theirs detracts from Cunningham's. Newton's excellence, his great achievements, did not blot out the excellence of all his predecessors back to Pythagoras. It was Newton himself who said, "If I have seen further, it is by standing on the shoulders of Giants." By the same token, of course, Einstein's achievements did not invalidate Newton's excellence.

A particular excellence does not necessarily prove that a given individual is "supernormal," enviable, or extraordinarily different—not least because the man of excellence is often possessed of but a single superb talent. (Because Saul Bellow is a Nobel laureate, would you hire him, sound unheard, to play the organ at your daughter's wedding? Because O. J. Simpson is a sensational broken-field runner, would you ask him to design you a house? For that matter, would you have let Einstein do your income tax return?) Talents are broadly distributed, rarely bunched together, and the grantee of great talent in one area is usually much like the rest of us in most other ways. Moreover, talents are not distributed in an all-or-nothing fashion. Most of us have talents—musical, artistic, athletic, mathematical, mechanical, scientific—that may not be outstanding enough to make us stars, but that could be used for the benefit or enjoyment of ourselves and others. The truth is that most of us make no appreciable use of these talents. We have been taught that, on these dimensions, too, there are the superior individuals, the stars, and then there are the rest of us.

When I was a kid, it seems to me, almost every other family had a piano in the parlor, the five-and-ten had a counter that sold sheet music, and sitting down and playing the piano was not an activity reserved for the elite. The facts bear my memory out; it is not simply nostalgia. In the decade beginning in 1910, one new piano was produced in this country for every six or seven households; by the 1960s the output had shrunk to one for every thirty households.[34] Fifty or sixty years ago the Broadway theater season would see nearly two hundred openings, and many cities had not only flourishing amateur little-theater groups, but also a professional or semiprofessional repertory theater. Today the ever-growing commercialization of the performing arts, squeezing excellence into the narrow confines of a salable commodity, has virtually wiped all this out. The result, obviously, is a *loss* of excellence. Fifty years ago the theater supported hundreds of writers and thousands of performers. The drastic reduction in number has not apparently been the result of aiming for even greater excellence. Would anyone seriously claim, for example, that Neil Simon and Stephen Sondheim are unequivocally more talented than were Robert Sherwood, George Kelly, George Kaufman, Jerome Kern, and Cole Porter, let alone Eugene O'Neill and George Gershwin? Or would anyone claim that the replacement of all this by popular television shows represents a step up in excellence?

One can find the same pattern in sports. Although there were fewer major-league baseball teams fifty years ago, there were many more minor leagues and a larger number of professional baseball players.

Is it not reasonable to assume that the proportion of persons in the population with the talent to become playwrights, actors, or baseball players has remained unchanged and that with the doubling of the populace the number of such talented persons has doubled? Where are they? What are they doing with their talents in this world of "star or nobody," "hit or flop," "big leaguer or nothing"? Their talents are going to waste, are not being used or enjoyed, are not enriching *our* lives, because the big owners of the entertainment business, now much more commercialized and profit-oriented, have decided on new arrangements to enrich *themselves*. This is Fair Play?

In a real egalitarian society—a Fair Shares society—talent would not be a commodity to be sold in the marketplace, nor would excellence be only a crowbar for prying away wealth. The talented would be valued and esteemed as examples of human excellence. They would not be given million-dollar contracts, but neither would they be thrown into the arena with their fellow artists to see who could trample over the most bodies in a wild, envious competition for a star on the dressing-room door. Excellence and talent would not be buried and thrown away in order to keep the supply down and the price up. It would be assiduously sought, everywhere and in as great numbers as possible; and tenderly nurtured—not for the profit of a few individuals, but for the benefit of us all.

4

Help the Needy
and Show Them the Way
IDEOLOGY AND SOCIAL POLICY

I   WHO HELPS WHOM HOW?

One's tendency to lean toward either the individual-different-internal perspective or the collective-similar-external perspective affects one's assumption about matters other than the specific question of Fair Play versus Fair Shares. Using the same approach, we can analyze questions that are not directly related to attitudes toward equality as such. This is so because, as I pointed out before, the questions from which these three dimensions themselves were derived are very broad and general; they are questions that have long been debated in the history of Western thought. Responses to them reveal relatively enduring assumptions about the very nature of mankind and of society. The set of answers that leads to a strong Fair Play point of view about equality will lead to corresponding attitudes about other matters, attitudes that are consistent with, and complementary to, the Fair Play ideology. The person holding a strong Fair Play point of view will base his analysis of social problems on the same premises. His viewpoint about social problems, then, will be consistent with his viewpoint about the equality issue. As he views equality as a matter of equal opportunity for *individuals* to freely exercise the *internal* qualities that *differ* from one person to another, so he will view, for example, mental illness as the consequence of *internal differences* among *individuals* (such as genetic defects or weak egos). The person with a Fair Shares viewpoint, on the other hand, will think about mental illness, as he thinks about equality and most other human issues, more in terms of collectivity, similarity, and external factors. He will be concerned about the overall mental health status of the community, the state, or the nation. He will think of emotional disturbance as something that manifests itself among persons, essentially similar to everyone else, who are being buffeted by stressful experiences in their own lives and in the world about them. There is, then, one view of emotional disorder that is directly analogous to the Fair Play perspective on equality, another that corresponds to the Fair Shares perspective. This is not to say that either the Fair Play or the Fair Shares viewpoint itself produces the specific set of ideas about emotional disorder, but rather that one's sense of the nature of the issues with respect to both emotional disorder and equality reflects the same more basic and more permanent preconceptions about human beings. This cluster of attitudes springs from the same source and forms an ideological pattern that has internal consistency, that knits together ideas and attitudes about ostensibly disparate matters—be they political, social, psychological, or moral.

A number of these areas of human concern are related to the issue of equality or, more narrowly, to that of poverty. I shall attempt an analysis showing the relationship between views about human nature in general and about equality in particular, as well as consequences of those views with respect to the movement toward greater equality.

Good men and women have always agonized over the presence of want in the midst of wealth. Many have spent enormous amounts of time and energy and much of their own treasure in trying to alleviate poverty and its associated evils. They have been the reformers and philanthropists of our society, and among their numbers are some great and noble names.

The problems they addressed were defined for the most part as poverty and its supposed concomitants, consequences, or causes—crime, insanity, family breakdown, drunkenness and other vices, ignorance, disease, and overpopulation. They established an enormous variety of methods for lifting the poor out of their state of want, ignorance, and vice into one of self-respect and self-support. They built mental hospitals and penitentiaries; they campaigned against the use of rum and whiskey; they founded orphanages; they persuaded the states to provide free education for all children; they extended the franchise to the propertyless and to women; they gave soup and sermons to derelicts; they saved fallen women from their lives of sin and disgrace; they campaigned for antitrust laws and the graduated income tax; they set up private charitable organizations from whose offices "friendly visitors" went to the homes of the poor, offering sound advice and moral guidance, as well as food, fuel, and even cash; they tried to help workingmen organize into unions and supported great and bloody strikes; they campaigned for birth control; they agitated to abolish chattel slavery of black people; they helped to legislate social security pensions and unemployment compensation; they declared war on poverty and manned the barricades of compensatory education and adult vocational training; they organized welfare recipients and slum tenants; they marched, boycotted, and sat in for civil rights—one could extend the catalog for pages.

A number of observations can be made about these efforts and about the myriad actual and proposed measures and programs that exist today. For one thing, while none has resulted in any dramatic reduction of inequality in America, some have had a measurable effect. Others have had no noticeable impact at all. One can also discern drastic differences in the styles of these approaches—compare the "friendly visitor" with the union organizer; or compare the mental hospital with the unemployment compensation office. Such differences suggest that approaches to social reform are almost as numerous as the approachers. Indeed, this vista of pluralism gone wild has been institutionalized in the idea that poverty is a many-faceted problem with an intricate pattern of multiple causation. From this it follows that poverty (and note that it is usually poverty that is being addressed, rarely inequality) must be approached only with an equally diverse set of "treatments."

It is my contention that the attribution of convoluted complexity to the issue of poverty is essentially a process of mystification and that the many approaches to poverty and social problems can be better understood through ideological analysis. That is, one's efforts to lessen inequalities that exist among men are predicated on, and shaped by, the implicit assumptions one holds about mankind and human existence.

This chapter, then, will undertake the task of an ideological analysis of the various proposed solutions to social problems in America. I will argue that the differences in style and those in effect are intimately connected, and I will try to show that approaches to social problems can be broadly divided into two parts—a larger part, consistent with the Fair Play ideology of inequality, that produces no change, and a smaller part, compatible with the Fair Shares ideology of equality, that at least has the potential for producing change and sometimes does. These two approaches have existed side by side in America, the former always larger and dominant but the latter gradually growing more influential.

Consider a typical case of income inequality: a man and wife in their late sixties, retired voluntarily or involuntarily, and therefore deprived of their previous source of income, the wages of the man. If nothing happens, that couple will rapidly be impoverished and will join the pool of persons at the bottom of America's income ladder. How is this outcome to be avoided?

Aside from personal or family provisions (saving money for one's old age, living with one's children), we now have three mechanisms: one is similar to the savings option in that it represents deferred income in the form of a private pension; the other two are governmental programs that illustrate the two opposing styles of solutions to social problems.

One of these programs provides Social Security retirement benefits, the other welfare benefits (formerly called, bluntly, Old Age Assistance, now renamed Supplemental Security Income—SSI). Why should there be two different programs to meet needs that are essentially the same? How is it determined whether the couple is to be placed in one program or the other? The basic criterion is work history. If a person has *worked* in what is termed "covered" employment for a sufficient period of time, has paid into the Social Security program, and has reached retirement age, that person is automatically eligible for retirement benefits. If he is not—usually because he worked in jobs that were outside Social Security coverage—he must ask for public assistance ("welfare," "relief"). Although today over 90 percent of all civilian workers are in the Social Security system, as recently as thirty years ago only two-thirds were covered. So it is that although over twenty million persons receive retirement income from Social Security, there are still about two million who need to turn to public assistance and ask for SSI benefits.

The general view of these two programs is that a person "earns" Social Security, by paying into the insurance system, much as one would purchase an annuity. Welfare, on the other hand, is seen as public charity. In fact, although one's Social Security deductions are listed as "contributions," they are much more similar to taxes than to insurance premiums, and if a retired person were to get only what he "earned," he would get very little indeed. It can be calculated that if a person had in fact purchased an annuity with his "contributions" to Social Security, he would be receiving an income equal to about one-fourth of his Social Security check.[1] The other 75 percent of his grant comes from other people's money—other people's current "contributions" to Social Security. Those now working are paying for most of his retirement benefits, just as he paid for the previous generation of retired persons.

SSI, as an income maintenance program, on the other hand, is financed directly by general tax revenues; there is no camouflage about "contributions." Most recipients of SSI, of course, worked and paid income taxes, which helped to support the previous generation of recipients of Old Age Assistance, as persons now working are paying, through their income taxes, for their benefits. The generation of the children support the generation of the parents. The Social Security retirement program has aptly been called an "intergenerational compact." But the SSI program for the aged is just as much an intergenerational compact. The main difference between the two programs is that the money goes into and comes out of different accounts.

But think about the consequences of the way the two programs are structured and defined in the public mind. And think about the tremendously different impacts on the families involved. Purely on the basis of which kind of check they receive, we have been led to believe that there are really two different kinds of older persons, and we are convinced that the two categories are implicitly defined by the manner in which the government is providing them with income—Social Security and SSI. Moreover, we go on to construct quite different definitions of the two groups, toward whom we have quite divergent attitudes. (It should be added, for the sake of completeness, that in practice there are many elderly whose Social Security checks are so small that they must be provided with additional help through SSI; they tend to be bracketed with the welfare recipients.)

What are our attitudes toward these older people, toward the processes by which money is provided to them, even toward the almost indistinguishable checks they receive? We have been trained to view the Social Security group as self-respecting old-timers (perhaps with full heads of white hair and healthy complexions—in extreme cases, the man is fishing, the woman is baking cookies for her grandchildren). In a disgracefully large number of cases the checks they get are far too meager to meet their needs, and they are forced to live in as respectable a state of poverty as they can manage. In other cases, the checks are a good deal larger and may be supplemented by a pension or by savings. Whether or not they *need* the checks is not a relevant question. They may be paupers or millionaires; they may rent a furnished room or own a block of apartment buildings. It doesn't matter. No questions are asked. The green checks come in the mail every month, and they take them out of the mailbox gladly, even proudly. They earned them. It's their *right*.

And how do we view those receiving Old Age Assistance? We begin to understand this by looking at how one gets to be a recipient. The retired couple receiving Social Security simply lets it be known that they are sixty-five and have retired, and their checks start rolling in. The Old Age Assistance route is more complicated. There is, first, the problem of eligibility. They must not simply be old and retired but also poor—and, what's more, certifiably poor. They have to prove that they need extra income. They must be investigated. If they have property, they must permit a lien to be placed on it; if they have savings, they must use them up. In former years, their children would have had to participate in the certification process and to show that they were unable to support their old parents. The applicants would also be required to demonstrate that they had been residents of the state for a specified period of time. When they have thus branded themselves as needy and pauperized, the city or county or state welfare department will arrange for them to get a tiny check, in an amount that is scaled to insure that these people remain unmistakably poor. In 1978, nationally, the average monthly SSI check for an elderly couple (excluding vendor payments for medical care) was $200; the average Social Security check came to $436 (excluding Medicare benefits).² The image, then, of the Old Age Assistance recipient is very different from that of the upstanding ruddy-cheeked Social Security beneficiary. One is inclined to picture him as gaunt, shuffling, and definitely bent over—in a word, as defective. He is perceived differently, given a different social definition, and treated differently.

Let us look at a second example of the two contrasting styles. Perhaps the most blatant differences in treatment occur in the cases of women who have lost their husbands and are left with the care of small children. For purposes of social policy, these women are placed into one of two groups—the sheep and the goats, so to speak—solely on the basis of how they lost their husbands. If her husband *died*, the woman can breathe a sigh of relief; by that criterion she is considered a respectable, worthy, and upstanding citizen. She's a *widow* and her children are *orphans*, and we know all about widows and orphans. She takes her place on the right side, among the sheep. But if her husband ran away with another woman, if she is separated or divorced, or if, God forbid, the father of her child never married her, she definitely belongs among the goats, along with the rest of the usual suspects. She's not a respectable, worthy widow; she's just a woman without a man—who let him get away or never caught him in the first place—and God knows what she's up to. In the section on the five families in Chapter One, this difference was illustrated in the case of Judy, whose husband ran off and who eventually had to turn to welfare, AFDC (Aid to Families with Dependent Children). Elaine, on the other hand, when her husband died, was eligible for survivors' benefits under the Social Security program. Judy had to prove she was penniless, had to undergo constant scrutiny and degradation. Elaine, though comparatively well off, simply filed her claim and began receiving her checks. Their situations were essentially identical, but the answer to a single question—where is your husband?—determined that one was a noble widow with orphans while the other was a questionable female-headed family. The latter constitute perhaps the most scapegoated group in our society. They are the first to be nominated for human sacrifices when politicians start thinking about budget cuts. National leaders like Senator Russell Long feel free to call them "welfare sluts." They are branded with the public image of incompetent, shiftless, thieving, promiscuous women.

In 1978 the average monthly grant for an AFDC family (typically, a mother with two children) was $254; the size of the payments ranged from $61 in Mississippi to $375 in New York. The revered widows and orphans, on the other hand, received in the same year average Social Security survivors' benefits—for a mother and two children—of $508 a month, and this figure did not vary from state to state. Our public policy and attitude toward them are perhaps more reasonable and enlightened than they are toward any other social group. We consider this possibly the most successful and desirable program among all the desirable and progressive programs under Social Security, and no politician would dare to propose cutting this budget, at least not if he was planning to run for reelection.

Here again, we have two drastically different modes of solving essentially the same problem, accompanied by diametrically opposed images of, and attitudes toward, the two groups we have artificially contructed.

Still another example: a man is unemployed and cannot feed his family. The average man in that situation gets himself down to the employment security office as quickly as he can, files a claim for unemployment compensation, and soon starts picking up weekly checks while he is looking for another job. Of course, the check is a good deal smaller than the regular paycheck he is used to—nationwide, in 1978, the average was $83.67 a week—but this income usually makes it possible for him to get by for a while, until he can find a new job or until his old firm rehires him. In many cases, his wife is working and the continuation of her paycheck eases the burden further. So, while unemployment is undoubtedly a disaster and requires a good deal of belt tightening, the cushion of unemployment compensation makes a tremendous difference. Most important, he can walk in and collect his check without cringing or fretting about accepting charity. It is widely accepted that this check is a right. He is entitled to get it every week for a number of months, and during that time he usually finds a job. The average beneficiary of compensation payments is out of work about three months.

But sometimes he doesn't find a job—as hundred of thousands of workers have been discovering in recent years—and his entitlement to his unemployment check runs out. His right is terminated. In recent years this has been happening in about one out of every four cases. Obviously, in the week after his claim has terminated, his situation has not changed; his problem remains the same. But the solution changes drastically. He is moved into a different category, joining those, for example, who worked in jobs not covered by unemployment insurance; who are not covered, because they quit working without an officially acceptable reason; who are not getting checks, because they are on strike; or who are not working because of a prolonged illness that is not permanently disabling. These are the *ineligibles*. Their rights are sharply limited. Attitudes toward them and the social definition applied to them are very different. He is now in a situation similar to that of the retiree receiving SSI rather than Social Security or of the husbandless wife receiving AFDC rather than survivors' benefits. Programs available to this group of persons are few indeed, mostly general relief or veterans' aid. These programs are operated and completely funded by state or local authorities, without matching federal funds.

Now that his entitlement has run out, the unemployed man must do a good deal more than simply report to the unemployment office and put in his claim. Like the retired person getting Old Age Assistance and the woman on AFDC, he must demonstrate that he is destitute, must proclaim his pauper's estate, and must be scrutinized and certified as a fit subject for special consideration in the form of a check that, on a national basis, averaged only $36.63 a week in 1978. The check will be too small to allow him to buy gas, but that doesn't matter, because he may well have to sell his car. If he should be a skilled craftsman, owning his own expensive tools, he may be required to sell his tools before he is eligible for relief. He is, in short, pauperized. This means not only that his sense of self-esteem will inevitably be damaged but that his ability to get a new job will be very sharply limited.

These are examples of differences in *styles* of helping, of solving human problems. It should be noted that, despite the contrasting styles, one can perceive the underlying belief of most Americans that people in need of income must get some—they may not be allowed to starve. But there is a significant distinction. Some are clearly entitled, indeed, welcome to the income. It is handed out to them ungrudgingly, though usually sparingly. Others are made to crawl for it. Why do we make such radically different arrangements to solve essentially the same problem?

Or consider the problem of urban education. If there is one generalization that gains overwhelming approval among Americans, it is that we must do something to improve the city schools. Many persons are prepared to participate directly in trying to solve the problem. The differences of opinion arise around the proposed styles of the solution. Some solutions are seen as praiseworthy and practical; others as radical, destructive, and unrealistic. In the former category are Head Start, tutoring, after-school study clubs, and remedial reading programs. The radical and unacceptable group includes such proposals as drastic organizational and curricular reform, participation by students and parents in decision making and planning, and desegregation. In each of these three cases, there is broad agreement on goals. The consensus breaks down over the question of the style of the solution, which reflects underlying assumptions about the causes of problems in society.

Why do retired people need a new form of income? What causes a man to lose his job and therefore to be in need of another source of income? Why do so many children, particularly working-class and black children, do worse in school?

Contrasting viewpoints about the nature and causes of these situations directly produce a second set of assumptions about what kinds of programs or services should be initiated and about how they should be organized. Unemployment-compensation insurance, Social Security retirement pensions, and survivors' benefits rest on the idea that everybody who works might easily be one of those who goes without work during short or long spells of "hard times" and that when the time for retirement comes or when tragedy strikes, essentially every family will need a new source of income. On the other hand, Old Age Assistance and general relief, as well as other forms of public assistance, reflect the belief that each case is special, different, individual, and should be diagnosed and dealt with separately, beginning with the overriding need to certify that this particular case is really different in the sense that it is one of true poverty.

II THE IDEOLOGY OF BEING HELPFUL

When we analyze ideas about poverty along the three ideological dimensions, we can begin to see the extent to which they are congruent with the Fair Play or Fair Shares viewpoints.

Take, for example, the relationship between the conception of poverty and inequality itself. As Miller and Roby and others have shown, what we tend to call the problem of poverty is in reality only an aspect of the overall problem of inequality.[3] The highly distorted structure of the distribution of resources in our society is such that, at any given time, a proportion of the population is in an extremely deprived position. When that subgroup is looked at separately, isolated from the overall structure, it tends to be called the "poverty group," and the problem is seen as the task of getting the members of that group "out of poverty." However, a consideration of the total inequality structure suggests that, even if all the members of the group were lifted above the "poverty line," as long as the structure itself remained unchanged there would still be a subgroup—perhaps with an entirely different cast of characters—that would be extremely deprived of resources. Those who look at these issues while emphasizing the individual, the different, and the internal tend to think about the "poverty group" in terms of lack of skills or education, deficiencies in character, adherence to a dysfunctional cultural pattern, illness or disability, accident, misfortune, and absence of intelligence or virtue. This categorization of poverty encompasses all definitions of social problems as the result of individuals' being internally different or deviant: poverty, crime, and vice result from idleness, lack of discipline, and weakness of character; poverty results from unrestrained reproduction and the consequent need to feed too many mouths; a low level of education results from genetically based lack of intelligence or immersion in an anti-intellectual family and community culture, and so forth.

If one's assumptions tend toward the collective-similar-external end of the dimension, on the other hand, one is likely to view poverty, not as an isolated problem, but as an aspect of inequality itself, to be aware that, in looking at poverty, one is seeing only a facet of the maldistribution of wealth and income. From such a viewpoint, for example, one can perceive poverty as a necessary social byproduct of wealth, and one does not, of course, pay primary attention to individuals, nor does one propose programs aimed at correcting the internal defects or deficiencies of individuals. Since our particular structure of inequality is such that a certain number of persons are at the bottom of the distribution, by the nature of the distribution itself, it is not a matter of urgent priority to determine which particular individuals are filling those particular slots. In time, new individuals (mostly their children) will be in these slots, and if in the course of a single generation some move into significantly higher positions, their slots will be filled by others. Inequality, then, is a condition that refers to events that are occurring in a collective, a whole society. It is the latter that must be considered if inequality is to be reduced, not the presumed deficiencies of individuals who are poor or who "have" something—in the sense that one "has" pneumonia or cerebral palsy—that is said to be making them poor.

From these analyses of ideas about causes, we can begin to infer something about the nature of the programs that are advanced as solutions. If particular problems are basically to be defined as being *inside individuals*, consisting of something that makes them *different* from the rest of us, it is logical to develop services for the persons who are different—the "slow learner," the "mentally ill," the "criminal," the "unskilled youth," the "unacculturated rural migrant," and so on. In other words, special categories of deviants are created who become the targets of these programs. From the opposite perspective, attention would be directed, not toward a deviant individual, but toward a group—the community, the society, the total population. If slow learning occurs in the schools, the question becomes, What is there about the schools that produces slow learning (rather than slow learners)? If the welfare of the community is harmed by high rates of unemployment among young people, it becomes, What is there about the nature of the economy that fails to produce reasonable work for our youth? If a segment of the population is suffering from high rates of emotional distress and disorder, it becomes, What is the nature of their situation within the larger society that might account for this?

So, when we analyze programs, our first measure is whether the program is directed toward *special groups* or toward *populations*.

Closely connected to this is the question of the goals of the programs. Is the purpose to correct, treat, cure, and rehabilitate individuals who are different or deviant? Or is it to promote the health, general welfare, and well-being of the population and to prevent disease and discomfort?

The second measure by which to judge programs, then, is whether they are *remedial* or *promotive* and *preventive*.

It follows, too, that if we concern ourselves with the correction of differences in individuals who make up relatively small categories of persons, it must be done principally by persons who are expert in understanding those kinds of deviances or abnormalities and who engage in such activities outside the mainstream of community life, in some kind of contractual relationship with the individuals affected. The "slow learner," for example, is thought to be out of place in an ordinary classroom led by a person with generic teaching skills. He must be taken aside and put into the hands of a person specifically trained to deal with his special problems. Such relationships—which include, among others, that between the psychiatrist and his neurotic patient—are viewed as unusual, voluntary in nature, private, confidential, and completely out of place in the arena of public affairs. The only exception to this last rule is that the *funding* of these processes with public money may be tolerable, but only if accompanied by the guarantee that there will be no meddling in the relationship between the expert and his client. The decision-making powers must be left in the hands of the exclusive group of experts and professionals who are thought to understand these matters best.

From the opposite perspective, undesirable processes (slow learning, emotional distress) are matters of public concern. The population of school children, for example, will in a few years merge with the larger community, and thus the problem of slow learning will affect the well-being of the total population. Decisions about these issues can therefore not be left in the hands of some exclusive group; they must be brought into the realm of wider decision-making processes that are established for such purposes. Moreover, this type of analysis does not produce program ideas that feature a scattering of voluntary relationships; the solution to the problem is planned collectively to produce a program that will make systematic changes, often involving public regulation or legislation.

We have, then, three additional measures that can be applied to services, programs, and public policy: whether the program is in the *private* or the *public* sphere; whether it is based on purely *voluntary* arrangements or whether it involves systematic *planning* or *legislation*; and whether the group of decision makers is *inclusive* or *exclusive*.

A sixth measure relates to scope. If the problems being addressed are unusual, unpredictable, even accidental, involving individuals who are deviant or different in some particular way, it would seem probable that the pattern of problems would vary considerably from one locality to the other and that each locality would have its own particular set of them to deal with. The opposite perspective would define these manifestations of problematic processes as inhering in the structure of the collectivity within which they occur, which is only rarely that of some small locality and more commonly that of the state, the region, or the whole society. The sixth measure, then, that can be applied in an ideological analysis of social programs and policies has to do with whether the scope of the program is viewed as purely *local* or whether it is defined as *regional* or *national*.

To summarize, we can ask six questions about programs and social policies the answers to which will help to illuminate the ideological base on which the policies and services rest:

• Are programs directed toward specific categories or toward a general population?

• Are they purely remedial, or are they oriented toward preventive and promotive goals?

• Is the program in the private sphere or the public?

• Is it based on voluntary agreements, or is there some larger base deriving from a systematic planning process or legislation?

• Is decision making exclusively in the hands of the few experts who are considered to be closest to the problem, or is it more inclusive, involving the population that is supposedly benefiting from the program?

• Is the program narrow in scope, concerned only with the particular issues within a neighborhood or a municipality, or is the scope much larger, extending to regional or even national boundaries?

Programs that are *remedial* in nature, directed at *specific* categories of deviants, operating *voluntarily* in the *private* sphere, under the domain of *exclusive* decision makers, and at the *local* level are those that are most consistent with Counterfeit Equality and with the Fair Play position. Programs that are more *preventive* in nature, directed at the entire *population*, subject to *inclusive* decision making, in the *public* sector, based on *planning* or *legislation*, and operating at a *regional* or *national* level are more consistent with movement in the direction of Fair Shares equality.

Ali Banuazizi and I first developed these six measures in a study of mental-health planning agencies. Perceiving them as expressions of a single underlying dimension, rather than an either/or pair of positions, we named this ideological continuum *exceptionalism versus universalism*. At that time we described this dimension, as applied to social problems and human services, in the following words:

> The Exceptionalistic . . . outlook perceives social problems and needs for human services as exceptions to the general run of affairs, as accidental, unpredictable, arising from special, individual circumstances. . . .
> The person with a Universalistic outlook, on the other hand, sees social problems as rooted in societal and structural contradictions, as general, regular and expected. . . .
> The Universalist tends to look more closely at the rule than at the exception; his framework is more often the collective, the group, the social system, whereas that of the Exceptionalist is the individual. The Exceptionalist is shocked by accidents; the Universalist expects the consequences of structural defects; the Exceptionalist wants to repair lesions; the Universalist seeks to prevent injuries;

the Exceptionalist wants to change attitudes, the Universalist acts to change laws. When he goes on an ocean journey, the Exceptionalist insists on seaworthy and well-stocked lifeboats, while the Universalist requires a precisely accurate compass and radar. In the darkness, the Exceptionalist urges each man to light a candle; the Universalist establishes a rule that everyone must contribute to the cost of a generator.[4]

The exceptionalist-universalist dimension was adapted, but with some expansion, from a similar dimension that Wilensky and Lebeaux had originated in order to analyze differing concepts of social welfare, which they labeled as residual versus institutional.[5]

The late Richard Titmuss, the acknowledged master of our time in the analysis of social policy, elaborated on Wilensky and Lebeaux's categories in what he called "models" of social policy, which he related to economic policy, to ideology, and to the specific issues relating to the administration of social programs:

... Tentatively, the three models can be described as follows:

MODEL A *The Residual Welfare Model of Social Policy*
This formulation is based on the premise that there are two "natural" (or socially given) channels through which an individual's needs are properly met; the private market and the family. Only when these break down should social welfare institutions come into play and then only temporarily. As Professor Peacock puts it: "The true object of the Welfare State is to teach people how to do without it." ...

MODEL B *The Industrial Achievement-Performance Model of Social Policy*
This incorporates a significant role for social welfare institutions as adjuncts of the economy. It holds that social needs should be met on the basis of merit, work performance and productivity. ...

MODEL C *The Institutional Redistributive Model of Social Policy*
This model sees social welfare as a major integrated institution in society, providing universalist services outside the market on the principle of need. It is in part based on theories about the multiple effects of social change and the economic system, and in part on the principle of social equality. It is basically a model incorporating systems of redistribution in command-over-resources-through-time.[6]

Roland Warren, in a study of the organization of Model Cities agencies in a number of communities, derived a very similar dimension with respect to differences in the formulation of problems and programs, which he named Paradigm I (similar to the exceptionalistic and residual perspectives) and Paradigm II (similar to the universalistic, institutional, and redistributive perspectives).[7]

In the United Kingdom these contrasting approaches to social welfare and social services have been the subject of an ongoing discussion and debate, using the terminology of "universal" services (those available in general to the total population, such as pensions and health care) and "selective" services (those that are available only to specific categories of persons and that are means-tested—that is, dependent on inability to pay).[8]

These contrasting approaches to human problems are, in themselves, relatively value free and complementary to one another. Their ideological import derives from the implicit claims made for them. If we consider highway accidents, for example, it is easy to imagine both universalistic and exceptionalistic approaches that are valid: e.g., speed limits or seat belts, on the one hand; efforts to repair broken bodies or broken cars on the other. No one in his right mind would argue against the exceptionalistic practice of setting the leg of an accident victim. One would, however, object if the physician mending the leg claimed to be participating in a program to promote highway safety.

Other kinds of programs can be readily categorized, using the six measures outlined above. For example, Social Security retirement and survivors' benefits and unemployment compensation would be put near the universalistic end of the dimension; SSI, AFDC, and general relief, near the exceptionalistic end. They are not pure examples, obviously. The universalistic examples exclude segments of the population, are limited to persons with certain kinds of work histories, and so on. (Our social security system is closer to Titmuss's Model B than to Model C.) And the exceptionalistic income maintenance programs, although targeted for specific categories of individuals who are defined as different and pauperized, do have the more universalistic features of being based on national legislation and involving public funding. It is equally obvious that the more universalistic programs—if only because of their greater benefits and range of coverage—do make some contribution to the reduction of income inequality.

In the next section, in which I will examine in some detail the problem of income maintenance, I will try to clarify the relationship between inequality and the ideological character of the large number of policies and programs that have been developed to deal with the so-called poverty problem.

III HOW TO KEEP THE POOR ALWAYS WITH US

Hardly a day goes by on which some expert doesn't remind us smugly that we really can't expect to cure social ills like poverty simply by "throwing federal dollars at them." These experts are apt to go on and explain that we're wasting billions of the taxpayers' dollars on social programs that don't do a damned bit of good. The tax Scrooges among them add the caution that this sentimental waste of good money is threatening to put us all in the poorhouse. In order to engage in any serious consideration of social-welfare and social-policy issues, one must pay some attention to the implications of this rhetoric and, in addition, acquire some knowledge of the relevant facts.

What is it, exactly, that these hard-nosed sophisticates want us to understand by these assertions? Let me try to make their claims a bit more explicit:

• First of all, they expect us to believe that we have been pouring hundreds of billions into social-welfare programs to help the poor. (In the minds of many, the broad term "social welfare" is directly absorbed into the everyday meaning of "welfare" or "relief.")

• They make the further claim that, despite these efforts, the poor remain poor, and their spoken or unspoken explanation is that this is principally because their individual problems or deficiencies cannot be remedied simply by spending money on them.

• Finally, they paint a grim picture for their audience, one showing that all this extravagant generosity to the poor is producing a mounting burden of federal taxes, which is bringing the average American to his knees.

What is the reality behind this rhetoric? While it is literally true that about half the federal outlay budget falls under the general rubric of social welfare, we must recognize how inclusive this category is. The fact is that about half of all this money is spent on retirement checks, mostly Social Security payments.[9] The large majority of the recipients of these checks do not belong to the group that most people have in mind when they talk about "the poor." Over twenty million senior citizens receive these checks on the third of every month, the average amount for a retired couple today being something over $500. It must be fairly obvious that the majority of these older persons stay afloat somewhat above the official poverty line precisely because we throw these federal dollars at them.

The two next-largest chunks of the money listed under social welfare are payments to the providers of Medicare services (hospitals, physicians, druggists, and so forth) and grants to the states to help support health, education, and social services—ranging from foster home placement to crippled-children's programs to school lunches.

When we get down to the amount of federal money that goes to welfare recipients, the "poor" in most people's minds, the figure gets quite small. In 1977 it was a bit over $12 billion, out of a total "social welfare" budget of over $250 billion; currently, it is probably about $15 billion. About half of the recipients of this largesse are children in AFDC families, the other half are the aged, blind, and disabled who are not eligible for Social Security. This munificent sum represents, not half the federal budget, but a bit more than 2 percent of it. So, it can be seen that what we call "throwing dollars at poverty" represents only a tiny slice of the budgetary pie. Even during the height of the so-called war on poverty, when the federal budget was racing past the $200 billion mark, the Office of Economic Opportunity, which administered the antipoverty programs, never had an annual budget as large as $2 billion.[10] When it comes to throwing dollars at poverty, there aren't many dollars left, and it doesn't take anyone very long to do the throwing.

Is it true that this spending on social welfare is extravagant and useless? As I argued earlier, some of these programs are effective in reducing inequality somewhat, while others have little or no effect. (Many included under the heading of social welfare are not really relevant to the issue; these include the costs of medical care to members of the armed services, research grants to social scientists, and across-the-board subsidies to medical schools, calculated on the basis of the total number of students enrolled.) The items that are instrumental in reducing inequality to a measurable though relatively small extent are those that I have identified as the relatively "universalistic" social-insurance programs, such as Social Security and unemployment compensation. Cash Social Security benefits to the retired, the disabled, and the surviving spouses and children of breadwinners who died young and weekly compensation checks to the unemployed amounted in 1978 to over $100 billion. Analogous programs—military and civil service retirement, veterans' pensions, railroad retirement pensions, the black-lung program for disabled miners, and the like—add another $30 billion. Medicare accounted for an additional $25 billion. That was almost $160 billion in direct and indirect benefits, going to over 35 million persons. Again, it must be quite obvious that, without this kind of support in the form of social-insurance benefits, most of those 35 million would be in very bad financial trouble indeed. Just considering the elderly, it is beyond question that there are millions of senior citizens, now supported at some minimal level of dignity and security, who would otherwise be living in unbearable poverty. That is the human meaning of throwing one kind of dollar at social problems. To say that all this has no effect on income inequality and the elimination—or, better, the prevention—of poverty is simply ridiculous.

The exceptionalistic programs, such as welfare and SSI, it is quite true, don't even begin to eliminate poverty. The reason is plain to see: we don't throw enough dollars. To the hapless people dependent on these programs, who number over fifteen million, the majority of them children, we are shamelessly, cruelly stingy.

Of all the individuals who receive benefits from social-welfare programs, a bit more than two-thirds receive some kind of social insurance; the rest receive welfare. We spend ten times as much on social insurance as on welfare. It is rather remarkable, when you come to think of it, that Americans do not appear at all to begrudge the huge amounts we spend on social insurance (essentially to *prevent* poverty) but are brought to the point of outraged frenzy by the relatively small amount we spend on welfare recipients whom we *imprison* in poverty. I say "imprison" advisedly because, obviously, the level of welfare grants guarantees that those who receive them will remain in the lowest depths of poverty.

The grain of truth, then, in the "throwing dollars" charge is that inadequate public assistance—the tiny neglected corner of social welfare—far from solving the poverty problem, is one of its main causes.

The argument that social spending creates spiraling federal taxes, which are bankrupting the average American, is also fallacious. First of all, federal income taxes are not, as we are so frequently told, spiraling up and up. They have remained remarkably stable in relation to income. In absolute figures, of course, taxes go up every year, but they do so at just about the same rate as does gross income. In 1960 federal income taxes were equivalent to 10.5 percent of all personal income; by 1970 the figure had risen to 11.0 percent; by 1977 it had dropped back to 10.6 percent; in 1978 the figure again stood at 11.0 percent; in 1979, at 10.9 percent.[11] In other words, the scarecrow of ballooning federal taxes is a myth.

As for the share of the federal tax burden specifically earmarked for public assistance programs, the average family earning $350 a week spends about $4 a week for all public assistance programs combined (as compared, for example, with $15 a week for national defense).[12] To suggest a more concrete measure of our spending on welfare, for every federal and state tax dollar we spend to support the 7.5 million children on AFDC, we spend over two on liquor and over fifteen on gasoline. This is not to deny that these children are, in fact, a tax burden to the average worker. Many people argue that this is unfair, that it is the responsibility of the natural parents to support these children. But I wonder how long the argument would rage if we all realized how light that burden is. For the average worker, earning $250 a week, the money taken from him for AFDC to support "other men's children," by way of the federal tax deduction, is about fourteen cents a day[13]—the cost of about four cigarettes. All this venom and rage over the price of four cigarettes a day!

This, then, is the general background. Three questions come to mind:
• How did all this come about?
• What is the purpose of retaining what Alvin Schorr called our two-tiered social-welfare system[14]—universalistic social insurance for the majority and exceptionalistic welfare programs for the despised minority?
• If Americans are ready to support universalistic programs with relatively little grumbling and resentment, why have we not been able to move even further in this direction (as every other industrialized country in the world did long ago)?

The first question can be answered briefly by sketching vignettes of three periods in the history of American social policy—the long period before

1929, the years of the Great Depression in the 1930s, and the decade of the 1960s.

For generations, relief—as it was called—was meager, fragmented, localized, and directed at persons who apparently couldn't make it in the hurly-burly of the free market. Some of these unfortunates were seen as relatively blameless—the ill, widows and orphans, the elderly without families. Others were seen as incompetent and lazy—the drunkard, the malcontent who wanted higher wages than employers were willing to pay, the "town bum," who was found even in the smallest village. The most basic survival needs of such persons (excluding, whenever possible, the incompetent and lazy) were met primarily by private charities, supplemented by a small amount of local tax money, spent in part for small cash grants, in part to support the grim institutions known as poorhouses or county farms—institutions that remain alive in the memories of many living persons. In 1890 the total amount of tax money spent for such purposes in the entire country was $41 million,[15] mostly by local municipalities.

During these years, the Fair Play ideology was riding high and was closely mirrored in most social arrangements, including philanthropy. The poor, the ill, and the aged, worthy and unworthy alike, were the losers in the great race of life. There were prominent professors and intellectuals who argued that these misfits, nature's marked losers, should simply be allowed to die "for the good of the race,"[16] but the great majority of Americans rejected so harsh a solution and made a half-hearted commitment to keep the poor from actually dying of starvation.

It took the Great Depression to bring about a major change both in social-welfare-policy thinking and also in the attitudes and beliefs of the average American. All through those grim years everyone knew many solid, hard-working, righteous people who were unaccountably (and, it began to seem, permanently) impoverished. The able-bodied pauper became commonplace; he was one's uncle or cousin or friend or neighbor and could hardly be branded as improvident or shiftless. There was only one way to distinguish him with certainty from the town bum of one's childhood, and that was to clearly establish a new and more respectable category—the *unemployed*.

In this way the problem of pauperism and idleness—of deviant men who *wouldn't* work—was distinguished from the problem of unemployment—of righteous men who *couldn't find* work. The issue of impoverishment was evaded. The issue of equality never even came up. The issue of jobs was made central, and joblessness was redefined in much more universalistic terms—as a mass phenomenon unrelated to personal characteristics and clearly the result of events external to the individual unemployed person. Programs were rapidly developed that were public, legislated, national in scope, and often directed toward a much larger segment of the population than those traditionally seen as "the poor." The federal government entered for the first time into the arena of cash relief payments. Federally funded programs to provide work were established, such as the Public Works Administration, the Works Progress Administration, and the Civilian Conservation Corps. The implicit *duty* of all to work was becoming something like a *right* to work (for a very low wage, of course).

The Social Security Act of 1935 included near revolutionary provisions for income cushioning that were designed ultimately to protect almost the entire *working* population—social security and unemployment compensation. Both programs were directly related to the experience of work—unemployment insurance if you were laid off from your job, social security pensions based on your having worked most of your life until the age of sixty-five.

For the poor who could not reasonably be defined as able-bodied and eligible for work—again, the traditional widow with small children, the aged, the disabled, the blind—means-tested categorical assistance programs were included, now organized in a more universalistic fashion in some respects, but retaining all the exceptionalistic features of old-fashioned relief.

During the same years, an equally significant piece of legislation, the Wagner Act, guaranteeing labor unions the rights to organize and to engage in collective bargaining, finally gave full legal recognition to the reality that employer-employee relationships were not a series of one-to-one contracts, but that the work force of a firm was a collective entity that could act as such.

The crisis of the Great Depression, then, produced a remarkable upsurge of universalism in thinking about social problems and a dramatic alteration in developments in official social policies. Even the essentially exceptionalistic programs established at that time, and still with us as our public assistance welfare programs, were pushed in the direction of universalism, in that after 1935 the welfare program was national in scope, under federal supervision and with a dramatic increase in public funding.

The next major event, the so-called war on poverty, occurred in the 1960s, following a rediscovery of want in the midst of affluence and the growth of the civil rights movement. The theorizing and the rhetoric accompanying the declaration of war against poverty were, interestingly enough, deeply imbued with universalistic themes. There was a rapid jelling of a consensus about the target to be attacked, namely, the "opportunity structure," the structural barriers built into the fabric of society that kept the poor penned in poverty.[17] But, as the experts translated the rhetoric into actual programs, the target changed subtly but dramatically. All the major poverty programs—Head Start, Adult Education, Manpower Training, Concerted Social Services—were specifically aimed, not at the "opportunity structure," but at the poor themselves. The goal, of course, became the elimination of undesirable internal deficiencies of individuals. The war on poverty was announced in ringing tones with the vow that we would pursue the war to its bitter end. The bitter end was that poverty won.

For forty years now, since our brief romance with openly universalistic programs, we have persisted with our two-tiered social policy, while the rest of the world has far outstripped us in developing social insurance and other universalistic approaches. And it is important to note that variations of this two-tiered system are evident in many other areas of our life. Take housing, for example. Public housing and its alternatives, such as leased housing and rental assistance, are straightforward means-tested programs for the certifiable poor. For middle-income and well-to-do people we also have housing-assistance programs, but they are almost invisible in their universality—I refer, of course, to income tax exemptions for mortgage interest payments and real estate taxes. These are available to everyone, with no test of eligibility (other than the minor matter of financial capacity to own one's home), and the consequent savings are a direct subsidy to the homeowner from the federal government in precisely the same sense that the relatively low rents in public housing projects are a subsidy to their tenants. The tax deductions that constitute a subsidy to homeowners, however, involve a far greater sum of money than the amount invested in the housing-assistance programs for the poor. But, of course, we homeowners simply take this as our right, our natural entitlement. It never occurs to us that the government is giving us something for nothing.

Transportation offers another example. Public investment in transportation for the poor—that is, public transportation systems—has been minuscule in comparison with the enormous investment in subsidizing interstate highways, airlines, trucking companies, and expressways that conveniently carry commuters to their suburbs.

The general principle seems to be that if a service or social program benefits the well-to-do at least as much as the poor, and preferably a good deal more, it will be organized along universalistic lines. The development of public fire and police departments, of state and national parks and other recreation areas, of polio vaccination, and of sewage disposal systems illustrates this point.

Movement toward universalism, on the other hand, is aborted, transformed, or somehow thwarted and crippled, when it involves any threat of real advance toward greater equalization in the distribution of economic well-being, or even toward the lesser goal of eliminating extreme poverty. I don't believe that public attitudes account for the persistence of exceptionalistic programs. For one thing, as I suggested, the public is dramatically more positive and generous in its attitude toward our universalistic social-insurance programs. In discussions of them we rarely are confronted with the spitefulness that almost always emerges in reaction to any mention of "the poor" or of "welfare people."

Although Americans have been confused and deceived in various ways, they seem almost instinctively committed to universalistic approaches to social policy. Social Security, for example, is now a sacrosanct institution in American life, and any proposal to alter its nature—to make it a voluntary rather than an all-inclusive legislated program, for example—meets with violent disapproval. For as long as there have been records of public opinion on the issue, at least fifty years, Americans have been overwhelmingly in favor of some national program of medical care like federal health insurance.[18]

So true is this that many exceptionalistic programs, designed intentionally or unintentionally to preserve inequality, are set before the public as univer-salistic schemes. A good example is the Nixon administration's Family As-sistance Plan, devised by Daniel P. Moynihan as a substitute for our present public assistance program, and presented to the public under the guise of a "reform" that would institute a "guaranteed annual income."[19] It was, of course, nothing of the kind; it was even more selective than our present system, included provisions for what amounted to forced labor at less than minimum-wage rates, even for mothers of young children, and set income levels far below the government's own poverty line. It was, however, deco-rated with some universalistic ornaments, such as national administration and standards, the elimination of specific categories, and the inclusion of the working poor, and those universalistic features were its major selling points. The scheme—one of the most insidious attacks on poor people in our his-tory—was narrowly defeated, primarily because of intensive lobbying efforts by poor people's organizations led by George Wiley, yet to this day it is referred to by political columnists and other observers as the progressive Nixon-Moynihan guaranteed-income plan. This probably illustrates why truth-in-labeling laws are so necessary for the protection of consumers.

Nevertheless, gradual movement toward more universalism in social-pol-icy and social-welfare programming contains within itself the seeds of change, the potential leverage for increased equality in our society, depend-ing on the acuteness with which the programs that ultimately emerge are analyzed and explained to the general public. The growing demand for some kind of national health-care program, and the increasing response to this demand on the part of politicians, is a case in point. Such a universalistic program would almost certainly reduce inequality in two ways—it would help to equalize the health *status* of all, and it would reduce the *economic* burden of health care for the great majority of the population. What would such a program look like, and how would it be distinguished from the typical exceptionalistic abortion that results from the program planning and poli-cies of well-intentioned liberals?

IV FAIR SHARES OF HEALTH

The three basic ideological dimensions and the six program dimensions previously described provide the analytic tools that enable us to distinguish between a universalistic health care program and one that is marred or, more likely, fatally wounded by exceptionalistic features. Let us quickly run through such an analysis.

Similar versus *different*   Does the program focus its attention on illness (difference) or health?

Internal versus *external*   Is the program designed to follow the American model of medical care, in which attention is paid primarily to existing internal events (e.g., the presence of infection or growths) and practice is directed toward internal intervention, or is consideration given to the external sources that produce the internal changes (sanitation, environmental pollution, automobile safety, atmospheric and mechanical dangers in factories)?

Individual versus *collective*   Is the program directed only toward individual persons who can be defined in some way as patients, or does it encompass some relevant collective—the municipality, the state, the nation?

The program equivalents of these dimensions become readily apparent:

Private, voluntary versus *public, legislated, planned*   Does the program simply subsidize the existing practice of professional entrepreneurs and of the private medical insurance industry (as is the case, for example, with both Medicare and Medicaid), or does the program propose a *public*, that is, governmental, health service? The scare word here is "socialized medicine," meaning governmentally operated programs. Resistance to this idea is couched in terms that try not only to trigger negative responses to words like "socialism," but also to call up the image of the sacred (private) doctor-patient relationship, based—God only knows why—on the principle of fee for service. It is interesting, however, to notice how presidents, cabinet secretaries, congressmen, and senators do not seem to shy away from the benefits of socialized medicine, when they take advantage of the opportunity to use the services of government-operated medical programs and enter government-run hospitals like Walter Reed or Bethesda Naval. I don't recall any of them indignantly rejecting such an opportunity and insisting on their God-given right as American citizens to pay out of their own pockets the high rates of private hospitals and the high fees of private doctors.

Specific categories versus *total population*   This principle involves two issues—eligibility and scope. The application of any mechanisms related to the ability to pay, or of means tests of any kind, would almost certainly guarantee that a national health program would be a second-class program for second-class citizens. The second issue has to do with the previous question of whether the program addresses only those who can be defined as sick, as patients, or whether it is intended to maintain and improve the health of a total population.

Remedial versus *preventive*   Another version of the same question is whether the program provides only treatment of existing internal processes or whether it devotes a major portion of its resources to prevention, including health education, but, more important, focusing on external, environmental sources of illness. It is now agreed by most experts that the overwhelming majority of cancers, for example, are environmentally caused, by pollution and radiation in the atmosphere, by food and its additives, by cigarettes, by medications, and by industrial hazards. Like any other major disease, cancer can be overcome only by preventive strategies, and a national health program must have the authority and resources to develop and implement preventive strategies.

Exclusive versus *inclusive*   Does the program provide for decision making only or largely by medical professionals and other experts (insurance and drug companies, for example) whose vested interests and livelihoods are dependent on *disease*, whether they realize it or not? Or does it provide for decision making by those whose continued good health is the presumed objective—that is, the public at large?

Local versus *national*   Is it truly a national program with equal coverage for all the population—rural as well as urban, inner city as well as suburbs, Southerners as well as Northerners—or does it allow significant local variation both in allocation of resources and in program development?

Such a series of questions, growing directly out of the application of the ideological dimensions I have discussed, does two things. It gives us a prescription for what a national health program should look like, and it gives us early warning with respect to the kinds of exceptionalistic distortions that will be proposed and that, without massive opposition, will be included in any program that emerges.

A national health program, by these criteria, would be government-operated, under a broad legislative mandate that would include authority and resources for major preventive intervention as well as treatment programs; it would be available to all residents of the country without tests of eligibility; its goals would be to promote and preserve the health of the entire population, as well as to provide services to the ill and injured that would be of uniform quality and equally available to all persons regardless of where they lived.

And what would we have to watch out for as the lobbyists, amenders, and distorters went to work on a national health program? First of all, of course, anything that resembled limitations of eligibility or means tests. Second, any emphasis on the preservation of medical care in the private, voluntary domain, such as funding mechanisms that involved the payment of fees of private practitioners, or that subsidized insurance premiums of private companies, or, more innocuous, that allowed for the contracting out of program elements to voluntary, nonprofit organizations. Third, any elimination or whittling away of authority and resources for preventive intervention. And, finally, the exclusive focusing of auditing or evaluation functions on the utilization of facilities and services—as opposed to an evaluation based on indices of the health of the population; a national health program would not be successful simply because it allowed for a larger number of visits to the doctor's office or to the hospital by a broader range of people; its success would be measured by the reduction of illness, injury, and death in the nation, by the improved health of its citizens.

Similar analyses can be applied to any social program, any social-welfare proposal, any social-policy component. Similar analyses were applied, for example, to the programs of the war on poverty by myself and by others, and, by these criteria, these programs were found wanting. As a consequence, predictions were made that the war on poverty would fail. This, in itself, is nothing: none of us were competing as prophets, trying to outpredict Criswell or Nostradamus. That is not the point. The failure of social programs, and particularly the failure of those ostensibly designed to reduce poverty (which is to say, reduce inequality), provides further justification for the continuation of inequality. "We tried and we failed. Poverty and inequality are apparently not susceptible to anything we might do; they are inevitable; they are permanent; let's relax and enjoy it." We must prevent that lie from being transformed into a permanent myth.

5

Dishwashers Trained Here

IDEOLOGY AND EDUCATION

I THE GREAT UNEQUALIZER

As we have seen that ideological assumptions saturate thinking and planning in the realm of social welfare and social policy, thereby producing programs consistent with the Fair Play viewpoint and with Counterfeit Equality, so we can find the same phenomenon in many of our major social institutions. In this chapter, as an illustration of this point, I shall apply the same kind of analysis to one of the most significant of these institutions— education.

It is particularly important to stress the reality that one of the principal functions of schooling is to maintain inequality, because we have long and vehemently been taught precisely the opposite. Education is said to be the great equalizer, the path lying always open to the poor, the immigrant, and the children of factory workers, by which they can climb up to achieve equality with those above. The basic argument is that, if young people would stay in school, study hard, and develop skills, they would get better and better jobs, poverty would be eliminated, and the huge income gaps that are a major sign of inequality would grow narrower and narrower.

Now, to anyone who thinks about it for a few moments, it must be obvious that education has not produced these magic effects. For example, at the turn of the century, most young persons left school when they finished grammar school or before. Fewer than 10 percent graduated from high school; only 2 or 3 percent graduated from college. The *range* of education they received—defined as the number of years they attended school—was relatively large, while the *average* amount of schooling was quite small. Today's generation, in marked contrast, includes only a minority who don't finish high school—approximately 80 percent of young men and women get a high school diploma, and 20 to 25 percent of them go on to receive a college diploma.[1] The *amount* of schooling has increased tremendously and the range from top to bottom has decreased dramatically. Nevertheless, although the *absolute* standard of living has improved greatly for almost everyone, *relative* shares of wealth and income have changed only marginally in the direction of greater equality. The college graduate of today is about as well off in the economic structure as was his grandfather who graduated only from high school. (But the college graduate of today who is the grandson of a college graduate is likely to be much richer than his fellow graduates.) It is apparent that the change in the distribution of education has not produced any comparable change in the distribution of wealth and income.

The first thing we have to get into our heads, then, is that, despite all the mythology and all the rhetoric, education does *not* provide leverage either to greater and broader social mobility or to absolute equality. So what is education all about? Here we are, spending about $100 billion a year on our educational enterprises, most of that money in the form of tax dollars— about 10 percent of our national product. Are we to say that education doesn't work the way it is supposed to, that education is a failure? Not at all. It works extremely well. It always has. We have just been given answers that are somewhat less than candid to the crucial question of what our schools are for. They are not to help people rise, but to keep them in their places, to train young people to take their allotted positions in our inequality structure, particularly their occupational positions, without making a stink about it. As Bowles and Gintis and others have carefully documented, one of the major functions of schooling is to reproduce our hierarchically structured labor force.[2]

II   EMANATIONS FROM THE BELL-SHAPED MIND

If we look at the schools, then, from the perspective of their major social function, the nonviolent perpetuation of inequality, it is much easier to understand many things that seem inexplicable. Take the question of reading, for example. There are substantial numbers of young people with eleven or twelve years of schooling under their belts who can scarcely get through a fifth-grade reader. How can this be? Twelve years times 180 days a year times 5 hours a day, is 10,800 hours! How can any boy or girl spend all that time in school without learning to read fluently and easily? It seems incredible, particularly when you remember that they all came to school with a quite thorough and sophisticated command of a rather difficult language. How could they pick up a good *speaking* knowledge of a language in three or four childhood years, without any special instruction, and then fail to learn to *read* that same language? Becoming proficient in reading, despite all the educational mystification and artificial technicalities that have been attached to it, is a relatively easy task. Most illiterate adults can be taught to read their own language in a few months without any trouble at all. Anyone who has studied an alphabetic foreign language not written in our familiar roman system—such as Russian, Hebrew, Greek, or Arabic—knows quite well that it is much easier to learn to pronounce the words than to understand the language. It's only a simple code, which one can usually learn in a couple of weeks. The only possible explanation I can think of is that rather than teaching them to read, the schools discourage many children from learning. How is it possible to prevent children from learning that simple code even when one pretends to teach it to them for what must seem like countless years?

We are just beginning to learn the details of how this trick is carried off. There are several elements to the process, beginning with the assumption, drummed into teachers during their training, that all human qualities and measurable behaviors are, as they say, "normally distributed"—that is, measurements of these qualities and behaviors fall naturally into the well-known "bell shaped" curve, with most persons clustering in the middle, the proportions falling off sharply and symmetrically in either direction. The second element, directly contingent on the first, is the transformation of ideology into effective action. Teachers are trained to direct their teaching at the *individual*, emphasizing *difference* and concern with *internal* events. This is true both at the manifest level of classroom interactions and at the latent level of the structural organization of the schools.

The third element is the actual *sorting* process itself, the continuing sifting and grading of young people and the official labeling of those with greater or lesser merit.

The fourth, and perhaps most insidious, element is the legitimation of these processes in the minds and feelings of the students, teaching them to accept the underlying ideology and value system that the school system reflects and, more painful, to accept the grade that the school stamps upon them—prime, choice, good, or utility.

Teachers, principals, guidance counselors, and other educators act as if they believed that God invented the normal, bell-shaped curve shortly after he created Adam and Eve and that Moses worked out the statistical parameters of that distribution. In particular, they believe that "aptitudes" and "achievements" are precisely distributed across a collective of human beings in accordance with the immutable laws of probability. This is obviously not so. Take a simple thing like speed. Assume that we plotted the time it takes to run a hundred yards for a representative sample of the total population. The range would probably be something like ten to thirty seconds for the great bulk of the participants, but only a tiny fraction of them would be able to run the distance in less than, say, fifteen seconds, and the great mass of them would probably pile up in the range of twenty to twenty-five seconds. The distribution wouldn't look anything like a "normal, bell-shaped curve."

While it is true that many human characteristics and bits of behavior *are* "normally"distributed—e.g., height, weight, and shoe size—many others are distributed in a highly skewed fashion—visual acuity, sense of musical pitch, capacity to lift heavy weights, and so forth. With respect to the question of education, however, the crucial issue is how "aptitudes" and "achievement" are distributed. If one uses IQ measures as an index of aptitudes, the bell-curve fans seem to have won hands down: every IQ test has a mean IQ of 100 and a standard deviation of 15 (which means, approximately, that slightly over one-third of the population scores within one standard deviation *above* the mean, the same proportion within one standard deviation *below* the mean, the remainder being evenly divided in a more sparsely distributed group above and below the one-standard-deviation mark). The same thing is true of achievement tests. The Scholastic Aptitude Test, the Graduate Record Examination, and similar examinations are scored on the basis of a mean of 500 and a standard deviation of 100—half the tested population falls below 500, 34 percent of it falls between 500 and 600, about 14 percent between 600 and 700, and about 2 percent above 700. It seems unequivocally true that aptitudes and achievement are distributed almost precisely according to the structures of a normal distribution.

There is only one fly in the ointment: the tests are scored on the *assumption* that persons will fall into a normal distribution on the IQ or aptitude scores. In other words, the raw scores of the tests are transformed into a normal distribution—all the irregularities, skewed distributions, and inconsistencies that are evident in simple raw-score performances are adjusted until they fit into the normal distribution of the IQ scores themselves. For example, on an SAT type of test, let us say there are one hundred questions. As you recall, the "average" score on this sort of test is set at 500. What does a test score of 500 equal in terms of numbers of questions answered correctly, that is, the so-called raw score? Is it set at 50 percent or 70 percent or some other figure? The answer is that we don't know what number of right answers, what raw score, equals a particular standard score (500, 600, etc.) until *after* the test is "standardized"—that is, given to some representative sample (in the case of the SAT, high school graduates applying to college). A standard test score of 500 is defined as the midpoint of the raw scores obtained by the standardizing process. If half the group got more than seventy-five answers right and half got fewer, then seventy-five right answers produce a test score of 500. If only 16 percent got eighty-two or more right answers, the raw score of 82 then yields a standard score of 600. At the other end, it might be that 16 percent got fifty or fewer correct answers; a raw score of 50 then is equal to a standard score of 400. Thus, the "distance" in this case between a test score of 500 and 600 amounts to only seven wrong answers, while the "distance" between 400 and 500 is twenty-five wrong answers. This is, of course, an exaggerated and simplified example, but it illustrates the main principle that the eerily symmetrical distribution of the test scores does not necessarily reflect the reality of how the actual number of right and wrong answers is distributed. The bell-shaped curve that emerges from these manipulations is the result of arranging the raw scores, as it were, in the shape of a bell.

Lacking this technical information, seeing only the final product of IQ and achievement test scores, teachers and guidance counselors are naturally persuaded, without even thinking about it, that ability and school performance really are "normally distributed." The tests prove it and the grades allotted by the teachers should follow the same pattern. Somewhere, they come to believe, God has written that, say, 40 percent of the class should get C's, 20 percent B's and 20 percent D's, and 10 percent A's and 10 percent F's. If teachers grade correctly and conscientiously, and if performance is indeed normally distributed, this follows as the night the day. If, God forbid, say, 80 percent of the class get A's and B's, the teacher has obviously messed up the natural arrangement of things, committed a flagrant violation of natural law, possibly of felonious proportions.

The latter phenomenon is being criticized these days as "grade inflation." I began to hear about it a couple of years ago at Boston College, but it is apparently a national rather than a local malady. It consists of students' getting more A's and B's in their courses, and fewer C's and D's, than they used to. A lot of academic people are getting very worried about it and are trying to do something about it—to stop grade inflation as the Federal Reserve Board tries to head off monetary inflation. At first glance, it seems a little peculiar to worry about students' not getting *enough* C's and D's. These grades, after all, are undesirable; they are frowned on and often result in warnings and other forms of disapproval. One might be led to assume that an increase in the number of A's and B's would be welcomed and applauded. "What good learners our students are!" we might be saying to one another, or even, "What good teachers our professors are!" Nothing of the sort. When a large number of students in a course get very good grades, the professor is immediately suspected, not of teaching well, but of being "permissive," perhaps even subversive.

One begins to wonder what grades are supposed to be for. The naive answer is that grades represent an evaluation of how "well" the student did in a course, that is, how much he or she seemed to have learned, as well as one could judge by examinations, term papers, and other measures. One might also assume that the ideal goal for a teacher would be for every student in the course to get an A. Indeed, it might even be considered reasonable for a teacher to evaluate his or her own success in the course (and whether or not the students are getting a reasonable value for their tuition dollars) by the criterion of how many students did "well." The students, after all, are there for learning, and the professor is being paid—largely with their money—to teach. That's what college is all about, right? Wrong.

Upon closer examination, it turns out that universities are, in fact, engaged in a sorting and labeling process that has little or nothing to do with teaching and learning. When those whose brows are always wrinkled from worrying about grade inflation write long memos explaining their agitation and urging us to stop our inflationary grading, their concern becomes clear. They are fearful that our institution, our little community of scholars, our truth-and-beauty fan club, will get a bad reputation—that graduate schools, medical schools, corporations and other consumers of our products are being misinformed if we now label with a grade point average of 3.5 the kind of student who in the old days would have had an average of only 2.5. The meaning of our grades is being devalued and consequently so is the market value of our product—excuse me, graduates. After all, are we not being supported by society primarily for this function? Some we designate "superior," some "average," some "below average." If we are so unethical as to certify a student who is "really" average as a superior product, what will people think of us? They won't be able to trust us. They won't be able to believe us. How can we do such a terrible thing? Even more heinous, we are being unfair to the "really" superior student if we allow others into his category who don't belong there. It's not just. It's not fair. It might even be something for the Federal Trade Commission to look into.

The idea of a "normal distribution" of performance measures, or aptitude scores, or grades, or other gauges of human characteristics or behaviors, is the central concept of the "psychology of individual differences." Here we see, quite clearly, the ideological position upon which virtually all educational activities are based: namely, that psychological characteristics of an *internal* nature—intelligence, aptitude, motivation, learning—are best understood in terms of *differences* among *individuals*.

From this basic conception flow almost all classroom activities, almost all of the assumptions held by teachers about students, almost all of the formal activities of a school system, and almost all the central questions that are posed: Who is smarter than who? Who is more motivated than who? Who can spell better than who? Who can read better? Who will get promoted?

Who will go to college? The day-to-day activities of the classroom are geared toward answering these questions and toward achieving a convergence with respect to the answers—those with greater aptitude will achieve more, and the smarter can spell better and read faster.

I remember well how clearly and specifically all this was acted out when I was a kid in the second grade. There were spelling bees, for example, during which each member of the class would be eliminated from the competition as he misspelled a word, until only one triumphant champion of orthography remained standing—let's have a great big hand for the spelling-bee champion of Mrs. Powers's class! The class was, furthermore, seated according to Mrs. Powers's judgment of their relative "achievement." The first seat in the first row was reserved for the smartest kid in the class; the last seat in the last row for the dumbest. Mrs. Powers was doing very well what teachers do—determining, recording, and certifying individual differences in internal characteristics. After a few years of this sort of thing, Johnny Doyle, always seated in the last seat in the last row, became pretty well convinced of what lay ahead for him as he grew up; so he began looking out the window and dropping his books on the floor for diversion, as he waited until he was sixteen and could legally get out of that infamous seat and get a job as a stockboy in the A&P.

Every "reform" that has occurred in the history of elementary and secondary education—from the progressive movement of the 1920s to the idea of the comprehensive high school and that of the open classroom—has remained solidly within the ideological mold of *individual internal differences* and has, in fact, usually moved closer to the extreme ends of these dimensions. The villains that formed the targets of these so-called reforms—"lock-step" education, conformity to a standard mold, suppression of creativity, and so on—have never existed. Our schools have never attempted to produce a homogeneous product; they have always been an instrument for sorting and differentiating.[3] Seventy-five years ago the process was similar to the mechanical sorting of potatoes or oranges: as the small potatoes or oranges drop through the little holes, leaving only the big ones at the end of the winnowing process, so, in the early years of the century, did those with supposedly small minds drop out of school in the early grades, leaving only the big, juicy, superior minds with a high school diploma. It was only when everyone started to go to high school that the simple sorting process had to be replaced by more subtle and complex procedures, devised by the progressive and humanitarian reformers of the day. For example, the idea that schools should have as their goal the achievement of each student's full potential, which sounded so lovely and concerned, meant, first of all, that each individual was internally different with respect to his "potential" (some have the potential to be rich executives, physicians, or bankers; others only the potential to be machine operators, lab technicians, or bank tellers). Second, it meant that the schools shouldn't screw up the program by letting youngsters with the potential—something akin to destiny—of a machine operator trot undifferentiated alongside the youngsters who were obviously going to be running the factory. We could let them all go to high school, but we couldn't let them all get a high school education of the old variety. So we had "reforms": we got psychological testing to tell us—infallibly—what the potential of each student was, and we got separate curricula within what we still called a "high school"—the college preparatory curriculum, the business or commercial curriculum, the vocational training curriculum, the general curriculum, and so forth, sometimes subdivided even further into, for example, a high-class, advanced college curriculum and a low-class college curriculum. Ostensibly, these reforms were designed so that the new high schools would be "comprehensive," would meet the needs and abilities and interests of *all* children—something for everybody and to each according to his needs. Progressive educators bruised each other's shoulder blades congratulating each other on the incredible egalitarianism of it all.

Meanwhile, for some inexplicable reason, these wonderful reforms were not being adopted by the prep schools whose clientele were still almost exclusively the children of the rich. No one seemed concerned to find out whether these young people had the interests and mechanical dexterity that were the infallible signs of a "potential" to be a punch-press operator or a secretary. It was simply assumed that they were all going to go to college and then to do the same kind of work their fathers and uncles and older brothers did. So, it appeared, they were continuing in the old authoritarian, lockstep, uncreative, conforming, traditional curriculum—featuring Latin, history, mathematics, English composition, and French. All the poor little rich kids were being denied the wonderful new opportunities that were available in the comprehensive high schools. They couldn't learn how to take shorthand or how to run an adding machine, they were deprived of instruction in automobile repairing, and, rather than being allowed to learn long division three years in a row, they were required, willy-nilly, to learn algebra and geometry.

The underlying idea of the comprehensive high school—the differential training of young people to occupy higher or lower positions in the occupational hierarchy—was finally spelled out in an undisguised, almost ingenuous, fashion by James Conant, former president of Harvard, in his famous 1961 report *Slums and Suburbs*,[4] in which he called for the rational restructuring of education to perform its central task more efficiently and clearly— the task of preparing the children of the slums for blue-collar jobs and the children of the suburbs for white-collar and professional careers. Conant apparently thought that the children of the slums and their parents were quite conscious of what was going on in the schools, were in complete agreement that they had lower "potential" than their middle-class suburban fellows, and would be content with schooling that trained them more effectively for the modest and subservient roles that awaited them in real life.

More recent reforms like teaching machines and open classrooms again emphasize the idea of individuals and their internal differences; they stress the notion that each child should follow, as much as possible, his own individual interests and move "at his own pace," as they say. In other words, let the slow learner learn slowly (as slowly as possible), but let him do it by himself, sitting in front of a teaching machine, so he won't feel so bad when he sees how much faster his superior classmate is moving.

It is unrealistic, cruel, and reactionary, said the reformers, to expect children of low ability to grapple with *The Legend of Sleepy Hollow* or *Macbeth*. Let's find reading material that they can deal with, even if we have to be so radical and daring as to have them read the sports page of the local tabloid or even the comic books.

The mania for sorting by tracking was manifested in its most extreme form in my own experience when our daughter was in the seventh grade. This was in New Haven, to which we had just moved, and we discovered that the schools there had a system of testing children in the sixth grade, in order to "place" them with unerring accuracy when they moved on to junior high school—not, as one might expect, into two or three tracks, but into as many tracks as there were classes. Twelve seventh-grade classes? Twelve seventh-grade tracks, precisely sorted out, with the most able children in class VII-A, the next most able in VII-B, and so on, down to the thirty or so who were precisely the least able, caught in the drip pan at the bottom, the dread VII-L.

The most recent development of the sorting and tracking functions of schools is evident in the area of so-called higher education. Just as we reached the point in the 1930s when the majority of children completed high school, so we are now approaching the point when the majority of children will obtain education beyond high school. And we are restructuring our system of higher education to meet this contingency, just as we restructured our high schools in the 1920s. The purpose, naturally, is "to meet each individual's differing needs and abilities." We will have junior colleges and community colleges, primarily for the vocational training of technicians. There will also be state colleges that will train teachers, welfare workers, and higher-level technicians. And within the universities we will have different "schools"—business, nursing, education—as well as the elite liberal-arts schools, where we will go right on providing the old-fashioned college education that is not "functional" or "practical" for the average young person, who doesn't want to waste his time reading Shakespeare, books on European history, and other "irrelevant" material. No, they say, the average college student today wants to get a *real* education, a *relevant* education, that will provide him with "marketable skills" when he goes out with diploma in hand. Perhaps they're right. It seems that way. When the comprehensive high schools gave young people the opportunity to study bookkeeping and typing, rather than Latin and trigonometry, they similarly jumped at the chance to prepare themselves for the "business world." That's really meeting their individual needs and interests; that's really making useful education available to everyone.

At the same time that the educational system is meeting the special needs of every individual, it is miraculously meeting the needs of the labor market. Ten thousand new engineers? Coming up. Computer programmers? On the way. Not so many elementary-school teachers? We're already cutting back production. By some amazing coincidences, apparently, the schools manage to furnish business and industry with just the right mix of manpower, from janitors and dishwashers to accountants and managers. Whatever business wants, business gets, and the needs of business just happen to match the needs and talents of the individual students. An amazingly efficient system! We should wonder, perhaps, how schools manage to be so successful in producing a rather thoroughly sorted generation of children, almost every one of whom is quite reconciled, it would seem, to accepting his predestined niche in society, no matter how lowly it may be. It's not all that mysterious how the educational system trains someone to be a lawyer or minister; but how does it go about training someone to be a dishwasher or a janitor or a garbage collector? Or, for that matter, a clerk, a department-store salesperson, or a carpenter? How does this tracking and sorting system work so effectively? Let's look more closely at what happens in the classroom.

III EXPECT AND YE SHALL RECEIVE

There is an apocryphal story about an energetic teacher who was quite convinced that she gave her very best to every member of her classes and, in turn, got the very best out of each one of them. She was satisfied that this was so because, every year when school began, she would diligently collect information about the aptitudes of all of her pupils and keep their IQs—individual by individual—under the glass top of her desk, until she had virtually memorized them. At the end of every year, when she compared the achievements and grades of the students with their IQs, she found an almost perfect match—those with high aptitudes, with high IQs, did best; those with low IQs did worst. Every single child was performing to his capacity.

When a new principal came to the school, the teacher explained her system to him and demonstrated it in the classroom. She called on a pupil with a high IQ and he gave the right answer, and then on one with a low IQ, who gave a wrong answer. The principal was very interested and asked to borrow her list of IQs. The next day he came back to give it to her and said, "You're certainly right about the kiddoes performing just about the way these numbers say they should. I must tell you one thing, though. Instead of copying down your pupil's IQs, you've copied down their *locker numbers*."

This story illustrates the central mechanism in the classroom by which the miracles of sorting and labeling that I discussed in the preceding section are accomplished: human beings, and particularly children, act the way we *expect* them to act, because we unconsciously convey to them what those expectations are. The teacher in the story expected children with high locker numbers to perform well, and those with low numbers to perform poorly, and they did.

This process has now been demonstrated rather thoroughly in real life. Kenneth Clark and his associates in the HARYOU project, for example, concluded that Harlem schools were doing a poor job of educating Harlem children because the teachers in those schools *expected* the children to learn very little, and, naturally, they got what they expected.[5] A few years later, Rosenthal and Jacobson demonstrated this point in their dramatic "Pygmalion in the Classroom" experiment.[6]

This study has become very well known over the past few years, but I will summarize it very briefly. The experimenters were looking for the effects of expectations on behavior, the so-called self-fulfilling prophecy, and they tested it in the classrooms of an elementary school in San Francisco. At the end of one year, they administered a newly developed intelligence test to all the children in the school, but they gave it a meaningless high-sounding name, the "Test of Inflected Acquisition," and described it to the teachers as a new kind of test that would pick out children who were likely to show sudden intellectual improvement—"spurters" who would abruptly start to do much better in their school work. The test was obviously nothing of the sort, and they didn't use it for that purpose; rather, they just randomly selected 20 percent of the children—about five from each class—and casually informed the teachers that these were the ones the test had selected as potential "spurters." There was no intervention beyond this. At the beginning of the next year, they gave this false information to teachers in the hope of setting up expectations in their minds, before they even had a chance to see the children or get to know anything about them. Then they sat back to see the effect, which they measured by retesting the children later in the year and by getting personality and behavior ratings of the children from the teachers.

The results were striking. Most of the children who had been randomly picked out and labeled as potential "spurters" did in fact "spurt," particularly the younger children in the early grades, who showed tremendous gains on their tests. In addition, these children were seen by the teachers much more favorably than were their classmates; they appeared more curious and better adjusted, among other things. Finally, and in some ways most interesting of all, children *not* labeled as "spurters" who spurted anyway—who went *against* the expectations that had been set up in the teachers' minds— were viewed much more negatively, as showing undesirable behavior, being poorly adjusted, and so on.

Ray Rist followed up the Pygmalion experiment with a study in which he tried to find out more about how expectations form in teachers' minds in the ordinary classroom situation without any experimental intervention.[7] He focused his attention on a single class in a ghetto school, all black children, starting with them in kindergarten and following them into the second grade, stopping along the way for frequent formal and informal observations of the classroom goings-on and for interviews with teachers. Again, the results are rather startling.

On the eighth day of school, the kindergarten teacher was prepared to divide thirty children into three distinct ability groups. Two and one-half years later, in the second grade, ten of the thirty were still in the same building (others had moved, had not been promoted, or were in other second-grade classes in an annex). Of the ten, six had been in the top-ability group in kindergarten. All six were in the top group in second grade. The other four had been in the middle and low groups in kindergarten. All were in the middle group in second grade. (By the second grade, the lowest group was made up predominantly of children who were repeating the year.) What an incredible evaluating and prognosticating ability that kindergarten teacher had! Think of it: after eight days of school with thirty little five-year-olds she had never seen before—that is, after an acquaintance of not much more than thirty hours—this teacher was able to sort them out precisely in terms of their academic abilities in a manner that would hold up for at least two and one-half years (and, as we know from other studies, would hold up almost as well for the full twelve years of school).

Rist watched the teachers and the children very closely during that first year of kindergarten, and he found some interesting relationships. It was quite clear in the teacher's own mind how she went about dividing up the children: the nine children at table one, she explained, were her "fast learners," the other twenty-one, at tables two and three, "had no idea of what was going on in the classroom." How could she spot the "fast learners" so quickly? Rist did notice a number of objective characteristics and behavior that differentiated the "fast learners" from the others. First of all, the "fast learners," as she labeled them, were all neatly dressed in clean clothes; this was true of only one of the twenty-one other children. Second, the table-one elite all interacted readily with the teacher and each other. Third, they were more verbal and used standard middle-class English almost all the time; the others were much less responsive verbally and tended to use the phrases and syntax of so-called Black English. Finally, the children differed in a number of background characteristics that were known to the teacher from preschool registration: the parents of the table-one children had much better educations, jobs, and incomes than had the parents of the others. None of these families were on welfare, whereas six of the twenty-one others were. Only one-third of the table-one children did not have both parents living in the home, whereas the great majority of the others—sixteen out of the twenty-one—came from one-parent families. These and similar social-class characteristics sharply differentiated the three groups, even more than did relative cleanliness and verbal skills. Somehow, then, the teacher's estimation of a five-year-old's academic ability, whether or not he was a fast learner, coincided precisely with whether or not he was a neat, clean, verbal kid from a middle-class family.

At this point, we can consider three possible explanations of this uncanny course of events. The first is that the kindergarten teacher had an eerie, almost clairvoyant capacity to sense the abilities of five-year-olds and that the remarkable correlation between her judgments and the background of the children was purely coincidental.

The second explanation involves what might be termed the Coleman-Herrnstein hypothesis[8]—that, because of either genetic or cultural differences, middle-class children do indeed have greater verbal skill, greater learning potential, and that an accurate prediction of who the fast learners will be inevitably means picking out the middle-class children.

The third explanation is that the teacher has a preconceived idea of what "fast learners" look and act like (namely, like the teacher herself), that her expectations are based on these preconceived ideas, and that her teaching style is such that she treats children from different class groups differently, conveys to them her own evaluations and expectations, and thereby produces the anticipated results.

Rist's observations tend to support the last explanation. For example, although the three tables faced a blackboard that ran along the entire length of the wall, the teacher consistently tended to stand in front of table one and to write on the board directly in front of her "fast learners." She gave the overwhelming majority of her attention to the table-one children and usually called on them to respond to questions, to tell what they did on Halloween, to take attendance, and to act as monitors. In one classroom hour that Rist observed, the teacher communicated exclusively with the children at table one, except for two commands of "Sit down!" directed at children seated at the other tables. To sum up the year, it is quite clear that the teacher *taught* the children at table one, and either ignored, belittled, or disciplined the other children. At the end of the year, of course, the table-one children had finished all of their kindergarten work, and were ready for the first grade and the great adventure of learning to read. The teacher was still persuaded that these were the children who were most capable and interested in school and that the others were "off in another world" and basically "low achievers." The latter were, in fact, already behind, and when they went to the first grade, they were not *permitted* to start the first-grade reading lessons until they had finished up the kindergarten work that their teacher had neglected to teach them the previous year. The process continued into the second grade, the gap widened, and the differences among the children became more pronounced. As Rist put it, "The child's journey through the early grades of school at one reading level and in one social grouping appeared to be preordained from the eighth day of kindergarten."[9]

In addition, he noted that the belittling of the lower-track children was imitated by the high-track children, who gradually began to verbalize their own sense of superiority over those in the lower tracks. The labeling process was made quite manifest in the second grade, where the three different tables—instead of being called one, two, and three, as in kindergarten, or A, B, and C, as in the first grade—received characterizing labels that left no doubt in anyone's mind: the top group were the "Tigers," the middle group the "Cardinals," and the lowest group the "Clowns."

Other recent studies have discovered, with much more reliability and precision, the specific details of what Rist had been able to see so clearly at a more general level. Brophy and Good, and others,[10] have developed detailed procedures for observing and coding interactions in the classroom between teacher and pupils and have shown that, even when there is no substantial difference in the *quantity* of interaction between high-expectancy and low-expectancy groups, the *qualitative* differences are enormous. With students of whom they hold high expectations, teachers more often praise correct answers, or "sustain" the interaction if the answer is incorrect—that is, they repeat or rephrase the question, give a clue, and in general try to get the student to continue to work toward a correct response. With pupils of whom they expect little, teachers are more inclined to accept correct answers with minimal praise and to criticize incorrect answers. In addition, the teacher is much more likely to limit her interactions with these students to matters of class organization and discipline.

The summated data of all these recent studies appear to explain quite clearly how the tracking process works, mediated by teacher expectations. First of all, teachers always assume that some students will learn and that others will not. Second, they tend to take for granted that it is the children of middle-class background and characteristics who will be the fast learners, and that those of working-class background will do poorly. The teachers make their expectations come true—apparently not consciously—by their grossly different treatment of the children. Oversimplifying the vast array of available data, one might say that teachers instruct and praise the middle-class and upper-class children, making them feel superior, and that they discipline and criticize the working-class children, making them feel inferior. The result is that the former gain confidence, tend to like school, develop high educational aspirations, and act out the expectations conveyed to them; the latter also act out the expectations they perceive, by coming to believe in their own lack of aptitude, by disengaging from school, and by dropping out as soon as they decently can.

The saddest part of the whole process is the destruction visited upon the spirits and self-esteem of the poor and working-class children, many of whom are gradually convinced—by the behavior of the teachers and administrators, as well as by that of their peers who are labeled good students— that they are dumb, incompetent, unfit for intellectual activity, destined to be on the bottom of the heap in real life as they are in the classroom as little children. Sennett and Cobb, in *The Hidden Injuries of Class*,[11] have documented this ravaging of the spirit, which is one of the major functions of the school system.

IV   THE ADMINISTRATION OF INEQUALITY

One reason why so many students accept this unfair labeling of themselves as lacking in worth (although, thank God, there are many who remain unwilling to accept themselves as useless boobs and who rebel against the whole process) is that the schools, as well as the classrooms, are structured in a very authoritarian, hierarchical fashion. There is a series of ever more powerful authorities, who exercise the functions of prosecutor, judge, and jury in enforcing a seemingly endless and often apparently pointless set of rules and regulations, codes, prescriptions, and directions. One must walk on this side of the corridor, not talk in class, go up on this staircase and down on that, get hungry and eat during a particularly arbitrary twenty-two minute period of the day, get permission to get a drink of water or to urinate, and, while following all these dictates, constantly engage in—or appear to engage in—the endless individualistic competition with every other child in sight, in order to be labeled a bright, competent, quick, and likeable individual. Cooperation with your friends (they call it "cheating") is forbidden; only heartless and ruthless rivalry is allowed. Group activity not directed and led by an authority figure (but rather by a species of bad child known as a ringleader) is deemed a source of disruption that is probably breaking one or more of the rules. The whole process is arranged to teach the child that there is a natural hierarchy in this world, that he occupies a particular and unique slot in that hierarchy, and that he might as well get used to it.

This aspect of what has been called the hidden curriculum of the schools—that is, the task of readying and training children for the hierarchical, authoritarian world of work—was made clear to me and my wife one evening when we attended a meeting of parents, administrators, teachers, and children at Newton High School, a meeting called by a guidance counselor to "improve communications." Against our better judgment we went, because the counselor was obviously very sincere and eager somehow to improve the climate of the school.

During the course of the discussion, the subject of tardiness came up, and we learned about Newton's rather bizarre policy regarding tardiness. If a child came into a class late, he had to go up to the teacher, who filled out a late slip, which the child had to take down to the housemaster's office for a countersignature; then he had to return to the classroom and give the late slip back to the teacher. I could hardly believe that any sane person could dream up such a crazy ritual, and I asked what its purpose was. One of the teachers explained to me that if a child came into a classroom late two terrible things occurred: he disrupted the class, and he missed three or seven or nine minutes of the precious wisdom being imparted by the teacher. In order to discourage this, the late slip system was invented. Still speaking as reasonably as I could, I said it seemed to me that the procedure not only did not minimize the disruption and the deprivation of the teacher's wisdom, but apparently had the opposite effect. Instead of slipping in and sitting down quietly, the child was *required* to disrupt the class quite thoroughly in order to have the teacher fill out the late slip. Then he was *required* to miss an *additional* ten or fifteen or twenty minutes of wisdom dispensation, as he went on his journey back and forth to the office; at the end of all this, he was *required* to disrupt the class a second time in order to return the late slip to the teacher.

The teacher admitted there was a certain truth to what I was saying but pointed out that I was overlooking one of the main purposes of school. When children got out of school, they would be expected to get to the office or punch the factory time clock punctually; this punctuality was one of the things they were supposed to learn in school, and they would never learn it unless tardiness of this sort were dealt with in some dramatic and memorable fashion.

I acknowledged that he had me cold.

Our schools, then, are not the great equalizers they are made out to be. They are not springboards to social mobility, where individual merit is unerringly identified and nourished. They are, in fact, major social institutions that serve at once to sustain and cement inequality and to prepare a relatively docile work force for various levels in the hierarchy of labor. Its task is not to open the mind of youth to the glories of eternal truth and beauty, but rather to artificially enhance the egos of the children of the well-to-do and brutally assault the egos of the children of workers and poor people.

Above all, schools are ideological instruments, institutions for teaching by endless example and repetition that individual human beings are all different and, in particular, that the major difference is that some are superior and others inferior, as a consequence of their different internal qualities. Schools are places where competition by individuals striving to defeat one another is exalted, where cooperation by groups to help one another is condemned, and where reading and writing and arithmetic are merely the tools of the moment by which we can be taught to play out the great American game of survival of the fittest.

6

Black Like Them

IDEOLOGY AND RACISM

I   A DIFFERENT DIFFERENCE

In America, one of the most dangerous ways to be different is to be black. From the days when captured Africans were unloaded from the slave ships in Charleston until today, black men and women have always run the kinds of risks that the majority of whites know very little about—of being killed, of being brutally exploited, of being allowed to sicken and die before their time. We can acknowledge with some pride that, over the centuries, things have changed greatly for the better, as long as we also admit, with shame, that they are still very bad and that racism still towers highest among all of America's unsolved problems. We cannot talk about inequality in general without focusing on racial inequality in particular; any proposed remedy for inequality can be judged valid only if it also promises an end to racial inequality. More specifically, any discussion of inequality in the 1980s is incomplete unless it deals with the central racial issue of the times—affirmative action.

In this chapter, I shall apply to racism the analytical tools developed in the preceding chapters, in an effort to clarify the dynamics of it. To begin with, we have to recognize an anomaly about racial inequality, the fact that in both practice and ideology, racism is old-fashioned. By that I mean that most fundamental racist thinking has not kept pace with the modern exclusive emphasis upon the individual. Blacks have been, and continue to be, treated and kept down as a *collectivity*, with a primary emphasis on difference and only a secondary one on presumed internal aspects of individuals. This latter point is not immediately apparent, since racism seems to be based on surface characteristics (skin color, facial features, and the like) that probably, three centuries ago, reliably differentiated enslaved Africans from the homogeneous Northern European white colonists. Today, however, they can no longer surely differentiate the black minority. There are millions of "blacks" whose skin is lighter than that of millions of "whites," for example, and a large minority, if not an actual majority, of blacks now have some white ancestry, and a substantial minority of whites have some black ancestry. Race, then, has become completely a social rather than a physical category, and the supposed physical signs of membership are now taken as external signals of significant *internal* qualities of the *individual* members of the category—intellectual, moral, temperamental, and so forth.

The mythology that justifies racial inequality, then, is more complex than the one that supports more general social and economic inequality. Blacks are, so to speak, caught in a crossfire: they occupy a position in which they are the objects of two types of oppression and exclusion that overlap in such a way as to include only them. (There are other minorities—notably American Indians and Hispanics—whose positions are very similar, but for somewhat different historical reasons. The dynamics of sexism, however, are very similar to those of racism.)

The reality that blacks have tended to be kept at the very bottom of the inequality ladder and have been the most vulnerable among the vulnerable majority stems from the formulations of racism in collective terms—literally applying the standards of internal individual differences to a group in occupational situations, that is, the segregation of blacks into the most menial and low-paying jobs.

To some extent, this doubling of inequality jeopardy helps to explain the conflicting views deriving from the Fair Share and Fair Play perspectives. Those who view the race situation from the Fair Play point of view focus almost exclusively on the fact that blacks are defined collectively as inferior, which is a clear violation of the principles of equal opportunity for the individual and placement by merit. Those who approach it from a Fair Shares perspective, on the other hand, are far more impressed by the fact that blacks, as a group, have been blatantly and systematically deprived of access to resources through the mechanism of occupational segregation.

II UNTOUCHABLES

One way to gain insight into the unusual nature of the problem of racism is to compare the situation of blacks in America with that of the lowest stratum in an overt caste system (such as prevailed in India and the residue of which still affects the lowest caste, the so-called untouchables). In many ways, Americans have treated blacks as if they did indeed constitute the lowest caste in our society, and it is, therefore, useful to think about racism in America at least partly in terms of the conditions and consequences of a caste system.[1]

In the beginning, as slaves, blacks were considered to be so different as to be essentially nonpersons. Virtually all the elements of racist thinking, focusing on the imputed internal factors that determined blacks' supposed differences from and inferiority to whites, were developed during the period of slavery, specifically as a justification and explanation for slavery. After emancipation and the constitutional amendments that changed their formal legal status, blacks were still defined in the same racist terms, and their legal status as slaves was replaced by the post-Reconstruction network of Jim Crow laws and Jim Crow customs that virtually had the status of laws. At this point, though technically free, blacks were treated as a quasi-caste, the lowest caste in our society.

In a caste system, to cite two of its distinguishing features, members of particular castes tend to follow particular occupations and there is a substantial degree of ritual purity in the official separation of members of different castes. Members of a lower caste are said to be able to contaminate or defile members of a higher caste by coming into direct contact with them— as if they exuded some sort of spiritual bacteria.

Both of these conditions have been true, in general, for most black people in America. They have been closely associated with the roles of servants and unskilled laborers, particularly agricultural laborers ("hands"). Dozens of stereotypes spring to mind that are based on unpleasant reality—"George," the Pullman porter, the black maid, the black doorman. And until recently, of course, it seemed almost as ecologically inevitable for black people to be in cotton fields as for boll weevils. The dirtiest, most menial, and most servile jobs were explicitly labeled "nigger jobs."

The pettiness of Jim Crow laws—laws insisting on two sets of everything, from toilets and drinking fountains to schools and swimming pools; laws prohibiting blacks and whites from sitting side by side, on church pews, soda fountain stools, or bus station benches; laws forbidding social relationships, particularly intermarriage—this can only be understood as efforts to instill in the minds of people, deeply and permanently, ideas, attitudes, and motivations regarding ritual purity and pollution.

Not only ideas and attitudes were affected by this obsession with pollution. Ritually determined behavior was epidemic, ranging from the horror of lynching a black man accused of defiling a white woman to the stupidity of boiling a glass from which a black man (at the back door of a white family's house) had drunk some philanthropic water. There also exist endless stories of caste-linked occupational assumptions, such as the one about the black doctor in a hospital who is taken for an orderly.

Although virtually all white ethnic groups in America have experienced, and many continue to some extent to experience, discriminatory treatment, none have been accorded this particular castelike status. In the final reckoning they have been counted as white. One might not like them, their ways, or their speech. One might prefer not to have them as friends or as in-laws. But, in the end, they were grudgingly acknowledged to have the right to be "Americanized," "naturalized," and ultimately to pull themselves up by their own bootstraps, if they could find them.

With respect to *race*, however, discrimination and separation have been officially and legally established as public policy. Only one other oppressed group in America has been treated unequally under the umbrella of law and justice—women. There are "women's jobs" and "women's work" and "women's place" and specific, legal restrictions on women's rights. There are such things as racism and sexism, definable by particular laws and widespread, long-standing customs that have almost had the force of law. But despite group prejudice and stereotyping of the crudest and vilest nature, there is not, in the same sense, such a thing as "ethnicism."

The major distinction between discrimination against blacks and that against hyphenated Americans is precisely the history of castelike treatment. In my generation, and presumably even more in earlier ones, black men and women were almost never depicted in movies, magazines, and other public media in anything but servile roles—those of maids, janitors, waiters. No one undertaking a train journey seemed to notice, or be interested in, the fact that redcaps, waiters, and sleeping-car attendants were all black and that engineers, conductors, brakemen, and ticket salesmen were all white. It was as if to say: that's the way God made the world—a lot of whites to do the important things and a few blacks to wait on them.

There were other occupational stereotypes, but none of them had this servile, castelike quality. The Irish cop in the movies, though hilariously dumb, was an authority figure. The Greek restaurant owner on the radio, though amusing to us because of his excitability and his broken English, was a prosperous small businessman. The Italian gangster, though evil and dangerous, was a man of power and effective action.

The dimension of caste, then, is one axis of racial inequality; the other, although largely a consequence of the first, is analytically separable from it—the position of blacks with respect to command over resources. There were, and still are, essentially no blacks among the very wealthy, the owners, those who control America's resources, the "ruling class," the small minority at the peak of the inequality pyramid. This is virtually an all-white preserve.

Almost all blacks are workers, completely dependent on paychecks for survival, situated within the vulnerable majority. In 1977, for example, 24 percent of the white families in America received incomes in excess of $25,000, but only about 9 percent of the black families earned that much. The median income, of about $16,000, divided American families as a whole into the half above and the half below that line, but among black families 72 percent fell below this midpoint. At the low end of the scale, only 7 percent of the white families had incomes of less than $5,000, but about one-fourth of the black families were in this group.[2]

Virtually all blacks are members of the vulnerable majority, and in general they are the most vulnerable, being concentrated most heavily at the lower ends of the income and occupational scales. They are, in a sense, an especially vulnerable minority within the vulnerable majority.

It can be seen, then, that racial inequality has three important features. First, there is the effect of a semicaste status, as manifested in continuing gross racial discrimination. Second, there is the absence of wealth; few black parents can, simply by means of a last will and testament, ensure the economic security of their children. Third, there is the consequent reality that blacks, as a collectivity within the larger one of those who work for salaries and wages, are relatively worse off than the total group. One way of thinking of this is to note that the least-well-off 85 percent of blacks occupy positions in the inequality structure approximately equivalent to the least-well-off 60 percent of the white population.[3]

There are three common analyses of these conditions, none of which is complete and accurate and none of which, in my opinion, provides an adequate basis for effectively ending racial inequality:

• The first, essentially the analysis that grows out of the Fair Play perspective, ignores the economic position of the black population as a whole and focuses on the residual effect of the caste problem on the individual black person, to the extent that this deprives him of "equal opportunity."

• The second, largely ignoring the caste problem, includes blacks in an undifferentiated way within the collectivity that I have called the vulnerable majority, holding that the achievement of overall equality will automatically eliminate racial inequality. This is a plausible position, but it provides no specific methods or safeguards to ensure racial equality.

• The third analyzes the caste problem in collective terms, but attributes the imposition of caste conditions and the continued discrimination against blacks to the activities of *all* whites as an opposing collectivity. This position omits from its analysis the larger structure of inequality which directly affects the great majority of whites. It particularly ignores the fact that a numerical majority of whites, those who are least well off, are in approximately the same economic position as the huge majority of blacks.

III ANALYZING THE ANALYSES

It is important to recognize and to acknowledge that virtually all progress toward eliminating racial inequality until the 1960s grew out of the first of the above three analyses, stressing the definition of racial injustice as the deprivation of individual rights to equal opportunity. Confronting what I have called the caste aspects of racism, advocates of Fair Play attacked the problem on much the same grounds on which they had attacked the outmoded structures of feudal inequality centuries before. In a sense, these aspects of racial injustice were remnants of that ancient system and thus susceptible to the same analysis and the same formulations for progressive change. And, as their ideological ancestors were a progressive force in overthrowing the feudal system, so Fair Players have been a progressive force in systematically attacking and destroying the legal and quasi-legal basis of race as caste. The ritual separation of the races is now broadly and firmly established as illegal in theory, and it has been diminishing in practice. This is visible in many areas of day-to-day life; blacks and whites sit side by side in all sorts of places that used to be monochromatic; they use the same soap and washbasin and drinking fountain. The kinds of ridiculous ceremonial rituals associated with separation are not only rapidly disappearing, but, even more important, they are being more and more clearly perceived as having been ridiculous in the first place. Now, one might snort at this and say, "Big deal!" But, trivial and ludicrous as it all was and is, to the extent that skin color has served as the equivalent of a caste mark in America, it is important that such practices be undermined and their disappearance be acted out as fully, publicly, and visibly as possible. Misguided assumptions and prejudices are formed through a process of experience and perception. People used to believe in the ritual separation of blacks and whites because, from childhood, that is what they had experienced and seen. The removal of opportunities to experience and perceive racial separation, then, will necessarily erode the basis of assumptions and beliefs upon which a castelike situation is founded.

Similarly, one can observe a gradual breakdown in the link between race and servile occupational positions, both in reality and in the presentation of black people in the media. It is a rare program or even commercial on television that remains all-white. It has also become more common—both in the media and, to a lesser extent, in real life—to see black professionals, skilled workers, business executives, or artists. Finally, there is substantial evidence to suggest that young persons—those who grew up during the years when legal caste barriers were being abolished one by one—are substantially less concerned about ritual separation and more committed to legal action against discrimination than are their elders.[4]

The weakness of the Fair Play position, of course, lies in its focus on the individual. This focus has been effective in winning legal victories, but it has little further contribution to make in actually bringing about the changes implicit in those victories. To eliminate the practice of racism, after the demolition of its formal, legal foundation, requires a fuller recognition of the collective nature of caste dynamics. Otherwise, the natural tendency is to pursue further victories on an individual basis, dealing with continuing discrimination on a case-by-case basis, which is fruitless and frustrating.

This can be more fully understood by examining the workings of government agencies charged with enforcing anti-discrimination statutes. For many years these agencies operated as if discrimination had indeed been a phenomenon directed against the individuals who were denied housing, work, and education, on the basis of race (or sex, age, or other criteria). This one-by-one approach was largely unsuccessful, in part because of logistics and the sheer limits of time, staff, and resources, in part because individual remedies were weak (by the time of the decision, the job or apartment had been taken and the complainant had to settle for other work or housing), but primarily because the process of discrimination is a collective, not an individual, phenomenon. A large real estate firm that discriminates in renting apartments, or a large employer who discriminates in hiring, does so by excluding blacks as a group, not as individuals. A firm of this sort could, did, and often still does maintain a pattern of activity that, when examined at the collective level, is found to be clearly discriminatory; at the same time, it can be dealing with an anti-discrimination agency in a most cooperative and conciliatory manner in regard to some individual case and even be offering humble apologies.

In the 1960s, here in Massachusetts, those of us involved as advocates with fair-housing or fair-employment cases would frequently find that the defendant company had been the subject of one complaint after another and that most of the cases had been settled and marked as "conciliated," with perhaps some nominal, symbolic remedy to the individual complainant and a fulsome letter of apology from the company, promising, cross their hearts, to be ever virtuous from then on.[5] We used to call them "I'll be good" letters. It was not until the agencies began to approach the problem at the collective level, examining *patterns* of discrimination and acting to eliminate those patterns by administrative remedies or class action suits in the courts, that these agencies began to make progress.

The second kind of analysis that I mentioned in the preceding section goes to the opposite extreme and attempts to explain racial inequality as being nothing more than an aspect of the overall state of social and economic inequality. That is, it does not take the caste problem into account at all. It is, of course, theoretically possible that an overall condition of equality could be achieved that would, by definition, entail the elimination of racial inequality as a by-product. However, prudence would suggest that it is equally possible that such an outcome could be fatally flawed by a continuation of discrimination and racial injustice based on the unresolved persistence of caste-linked attitudinal processes. The Founding Fathers, after all, were able to live with the contradiction of proclaiming that all men were created equal while, in many cases, owning fellow human beings as slaves. Are we so much more clever or unusual than they? If we try to move toward equality without specifically addressing the fact that continuing inequality of blacks seems "natural" to far too many of us, we might wind up with a society in which some are more equal than others. An analysis that omits the caste aspects of race, which is deeply ingrained in the American consciousness, seems to me weak and incomplete.

The third analysis, despite its emphasis on collectivities, is the weakest and most regressive of all. Formulating the issue simply as the collective white majority oppressing the collective black minority has two weaknesses: it implies unresolvable differences among all the members of the two groups, and, second, it draws incorrect conclusions from surface facts, without considering deeper structural questions. It is undeniably true that the great majority of whites are indeed infected with racist attitudes and expectations. How could this be otherwise in a racist society? It is also true that an uncomfortably large number of whites are prepared at least to support and often to participate in actions that are discriminatory and sometimes physically assaultive. Nevertheless, it is equally true that the majority of whites neither benefit from continued racial injustice nor originate the practices that maintain it. The role of beneficiary is filled by the well-off minority of whites, particularly the tiny minority of the very wealthy.

For example, in the case of housing discrimination, when a black family is refused the opportunity to rent or buy a home, it is the owners and the real estate network who are practicing discrimination, not the white family that ultimately buys or rents the dwelling at issue. It is the employer who actively discriminates in refusing to hire a black, not the white person who actually gets the job. While the white family that rents the apartment or the worker who gets the job does technically gain some marginal benefit from the proceedings, the primary culprits are the real estate operators and the owners of the discriminatory firms.

Or take another example: the mythology that the presence of blacks automatically reduces the value of homes in a neighborhood is a source of profit to the real estate interests, not to the white residents of the neighborhood. In fact, when the mythology becomes the basis of a carefully planned block-busting operation, the profits accruing to the operators come from the pockets of those exploited and manipulated whites.

In the realm of employment, the maintenance of a two-tiered job market in which blacks (as well as other minorities and women) are locked into a disadvantaged position—more frequently unemployed, excluded from better jobs, paid lower wages—not only does not benefit the average white worker, but it actually depresses his own wages. A regional labor market has a wage structure built on the foundation of the lowest going wage. The lower that base is, the lower the wages at the upper end of the wage structure. If, for example, in one area the average lowest going wage is $3.00 an hour, while in another it is $3.50, the effect is that the higher-paid worker who might be getting $9.00 an hour in the first area would in the second earn perhaps $11.00 an hour for doing the same work. The effect of discrimination against women and minorities is to reduce the foundation rate, the lowest going wage, and thereby to bring down the whole wage structure. Thus, although discriminatory practices affect blacks directly and visibly, they also have the more widespread indirect and invisible effect of keeping down the wages of all workers. The beneficiary is, not the white worker, but the white employer and the white stockholders, who exploit their white workers and doubly exploit blacks.

Blacks who act on this simple white-against-black hypothesis, without making any distinction between the wealthy white minority and their white fellow members of the vulnerable majority are, in my judgment, falling into the classical divide-and-conquer trap. Antiegalitarian propagandists try to exploit this simple white-versus-black formulation all the time in stirring up and nurturing racism among whites. A classical example of this can be found in Nathan Perlmutter's pamphlet *You Don't Help Blacks by Hurting Whites.*[6] Perlmutter presents a characteristic neoconservative Fair Play argument that says, in essence, that the solution to one group's getting a larger slice of the pie is to bake a bigger pie, on the grounds that you don't achieve equality by taking away from those who have more and transferring it to those who have less. Now this is obviously absurd. A way of *defining* equality is to picture a situation in which the monopoly of the rich over most resources is broken, in order to provide access to those resources for those who have less, namely, average working people. That's what equality is all about. The size of the *pie* doesn't matter a good goddamn. It's the size of the *slices* that counts, and the question is, Who gets a chance to eat what, and is one tiny group going to do the slicing in any way it chooses? Just as we must recognize that equality means taking away from the rich ("hurting" them) for the benefit of the rest of us ("helping" us), so we have to admit that in order for blacks to have greater access to resources, whites must necessarily give up their advantages in this respect.

But the significant question that gets blurred is, *Which* whites?

Data that I will present in the next chapter suggest very strongly that we advance toward equality, both racial and economic, by shifting the command of resources from the wealthy minority, virtually all white, to what I have called the vulnerable majority—which includes not only all blacks, but the huge majority of whites, as well. So we *do* "help" blacks by "hurting" whites—*rich* whites (and perhaps even a few rich blacks)—but we "help" most whites, ordinary working people, by the same process. Virtually all blacks, and the great majority of whites, are in the same boat and move toward equality together or not at all. And the bill for greater equality—economic *and* racial—is addressed to the wealthy.

An interesting point of rhetoric is raised by the use of a phrase like "hurting whites." In a way, one has to admire the propagandistic skills of those who phrase the question this way, implying (sometimes stating directly) that black advances are made at the expense of average working whites. They lay a seductive trap, offering to whites who are not well off the classical sop of being able to say, "No matter how bad things are, no matter how much we have to struggle, at least we're white and not black like them." And the idea that millions of persons are unemployed and millions more underpaid—disproportionately women and members of minority groups—is perversely twisted into a reason for a low-paid white worker to be grateful he has a job, obscuring from him the fact that unemployment and discrimination are two of the factors that keep his pay so low. In fact, as we shall see in the next chapter, not only does "helping" blacks (incidentally, an insultingly patronizing formulation) *not* "hurt" whites, it has precisely the opposite effect. So, this kind of propaganda, apparently so concerned about working-class whites, has the objective effects of dividing whites and blacks who have pretty much the same economic interests and of keeping them both vulnerable and deprived.

In the long run, blacks will best serve their own interests by joining with the majority of whites to transform our system of inequality and to work toward a Fair Shares society. In the short run, however, it is in the interests of both groups to give continuing high priority to the struggle against racial exclusion and injustice, in order to eliminate all vestiges of segregation and castelike disabilities, which are also injustices in themselves.

There are two important means to this end. One is full employment, which in itself erodes some of the economic effects of discrimination and minimizes the supposed significance of black-white conflict. The other is affirmative action, which takes direct aim at the caste problem. One cannot support Fair Shares equality without recognizing the significance of affirmative action, a fact that the majority of the leaders of organized labor, for example, clearly recognize, although they have not effectively educated their constituency about this matter. The average union member, like the average citizen, has been quite thoroughly taken in by the charges of the Fair Play crowd that affirmative action is "reverse discrimination." This issue, then, requires detailed consideration.

IV AFFIRMATIVE DISCRIMINATION AND NEGATIVE ACTION

Perhaps the most discordant clashes and the fiercest debates between proponents of the Fair Shares viewpoint and the Fair Play apologists occur over the issue that the first group names "affirmative action" and that the second criticizes as "reverse discrimination." It might be worth a moment or two to establish the nature of the concrete realities around which these arguments swirl. The typical story goes something like this: It has been determined that the present small number of blacks on the payroll of the Caldwell Manufacturing Company reflects discriminatory hiring practices. The company agrees to stop discriminating. In order to implement this good resolution, it is stipulated that the company undertake a program of "affirmative action." Such programs, whether undertaken voluntarily or as a consequence of governmental pressure or a specific court decision, are intended to be methods of transforming the words of laws, court rulings, or institutional promises into some semblance of reality. In essence, an affirmative action program sets down on paper a plan to end intentional or unintentional discrimination. It typically specifies procedures—such as broadened recruitment—that will be used in order to increase the proportion of blacks (and women and other minority groups) in the work force or some segment of it, in the student body, in the faculty, and elsewhere. It also sets specific goals such as dates and numbers that are defined as the targets being aimed at.

If the Caldwell Company establishes such a program and actually does make some efforts that are in any significant measure successful (an event considerably more rare than the new mythology would have it), then those who cry "reverse discrimination" assert that in deliberately trying to hire seven or nine or twelve new black employees, Caldwell must, in effect, make another parallel decision, the decision *not* to hire whites for those jobs. Critics charge that this second decision is unfair and discriminatory (hence "reverse discrimination") to the whites who, if it were not for the affirmative action program, would probably have been hired. This, they say (with, I think, varying degrees of sincerity), places Mr. Caldwell into an exquisitely complex and painful moral dilemma: he must either continue to discriminate against blacks or, if he abandons that practice, necessarily discriminate against whites. In the words of Tevya, we appear to be confronting enormously complicated "problems that would cross a rabbi's eyes."

In the following pages, I will be arguing that the problems are really not so complicated, not even complicated enough to cross the eyes of a bar mitzvah boy, let alone a rabbi; that these apparently delicately balanced moral dilemmas are the consequence of pure sophistry; that all the slippery supporting argumentation is, in the final analysis, simply a defense of existing racial inequality; and that the prevailing arguments, when examined even casually, could be persuasive only to those who are already committed to maintaining the status quo and who are looking around for impressive-sounding justifications.

As might be expected, we find that most of the arguments and rhetoric used in the attack against affirmative action have been supplied by the hard-working "neoconservatives," the Fair Play propagandists, notably by Nathan Glazer.[7]

Let me try to specify and comment on some of these arguments (which will, I hope, begin to sound familiar to the reader as the fruit of the viewpoint that stresses the individual, and internal differences).

1. "Preferential treatment" of blacks (or women or other minorities) necessarily forces the hiring, promotion, or admission of less-qualified persons at the expense of the more qualified.

2. A well-established constitutional principle holds that the law is "color-blind"; any treatment—negative or affirmative—that is based on color is therefore unlawful and wrong.

3. Through the use of "quotas," affirmative action introduces a totally new and wholly unacceptable principle into American life, the principle of "representation." All institutions and enterprises, they say, will have to meet arbitrary, contradictory, and unworkable standards requiring the "representation" of all conceivable racial, ethnic, age, sexual, and religious subgroups in the surrounding community. Absurd examples are offered of employers or college administrators who desperately but futilely run around trying to fill their "quotas" of nubile Polish-American Baptist women or of middle-aged black Jews of French-Canadian extraction.

4. Affirmative action programs dangerously violate fundamental American principles of equal opportunity and selection or advancement solely on the basis of merit.

5. In particular, critics of affirmative action point out that the "burden" of desegregation and the elimination of discrimination fall on the shoulders of the innocent, persons who did not participate in, and are not responsible for, the discriminatory acts that occurred. Critics are especially solicitous about how these programs unfairly affect working-class white families and thus increase white resentment and racism. They say this is particularly bad because it is futile, bringing no significant payoff. They claim, for example, that when schools are desegregated there is no improvement in the quality of education and that ending discriminatory hiring practices has no effect on segregated residential patterns, which are the real root of the problem.

I am surprised, to tell the truth, that these arguments have proved so convincing in practice. To me they seem like transparent defenses of inequality. But it turns out that they are extremely persuasive. The term "reverse discrimination" is used routinely, without explanation and without quotation marks. Polls show that the overwhelming majority are opposed to "preferential treatment" and "reverse discrimination." A growing number of politicians, moreover, are finding this to be a useful and popular issue. The arguments thus have to be answered in some detail.

Preferential treatment   The claim that affirmative action has created a situation in which unqualified blacks are hired, promoted, and admitted ahead of qualified whites is a serious one, charged with weighty moral and political overtones. If the second-class status of blacks can be overcome only by such methods, then we appear to face a politically explosive choice between two undesirable alternatives. But is this truly the case? Is there any evidence to suggest that unqualified blacks are being given preferential treatment over qualified whites?

A fundamental question to begin with is, Who has a job and who does not? For decades the unemployment rate for blacks has usually been almost double that of whites. If blacks are really receiving preference in hiring, such kindly treatment should have some effect on this disparity between black and white unemployment rates. What are the facts?

If, following Glazer's chronology, we take 1970 as the approximate time when affirmative action began to have some effect, we can simply look at the unemployment figures before and after that date.[8] In 1960 the unemployment rate among blacks was 85 percent higher than it was among whites (10.2 as against 5.5 percent). By 1970, there had occurred a tiny improvement, the black rate being "only" 82 percent greater than the white rate (8.2 compared with 4.5 percent). Then came affirmative action and, it is claimed, preferential treatment. What happened? By 1978, the black rate had climbed back *up* to a point that was 142 percent greater than the white rate (10.9 as against 4.5 percent). After eight years of "reverse discrimination," the situation of blacks relative to that of whites had gotten *worse*, was in fact worse than it had been in 1960.

Might this not be considered a rather strange outcome of "preferential treatment?"

But perhaps these broad patterns are too general to pick up what might be more subtle effects regarding the preferential treatment of the unqualified. We can then look at groups that one would presume to be about equally qualified, such as black and white high school graduates who have had no further education, and evaluate the relative successes of the two groups in obtaining good or bad jobs. If we agree to call white-collar jobs generally "good," and service jobs generally "bad," we can compare the situations before and after affirmative action. In 1960, about three out of five white male high school graduates were in white-collar occupations as against only two out of five of their black counterparts.[9] (I am quoting only the rates for males, in order to avoid the confounding effect of discrimination against women). By 1970 the situation had improved very slightly in favor of blacks: a slightly higher proportion of them had white-collar jobs, while a slightly lower proportion of white high school graduates were in comparable jobs. (The improvement was, as I said, not at all remarkable; the ratio of the percentage of whites to that of blacks in this job category changed from 59:39 in 1960 to 58:42 in 1970.) But then, we are told, came "preferential treatment" under affirmative action programs and more substantial improvement in the position of blacks. The fact is that by 1978 the position of blacks relative to that of whites had worsened (the ratio now being 53:34); it was slightly *worse* than it had been in 1960.

The picture of high school graduates in service jobs is the mirror image of those in white-collar jobs. In 1960 one out of five black high school graduates held service jobs, as compared with only one out of twenty-five white graduates. By the end of the decade the situation had improved considerably: only one out of eleven blacks, as compared with one out of twenty-two whites. Then came affirmative action, supposedly to give an unfair advantage to blacks. After eight years of this kind of advantage, the 1978 picture was as follows: black high school graduates in service jobs—one out of seven; white graduates—one out of sixteen. Again, under a program accused of giving "unqualified" blacks an advantage, the overall situation of blacks deteriorates. To some this might look like preferential treatment. I'll bet that it sure doesn't taste like it.

Another way of approaching the question of how the unqualified are treated in relation to the qualified is to take persons in different occupations and to compare some measure of their "qualifications." A widely used index of this elusive characteristic is years of education. Over the years whites have had a marked superiority over blacks on this measure (and, according to this kind of reasoning, were therefore more qualified). Several decades ago this edge in "qualifications" was substantial—whites had, on the average, three or four more years of schooling. Today they still are more "qualified"—but only by a tiny margin, by some two months of schooling. In most job categories we find the pattern one might expect—whites are more educated than blacks. In only one, that of professional and managerial jobs, is this pattern reversed. Not surprisingly, this is the highest category used by the Census Bureau. Here, if anywhere, we should find evidence of preferential treatment—of a lower educational level among blacks in such jobs than exists among whites. What are the facts? Looking only at men (again because they dominate this occupational group and because the extensive discrimination against women complicates the situation), we find that in 1959 black professionals and managers had an average of 14.8 years of education, that is, had 2.8 years of college, while whites had an average of 13.2 years, that is, 1.2 years of college.[10] By this measure, "preferential treatment" was clearly being provided to less "qualified" whites. By the end of the 1960s, we find that this differential had been completely eliminated. In 1970 both black and white professionals and managers had an average of 14.6 years of education, and they were thus equally "qualified." Then along comes affirmative action to work its benevolent magic, and six years later black professionals and managers have 16.6 years of schooling, whites only 15.8. In other words, after six years of what critics charge was blatantly illegal preference of unqualified blacks, we find that somehow, once again, the average white manager or professional was less "qualified" (less educated) than his average black counterpart. One begins to wonder why supposedly preferential treatment seems consistently to produce results that are just the opposite of the intended ones.

The picture in education is not so gloomy. The proportion of blacks in college has been consistently increasing. In 1978, for example, 10 percent of the students enrolled in college were black, at a time when blacks constituted 14 percent of the college-age young people.[11] This is down from the high point of 11 percent in 1976, but up from 7 percent in 1970. This is the change that occurred during the eight years of supposed affirmative action. However, between 1965 and 1970, the years *before* its implementation (but, as readers will recall, the years of the high visibility of civil rights action), the increase was from 4.5 percent to 7 percent. In other words, the *rate* of increase from year to year is now only half of what it was before affirmative action presumably began to work its preferential wonders. This does not tell the whole story, either. The increase in black college enrollment has occurred disproportionately in predominantly black schools. In the early 1960s about two out of five black students were in black colleges; by the late 1970s this figure had risen to three out of five.[12]

Still another part of the picture must be considered. Enrollment in college must, after all, be preceded by graduation from high school. As recently as 1960 the likelihood of a black youngster's graduating from high school was about half that of a white one's; today the odds are almost even, and there exists evidence that within a few years black students will be *more* likely to graduate from high school than will white ones.[13] On this last point we can look at data about high school dropouts.[14] In 1970 blacks made up 13 percent of all youngsters aged fourteen to seventeen, but accounted for 20 percent of the high school dropouts. In 1978 they accounted for 14 percent of that age group, but for only 12 percent of the dropouts. As of now, then, teenage whites are slightly more likely to drop out of high school than are blacks of the same age. To spell out the implications of this data, the proportion of blacks in the pool of *potential* college registrants (high school graduates) has been increasing very rapidly; the proportion of blacks among *actual* college registrants is increasing very slowly. Draw your own conclusions.

The upshot of all this is that, while we are supposedly being plagued by preferential treatment, blacks have been able to maintain most (but not all) of the momentum in education they had built up during the 1960s. But again we see that between the promise of education and the actual payoff stood the same barrier of discrimination. The occupational situation, which had improved so dramatically during the 1960s, actually worsened significantly during these years of supposed preferential treatment.

Some preference! Some treatment!

The myth of the preferential treatment of blacks (and a similar one regarding women) is simply not supported by the facts, by the events of real life. The origin of the idea that there has been such a thing as preferential treatment is a mystery. It is presumably based on anecdotal evidence, a handful of horror stories about the stupidity or rigidity of some affirmative action bureaucrats. It would be surprising if such incidents did not occur from time to time, but they are obviously not representative. And the indignant telling, retelling, and embellishing of such stories add little in the way of serious proof.

All the evidence indicates that preferential treatment still exists, that it is quite extensive, and that it is still preferential treatment of *whites*.

If the real situation has been accurately described in the previous pages, it becomes evident that complaints about reverse discrimination are not founded in reality at all. Rather, they are based either on mistaken assumptions and prejudices or on speculations about a pure abstraction—about a "what might have been" rather than a "what really was." To me this suggests further that the real concern of the Fair Play critics is not to protest unfair changes (which have not occurred), but to forestall *any* changes, to insure that things remain the way they are. The way things are is that in many areas, blacks are actually falling further behind.

With that perspective we can now go on to consider the other objections produced by these transcendental meditations about hypothetical events.

But first a final word about preferential treatment that, I believe, seriously calls into question the sincerity of the critics of reverse discrimination. To my knowledge there is *one* real open program of preferential treatment that has been in place for some time. This is the preferential treatment given to veterans in federal and state civil service examinations. Federal civil service practice is to add a specific number of points to a veteran's score on an examination—I think it's ten points. In Massachusetts all veterans who pass the examination are ranked above all nonveterans who pass, and disabled veterans are placed at the top of the list. So, for example, a veteran who there obtains a grade of 75 on his test will be placed above a nonveteran who gets 95. Is this a case of reverse discrimination, of giving preference to the less qualified, of violating the sacred laws of advancement solely by individual merit? If so, why do the Fair Play critics never discuss it, let alone attack it? Does it add any credibility to their arguments to know that they ignore this case of real and admitted preferential treatment and confine their polemics and hysteria to the purely imaginary problem of preferential treatment of blacks and women?

Color blindness and quotas   Let's return now to the general situation that usually precedes some kind of "affirmative action." The firm, university, or other institution in question has admitted or been adjudged to have discriminated, intentionally or unintentionally, and now there has been a decision to do something about it. The company has resolved (or been required) to repent and reform and mend its ways, and it announces that it is going to make an effort in good faith to increase black membership in its work force from 1 percent to 5 percent over a three-year period.

"Aha!" scream the critics. "Quotas! Reverse discrimination! Shameful retreat from the holy principle of color blindness!" (One is tempted to inquire where they were hiding their indignation during the years when discrimination was going on unchecked, but let's not be beastly.)

Now, everyone can agree in a moment that color blindness is a good, an end that we all want to see achieved as soon as possible. But there are certain logical problems. For example, how do you know whether or not you're color-blind? More concretely, how does anybody notice whether or not there has been discrimination on the basis of color in the first place? How does one *enforce* the principle of color blindness without employing color consciousness? What happens when the color-blind are leading the color-blind?

Let me illustrate by describing an imaginary but typical scene, familiar to everyone who has ever been active in efforts to combat discrimination. It takes place in the office of old Mr. Caldwell, president of the manufacturing company. The civil rights activist or the official from the antidiscrimination agency speaks:

"Mr. Caldwell, have you noticed that among the 897 people you employ only 4 are black? Did you know that last week 15 blacks and 38 whites applied for a job at your personnel office and that you hired 7 of them—all white?"

"Is that so? Really! I'm amazed!" exclaims Mr. Caldwell. "Of course, I wouldn't notice that sort of thing. Never think about the color of a man's skin myself. Wouldn't know if we had four colored or four hundred. Me, I'm color-blind. All I care about is a man's individual ability. Can he do the job? Yes? Hire him. No? Don't hire him. Only fair way, right?"

Now, the diplomatic answer to this is obvious. So is the real, though usually unspoken, response: "Ho. Ho. Ho. Tell me another."

In the old days, Mr. Caldwell would say that he was sorry about that, that he'd take care of things, that everything was safe in his hands, since he was, by his own admission, an utterly unprejudiced person. A year later, one would return, like a sneaky un-American cad, count up Mr. Caldwell's work force, and tell him that he now had 5 blacks and 902 whites.

"I know, I know," he replies ruefully. "Looked into that situation myself. Personally. Turned out we weren't discriminating at all. The colored who came to us just didn't have the stuff, couldn't cut the mustard. Now, if you people could find me some qualified . . ."

That's what used to happen and what still happens in too many instances, when the task of ending discrimination is put under the jurisdiction of the discriminators. It is an ancient philosophical, moral, and ethical problem, also known as leaving the fox in charge of the chicken coop or the goat in charge of the cabbage patch.

To move away a bit from that particular merry-go-round and to establish a criterion of numerical goals is simply to inject a rational procedure for checking whether, when Mr. Caldwell and others say, "I'll be good," anything happens. I sometimes speculate about what alternative procedures would be recommended by those so lately smitten by color blindness. If ending discrimination is not supposed to result in a larger proportion—an increase in *numbers*—of those who have been discriminated against, what, in the name of God, *is* supposed to happen? It would seem to me that an increase in numbers is a pretty good criterion for judging whether or not discriminatory practices have been ended. In fact, I can't think of any other that could be used. So, if this is a good, and perhaps the only, criterion, why shouldn't we use it?

He who says he is against both discrimination and "quotas" is very much like a judge who, confronted with a bank teller who embezzled ten thousand dollars, offers his opinion that the teller should really put the money back in the till, but that it would be rather ungentlemanly and uncharitable if the bank's treasurer proposed to count the money in the till to see if any of the ten thousand (the goal? the quota?) actually showed up.

Individual merit and group membership   The quotaphobics say, rather stridently, that it is illegal, immoral, unethical, and completely outside our traditions to make hiring or admission decisions with any reference whatever to membership in specific groups—racial, ethnic, sexual, or any other. They say that in opposing discrimination we should not, may not, advance any further than the equal-opportunity threshold. An all-white, all-male institution may be perfectly legal and moral, they say, if it can be plausibly asserted that the white males were chosen uniformly and solely on the basis of their superior merit and qualifications. (An assertion that does seem quite plausible to many white males.) They state or imply that discrimination can be exercised only against an individual and that nondiscriminatory treatment can be defined as one that treats an individual solely on the basis of his or her own abilities.

There are several objections to this argument. First, it is illogical. It is impossible to discriminate against individuals as *individuals*; it can be done only against individuals as members of a group. Racial discrimination does not consist of an unrelated series of discrete actions directed against a random group of individuals who happen to be black; it is directed against blacks in general, as a group. That is the essential nature, the definition of discrimination. If I don't like you for some specific reason—you're a loudmouth, you're ugly, you're hostile, or you don't laugh at my jokes—and if I treat you badly because I don't like you, that's not discrimination, unpleasant as it might be. When I decide that all women are loudmouths, all blacks are hostile, and all Jews lack a sense of humor and when I treat members of those groups unfairly, that's discrimination.

By the same token, antidiscriminatory efforts and actions must be formulated in group terms. The abandonment of discriminatory practices can be evidenced, witnessed, and measured only by the observation of *changes* in the distribution of members of different groups.

Second, there is the problem of deciding which individuals have merit and are qualified, an issue I dealt with in Chapter Three. Here let me reassert only that there are very few, if any, methods of determining with any certainty the answer to that question.

Those who rant against "reverse discrimination" are quite certain, I will grant without question, that they are supremely capable of judging the merit and quality of their fellow men and women. It is not, I hasten to make clear, their confidence in their own judgments that I question, but merely their accuracy.

Representation   Diatribes against "quotas" frequently go on to construct an even more malevolent scenario, in which multiple quotas are imposed, based on color, ethnicity, sex, religion, and so on. If such multiple quotas have ever really been laid down in any particular case, I am not aware of it, and I assume that such cases are either nonexistent or extremely rare. Nor have I heard any advocates of affirmative action propose such a principle of representation, requiring that all institutions be more or less exactly "representative" of the total community from which they draw their membership. In this sense, "representation" as a principle is simply one more imaginary demon invented in the febrile imaginations of the antiegalitarians. It is an absurdity that no one has seriously proposed and that no one would undertake to justify.

Where the question of representation does arise is in its use as an index of possible discriminatory treatment and as a criterion for the ending of such treatment. In this case, we begin with the *lack* of representation. Let me cite a simple example, not uncommon a few years ago. It is found that a supermarket operating in a black community has all white or almost all white checkout clerks. Here we see a lack of representation in a category of employment that does not, after all, require a Ph.D. or professional graduate training. It would seem logical that most persons could learn to be competent checkout clerks and that a substantial number of residents of the com-

munity served by the store should be qualified to perform that service. It is
hard to think of anything apart from discrimination that would explain the
lack of such representation. Therefore, agents of the community or of a
governmental antidiscriminatory agency would normally act to attempt to
end this discriminatory pattern and would demand, as evidence that it had
been ended, a visible change in the work force over some period of time, so
that, allowing for such factors as normal labor turnover, more and more
blacks would be hired for these jobs. The increasing representativeness, if
you will, of the group of checkout clerks would constitute the evidence that
discriminatory hiring practices were being abandoned. Note that the whole
operation would focus on racial discrimination. There would be no demands
that 46 percent of the checkout clerks be Methodists, 14 percent of West
Indian descent, 32 percent between the ages of forty-five and sixty, and 11
percent Elks. Such absurd demands for "representation" simply do not occur. The issue is almost entirely made up out of whole cloth.

In one aspect of affirmative action the question of representation does
figure indirectly—namely, in the question of admissions to institutions of
higher education. This was one of the specific issues involved in the *Bakke*
case. Although the Supreme Court ruled that the medical school of the
University of California at Davis did, in fact, admit students with a specific
numerical quota, not based on any remedial court order and therefore un-
constitutional, it also ruled that affirmative action admissions programs operated by universities with some principle of representation in mind were, in
fact, perfectly legitimate (as long as no rigid numerical quotas were specified) and that the admissions policies of universities had always been very
concerned with a variety of questions regarding representation. The decision
appears to have followed closely the argument presented in the *amicus curiae*
brief submitted jointly by several prominent universities, including
Harvard.[15]

Anyone familiar with university admissions is surely familiar with the
principles of heterogeneity or representativeness along any number of dimensions. An undergraduate college, for example, will typically receive
many more applications than it has places to fill, and a large number of
applicants will be well qualified by all the usual standards—grades, test
scores, references, interviews, and the like. If a college has, say, only 500
openings for new freshmen, how does it select the 500 to be admitted from
the 1,000 or 1,500 who are well qualified? Certainly not by grades and test
scores alone (at least not to my knowledge). Many other criteria are brought
to bear. Some colleges want to admit children of alumni in fairly substantial
numbers; some want broad geographical representation; some want to balance prep-school and public-school graduates. Most colleges also want to
assure themselves of a good supply of athletes, poets, musicians, debaters,
journalists, actors, and artists. A third-string high school quarterback with

high grades may be passed over in favor of a terrific tuba player with lower grades, because the college is up to its sacroiliac in quarterbacks, but has an empty tuba chair in the orchestra. For a college to add new criteria for the selection of its student body—a good representation of minority members or women—is in no way a deviation from the ordinary processes of decision making in admissions offices. No one objects to a "quota" of athletes to play on the football team or a "quota" of musicians to play in the marching band. Isn't it a bit odd that critics of affirmative action can swallow tight ends and bass drummers, but strain at blacks and women?

There's a simple question that helps to determine whether numerical targets are discriminatory, exclusionary quotas or antidiscriminatory goals: namely, Does the target number follow the phrase "no more than" or does it follow the phrase "at least"? Several decades ago, many institutions established discriminatory quotas against Jews—*no more than* a certain percentage of Jews. Today we are trying to establish antidiscriminatory goals—*at least* a certain percentage of blacks or women. The principle is not new; it is not discriminatory; and it is not unjust.

The "burden" of desegregation   The "burden" argument, as I outlined it previously, has three parts: (1) desegregation and affirmative action impose an unfair burden on working-class whites; (2) as a result, whites become frustrated, their racism increases, and they will probably run away to a whiter environment; and, (3) these actions serve no useful purpose—education does not improve when schools are desegregated, "real" integration in social life does not come about when affirmative action programs lead to the hiring of more blacks.

The smarmy hand-wringing and cooing about the poor working-class whites' "bearing the burden" smacks to me of hypocrisy. More important, it specifically revives the specter of ritual purity: the implication is that it is somehow offensive and degrading, for example, for white children to have to go to school with blacks. This is, of course, consistent with the purpose of segregation in the first place and reveals, I believe, the deeply rooted racism of those who make such arguments.

Finally, it is mischievous to assert that efforts to maintain racial inequality originate among the working class. All available evidence indicates that racial prejudice is at least as prevalent in the middle and upper classes.[16] It is insulting to talk condescendingly about working-class people's being violently opposed to desegregation but unable to express their frustration except by flocking to taverns or churches or by flinging rocks at yellow school buses filled with black children. Most people in such communities—here in my area the outstanding example is South Boston—are dead wrong about busing, for example, but they are not the primitive dummies they are being made out to be.

The white resistance argument is a peculiar one. First, the point should be made that the major prophet of "white flight," James Coleman, has been extensively and persuasively challenged by critics who say that his analysis is simply wrong.[17] More important, the argument seems to imply that whites are somehow exempt from adhering to the Constitution when it is uncomfortable or inconvenient for them to do so. If we push this argument up the scale of intensity, we can immediately see how racist it is. I don't think, for example, that a similar argument would be put forth regarding lynching— that efforts to put an end to lynching should be soft-pedaled because the potential lynch mobs would be disappointed and surly and resentful. Nor would anyone argue that recently desegregated neighborhoods, in which the homes of new black residents are stoned or burned, should be returned to their prior all-white condition in order to soothe the ire of the stoners and burners.

The argument that desegregation and ending employment discrimination do no additional good, bear no additional fruit, is specious. Why should that even be expected? The argument that school desegregation produces no educational dividends is simply irrelevant. (This is *not* to admit that the argument is factually correct; the weight of the evidence tends to contradict the assertion.[18]) It misses the whole point of desegregation. The purpose is to wipe out the *caste* implications of color. When drinking fountains were desegregated, no one expected the water quality to improve; when lunch counters were desegregated, the hamburgers and Cokes didn't taste any better; when bus stations were desegregated, the waiting room benches didn't get more comfortable. And no one expected black kids in desegregated swimming pools to start swimming faster or ministers in desegregated churches to preach more eloquently. Segregation itself unjustly inflicts pain and injury on black people. Desegregation is designed to stop that particular source of hurt; that's a good enough goal.

So, although improved quality of schooling is seriously hampered by segregation, there exists no automatic guarantee that desegregation all by itself is going to upgrade the educational process. In fact, one must be on guard against the possibility that resistance will continue after apparent desegregation, that internal resegregation, tracking, and other methods will continue to impede educational progress.

Desegregation must be defined as an end itself. Its effectiveness can be measured, not by changes in educational achievement, but by changes in segregation. This, of course, explains the need for numerical goals, or, as they say, "quotas."

The plain purpose of the "burden" argument is to persuade working-class whites that desegregation and affirmative action are aimed at them, that they are the targets of unfair tactics. The supposedly feared result—greater racial animosity—is actually the purpose.

Whether by intention or luck, this kind of rhetoric and propaganda uses an extremely clever tactic of ideological confusion, based on the similar-different dimension. Critics of affirmative action, of busing for school desegregation, and of similar policies, typically ignore the fact that these are remedial actions designed to correct past injustices. Rather, they directly define them as ways of giving special treatment to blacks, of regarding them as different and as deserving of privilege and preferences. This implies that the working-class whites who are necessarily involved are being accorded an inferior status, are being treated unfairly and unequally. This perverse, and largely unchallenged, definition thus gives whites an apparently legitimate reason to oppose remedies for inequality *on egalitarian principles*!

Unfortunately, advocates of desegregation and affirmative action often fall right into this trap and go along with the idea that blacks are indeed different and in need of special treatment, when they should insist that such efforts to overcome racism and discrimination are intended to *end* the special treatment of blacks as different, to wipe out perceptions of significant differences that have chained blacks into their roles as members of an inferior caste, and to institute practices of equal treatment of whites and blacks.[19] It is my own sad conclusion that liberal friends of black progress who accept definitions of antiracist and antidiscriminatory programs in the terms formulated by the critics of these programs are doing almost as much damage as open enemies.

If I were still a betting man, I would bet a bundle that the overwhelming majority of blacks really do not want to be seen as objects of "special treatment." They've had enough of it. Special treatment is what has produced the present situation. I feel fairly certain that they would settle for being treated in the same way that whites are treated.

But they long ago abandoned the fallacy of mistaking sweet words for sweet deeds. They would like to see a little evidence. And I don't blame them. I would too.

7

Making It Happen

THE INVISIBLE CLASS STRUGGLE

I INCHING TOWARD EQUALITY

Consider this riddle, if you will. In all public-opinion polls, the doctrine of Counterfeit Equality is an easy winner over the principles of Fair Shares. The Fair Play complex of ideas, expressed in terms of equal opportunity and meritocracy, is one of the most potent "ruling ideas" of our age. Yet the Fair Play proponents act unhappy. They seem almost unaware of the extent to which their pet ideas have dominated the minds of Americans. Indeed they often speak in the tones of harassed whiners in the wilderness. What in the world are they crying about? If the Fair Play party, as we might term it, is winning all the elections, why doesn't it open up the champagne and celebrate? What does it fear?

The answer is, I think, that the meritocracy mongers have become uneasily aware of three facts that threaten the hegemony of their Fair Play dogma. First, there *have* been some changes in the degree of inequalities of wealth and income in the United States. Second, these modest advances toward equality have occurred, not as a steady trend, but in the form of occasional surges toward equality during periods of concerted action by poor and working people. Finally, the Fair Play idea appears to be losing credibility. Examples of superior individuals who rise to the top by cleverness and diligence are getting scarcer all the time.

In this chapter I will consider the implications of these three facts for the struggle for equality. By analyzing what has happened to the movement for equality in recent years, we can perhaps begin to answer the question of what the effective means for achieving greater equality are.

That the last fifty years have brought significant, though small, shifts in the distribution of wealth and income seems hard to dispute. Of course, the actual extent of change has not been exactly dramatic, and, as many observers have cautioned, the richest segments of the population have forms of wealth and sources of income that do not get counted when the statistical tables are drawn up. Nevertheless a reading of these tables demonstrates two clear facts: the first has to do with the amount of the change, the second with its pattern and timing.

Most studies of changes in income distribution over time show the year 1929 to be the low point of income inequality in this century, the year during which the gap between the high-income group and the majority of working people was most extreme.[1] The ensuing fifty years saw a net change in the direction of somewhat greater equality, the high-water mark of equality being attained in the years 1968–1970. The change was not large, of course. For example, the share of total personal income received by the lowest three-fifths of the income distribution rose modestly from one-fourth in 1929 to one-third in the period 1968–1970. Nevertheless, it meant that the average family in this bottom three-fifths was getting over two thousand more 1970 dollars than it would have been getting if nothing had changed since 1929 (the difference between $9,000 and $11,000). This may not seem like much if you have it. It looks like a small fortune if you don't.

The second important fact is that this change did not occur in a gradual progressive manner. Rather, it was a back-and-forth, see-saw process—a series of advances by the vulnerable majority, followed by regression and at least partial resurgence by the high-income minority. The net gain over the decades is accounted for by significant surges in the direction of greater equality during four brief periods: the years from about 1933 to 1937; the years of World War II; the middle years of the 1950s; and the years from about 1964 to 1968 or 1970. During the years between these advances toward equality, the well-off minority recouped a portion of its losses. For example, in the past eight or nine years, there has been a sharp decline from the high point of 1970 to the equality balance of the early 1960s. (But the share received by the bottom three-fifths is still higher than it was in, say, 1950, and significantly higher than in 1929.) Again, it must be emphasized that these oscillations in the distribution of income are small—involving a net shift of less than 2 percent from the highest fifth to the lowest three-fifths.

The significance of this is not to be found in the disappointingly small net gain over a period of fifty years or in the fact that each movement toward equality was pushed back (and, in the most recent case, completely wiped out). Rather, I believe, it is important to focus on the fact that change in the direction of equality did occur and that this movement was condensed into four brief time spans. These facts lead us to ask, What happened during those four periods, and what can we learn from those experiences?

How did these changes in the inequality structure come about? It is the apparent answer to that question—rather than the relatively modest changes themselves—that is, I believe, threatening to the Fair Play perspective and heartening to those who subscribe to the Fair Shares viewpoint

Let us review three common explanations. The first, put forward by many economists, explains greater equalization as a by-product of our industrial system; as an industrialized society matures, increased productivity leads to an expanding prosperity that reaches larger and larger segments of the population. Such a theory implies that cyclical changes in degrees of inequality are correlated with the business cycle. In good times, equality spreads; in bad times, it contracts. This explanation sounds plausible, but it is completely at variance with the facts. Progress toward equality has occurred about as often during periods of recession as during periods of growth. The two periods of greatest movement toward equality in the last half century occurred at opposite points of the business cycle: during the years of the Great Depression and during the boom of the late 1960s. There is simply no relationship between changes in degrees of inequality and changes in the business cycle.

The two other explanations can be derived from the conflicting Fair Play and Fair Shares belief systems. The former accounts for greater equality by large-scale changes in internal individual characteristics, such as changes in educational attainment. The idea of advancement by education is, in fact, a standard corollary of the Fair Play perspective. Like the business cycle thesis, this explanation, at first glance, appears rather plausible. Certainly Americans in the 1970s were much more highly educated than had been the case fifty years earlier. But, as we saw previously, the overall change in income distribution is not at all proportional to the increase in educational attainment. For instance, during the first three decades of this century, there was a sixfold increase in the number of high school graduates, yet during those same years there was essentially no change—indeed, a slight change for the worse—in income distribution.[2]

We can observe that increases in educational attainment, like the uneven movement toward greater equality, proceed sporadically. But there is no evident relationship between the two patterns of movement. If anything can be deduced from a comparison of them, it is that there is a more rapid increase in education during periods of regression toward inequality. During two of the four surges toward greater equality—the World War II period and the latter part of the 1960s—educational attainment actually showed a slight decline![3]

This is not to deny the fact that, by and large, higher income goes along with more education. During the whole five-decade period, the average college graduate earned about one and one-half to two times as much as the average high school graduate. The difference, however, is that when graduation from college was a rare event the average graduate was near the very top of the income pyramid. Today the average college graduate doesn't even make it into the top 20 percent of the income distribution. In other words, when, for the most part, only the rich graduated from college, college graduates were rich. As a college education became more common, its presumed economic value as a license to riches was rapidly eroded.

Considering the evidence presented in this and previous chapters, it seems fair to say that the explanation that altering internal resources and characteristics of individuals, as exemplified by increased education, has led to greater equality is plainly contradicted by the facts. A Fair Play theory of how we move toward greater equality, then, does not fit reality any better than does a business-cycle explanation.

II   FAIR SHARES AND COLLECTIVE ACTION

A Fair Shares theory of how we move toward greater equality would emphasize *collective* rather than individual action; it would conceive of that action as directed toward *external* targets rather than toward the altering of internal characteristics; and it would assume that those engaged in collective action are essentially *similar* and are, therefore, seeking collective rather than individually differentiated benefits. If we try to find examples from the real world that fit this description, we think immediately of trade unions and of the kinds of public demonstrations developed by civil rights and welfare rights groups. The Fair Shares theory, then, can be simply summarized: greater equality is achieved by collective action.

The historical evidence supports this formulation quite well; precisely such actions were prevalent during the four time periods I have identified as marking surges toward equality. In *Poor People's Movements*,[4] Frances Fox Piven and Richard Cloward have described and analyzed in great detail the history of four such movements, two during the years of the Great Depression and two during the sixties, which were characterized by cresting waves of collective action. They point out that the success of such movements is attributable to intensive, widespread, collective action that produces a great deal of turmoil—strikes, demonstrations, disruptions of all kinds.

One can show this relationship between collective action and greater equality directly by looking at the correlation between the movement toward and away from equality and the waxing and waning of labor union activity. For example, a direct index of union organizing activity is the total membership of unions. During each of the four periods of significant income equalization, union membership shot up sharply:[5]

• In the seven years preceding the crash of 1929, union membership stayed constant at about 3.5 million. During the first two years of the depression it dropped below 3 million; then, reflecting the great organizing drives of the CIO, it soared to over 8 million, more than doubling in about five years.

• Intensive organizing was resumed as World War II started, providing leverage to the aggressive unions in the great war industries—automobiles and aircraft, steel, rubber, and so on—and the ranks of organized labor increased in four years to about 14 million.

• After the war there was a lull in activity and an actual decline in membership until the mid-1950s, which saw a leap to about 17 million members.

• The final major increase in union ranks occurred in the most recent period of activity, from the middle to the end of the 1960s, which brought a gain of another 3 million members, raising the total to about 20 million. Since then, as we have started to slip backward toward greater inequality, union membership has declined, even though the total labor force has been increasing rapidly.

The increase in labor militancy, as measured by strikes and other work stoppages, follows a similar pattern. As an index of this militancy we can select the proportion of the total work force that engaged in work stoppages during a given year.[6] During the four equalization periods, which, as we saw, were characterized by swelling union membership rolls, the number of strikes reached a high point; on the average, about one out of every twenty workers engaged in a strike during any given year. The corresponding figure for the intervening years of inactivity was less than half of this, about one out of forty-five. During the period when inequality was at its peak, from about 1927 to 1929, only about one worker out of a hundred went on strike in the course of a year.

It seems apparent, then, that collective action for collective benefits, as exemplified by increases and decreases in union activity, directly parallels movement toward and away from general economic equality. Perhaps even more important, these periods of intensive organizing and militant action by unions brought benefits not only to the members of those unions, but to all wage and salary workers. Precisely how this correlation might be interpreted is not, of course, implied by the correlation itself. It might be that the militancy of labor unions reflects the measurable aspect of a general sense of militancy among both union and nonunion members—a tip-of-the-iceberg phenomenon. Or it might be that all firms are pulled into following the lead of the unionized firms in granting wage increases. Whatever the dynamics, it seems clear that income equality spreads outward from centers of collective action.

Equality not only spreads; it is also unitary, at least with respect to general economic equality and more specific racial equality. During periods of greater equalization of income in the general population, the differential between the incomes of blacks and of whites, a rather straightforward measure of racial discrimination, usually diminishes. There is available for the last thirty-three years a precise measure of this discriminatory differential, an index of the ratio between the median family income of blacks and that of whites.[7] Over this period, the median income of black families has tended to be only a bit more than half of what white families receive—the ratio has averaged about .56. Over time the changes in this ratio match pretty well the ups and downs of income equalization. In the beginning of this period, in the years 1947–1951, the average income ratio was .52. It went up during the 1950s at about the same time that there was a surge toward general income equality, averaging .55 between 1952 and 1957. This period was followed by a regression toward more general income inequality, and we also see a slump in the racial index of equality; between 1958 and 1965 the ratio slipped back to an average of .53. During the great surge forward in the late 1960s, we find the ratio of black income to white income also leaping upward, averaging .63 between 1966 and 1971. Since then it has again slipped backward, to an average of about .58 in the last several years.

There have been not only parallel changes in the extents of economic and racial equality, but also corresponding trends in collective action on civil rights issues. As I suggested earlier, through the 1950s the dominant mode of action for greater racial equality reflected the Fair Play model. The emphasis was on equal opportunity, both in the courts and in the early direct-action events. The lunch counter sit-ins, the freedom rides, and similar activities were defined as efforts to gain equal access and to eliminate discriminatory barriers that affected black individuals.

But, even at the beginning, some of this activity had a new and different tone. In Montgomery, Alabama, an obscure Baptist minister, Martin Luther King, led a successful boycott of the buses by the great masses of the black community to gain something that might have seemed trivial to many: equality of seating patterns on buses. In this case, a professional lawyer did not take an exemplary case through the courts in order to win a new interpretation of the law—the most typical pattern of civil rights activity in the past. Rather, a black community was almost totally united in taking direct action, outside of the courts and the usual political process, to achieve a collective community goal. Not since the 1930s had this particular pattern appeared on the American scene; it was reminiscent of the sit-in strikes in automobile factories, of the Washington encampment of veterans fighting for their bonuses, and of the marches of the unemployed demanding jobs. In Montgomery, and later in St. Augustine, Birmingham, Selma, and other Southern cities, Dr. King repeated and refined his tactics, which involved rallies and marches of large masses of ordinary people, often countered by the arrest of scores, sometimes hundreds, of demonstrators. The beginnings in Montgomery had set the pattern: collective action by large numbers of people from a local community—frequently reinforced and supported by persons from other regions, even other states—directed toward the achievement of a collective goal, such as voter registration of black citizens, and involving public demonstrations rather than litigation or lobbying.

Other new or newly revived organizations were simultaneously undertaking similar kinds of activities, both in the North and the South, notably the Congress of Racial Equality (CORE) and the Student Nonviolent Coordinating Committee (SNCC). We began to see, rather routinely, many mass demonstrations—the picketing of discriminatory landlords and of firms that apparently discriminated in their hiring practices, school boycotts directed at continued educational segregation, rallies and marches of all types.

In the course of these activities, the idea of eliminating barriers to individual opportunity—the traditional goal of civil rights actions and civil rights organizations—began to change. Negotiations with employers who were charged with discriminatory hiring or promotion policies and who responded to mass demonstrations, picketing, and boycotts, focused on a change in the overall patterns. It was no longer acceptable, for instance, for a bank to say that it would in the future make every effort to hire "qualified Negroes" who applied for work. The demand was for action to change hiring patterns and for evidence in the form of a significantly larger number of black faces behind tellers' cages within some specified period. Collective action was in itself changing the idea of racial equality from an emphasis on opportunities for individuals to an emphasis on collective benefits.

During this period the Department of Justice began to keep track of and to count the occurrences of the most dramatic of these new forms of protest—civil disorders—and in its figures we find a pattern similar to the one that we saw with respect to strikes and union organizing.[8] During the years from 1963 to 1969 an average of more than 150 civil disorders a year were counted, almost three times the average for the preceding five years. As we moved into the 1970s and the movement toward equality began to be beaten back, there was a sharp falloff in this kind of collective activity, dwindling to only 17 disorders in 1973, the last year in which they were counted. In recent years, then, collective actions of this type have almost disappeared, and the gains made by blacks during the late 1960s have, at the same time, been almost completely erased.

It appears, then, that the movement toward and the regression from both racial and economic equality parallel each other strikingly, as do levels of collective action for working people in general and for blacks in particular. This suggests that, at least in terms of actions and results, racial inequality and economic inequality are linked issues.

In trying to solve the problem of what works to achieve greater equality, we come upon a seemingly clear conclusion. The Fair Shares outlook, translated into collective action, has consistently and successfully shaken the structure of inequality. We should be able to dig out some of the answers about how we can achieve greater equality from a further examination of these actions.

At the same time it is important to keep in mind the human content underlying all the numbers I have been reporting. It is easy to forget sometimes, when we use abstract terms like collective action, that we are talking about risky, painful behavior undertaken by groups of brave men and women. To young persons who read about them, the successes in the 1930s of the CIO do not, perhaps, seem very remarkable. To those of us who lived through the years of the Great Depression, they constituted an astonishing accomplishment and still do. I suspect it's not possible to appreciate from the perspective of today what it was like living through the Great Depression, although there is a book, Studs Terkel's *Hard Times*,[9] that captures much of the feeling of those days. The overriding, all-important issue in life was whether one had a job. Millions of persons, at one point almost one-fourth of the labor force, were without work, which meant, in those days, without income. Everyone knew someone—a friend, an uncle, a brother-in-law—who was first out of work, soon out of money, and then out of food. The lives of millions depended on the willingness of other millions to share. In those days, to bring home a pay envelope every single Friday was to be envied by many a neighbor, even if, when you shook out the envelope on the table, only twelve or fourteen dollars fell out. It was possible to make that last for seven days, and the following Friday would see another envelope.

In that atmosphere of pervasive fear, the willingness of millions of workers to band and act together, to go on strike, to sit down in the factory, and to risk being fired and changing places with the jobless man on the street grew out of a kind of collective courage and trust that was not to reappear on the American scene until the era of mass civil-rights demonstrations. And, as Piven and Cloward showed, these workers didn't wait for the CIO organizers, the "outside agitators," to bring them together; they acted on their own, and the organizers often had to run to catch up.

These bright periods of action demonstrate that those who are deprived of their fair share are not ignorant victims who stand still and take their punishment. They often do act, usually together, although sometimes they act with very little knowledge of the larger process of which they are a part, perhaps only dimly conscious that millions of others are acting at the same time. For example, how many of us were fully aware during the late 1960s that just when the civil rights and welfare rights movements were vibrant with successful activity, similar growth and action were occurring among labor unions?

Another argument, that there is little that can be done in the face of overwhelming entrenched power, is refuted by these examples of collective action. These were actions that appeared impossible. How in the world could anyone expect a few hundred workers in a factory to risk not only their jobs but a confrontation with the company police or national guardsmen? Who could reasonably expect a few dozen blacks in a Southern town, with a burning collective memory of the strange fruit of lynchings, with the experience of daily lessons in their own powerlessness, to confront the sheriff and his deputies? All must have known the dangers—of economic reprisal, of pain, of injury, even of death. Yet they acted. And they felt the consequences.

One remembers some of the great bloody strikes—the Pullman strike, the Homestead strike, the Little Steel massacre, bloody Harlan County, and the great battle of River Rouge, where members of the UAW were beaten bloody by the armed thugs of Henry Ford, yet won the seemingly inconceivable victory of forcing Ford to sign a union contract. We can recall great massacres of workers and the countless smaller battles where workers were beaten, jailed, shot, and killed by the police, by the National Guard, or by the private armies of the great masters of America's industrial machine.

And who can forget some of the horrifying scenes from the civil rights struggles of the 1960s? Frail black women being flung by powerful fire hoses through the streets of Birmingham, like garbage being flushed along the gutter; bodies stiffening in agony when shocked by powerful cattle prods; faces covered with rivulets of blood streaming from skulls smashed open by the clubs of the police; churches and homes burning unchecked. And the bodies. Dozens counted and named, perhaps hundreds unnamed, unknown.

The struggle for equality is undeniably costly. But it brings results. Even though there may be slippage after each advance, the next advance moves to a higher point. And along the way are planted legislative supports for equality. We still benefit from the Wagner Act of the 1930s guaranteeing the right to organize unions, and from the epochal Social Security Act of 1935, perhaps the single greatest economic victory for the vulnerable majority. World War II saw the establishment of the Fair Employment Practices Commission and left the legacy of a formally desegregated armed forces. The civil rights legislation that began with the timid Civil Rights Act of 1957 and the war on poverty are other examples, as are Medicare and Medicaid, which mark the beginnings, however imperfect, of the establishment of health care as a right of citizenship.

My main point is that those of us who are a part of the vulnerable majority will get nowhere by following the mirage of individual advancement by individual merit. At best, some of us toward the back of the bus will change places with some at the front. The driver will remain in the driver's seat. Acting as individuals, we remain vulnerable, and many of us will be badly hurt. We will remain vulnerable until we learn, fully and clearly, that we must act collectively, vigorously, and, when necessary, courageously.

III   ASSAULTS ON EQUALITY

A large question remains. Why do we find only sporadic progress toward equality, only brief waves of forward movement followed by years of no headway, and even of slippage? Why isn't there a steady trend? What happens in between, during the periods of stagnation and decline?

The general answer, I believe, is that, just as the great majority of working people are not simply passive and ignorant but do try to win larger shares for themselves, so members of the wealthy minority act to retain and if possible to enlarge the disproportionately large shares they have. There exists, in other words, a subtle and somewhat hidden conflict between these two groups.

This is a general proposition that can be found in various forms in the works both of radical economists and reformers (the Marxist notion of class struggle) and of conservative thinkers and conventional economists (the general idea of rational action to maximize one's own gain). A specific formulation of these dynamics of conflict as they appear in the welfare system, for example, has been suggested by Piven and Cloward in their book *Regulating the Poor*.[10] They argue cogently that there is a cyclical process of expansion and contraction in the size of welfare benefits and in the numbers of welfare recipients, reflecting a parallel process of social unrest and disruption by low income groups, and then a reaction by the state in the form of tightening eligibility requirements, cutting benefits, removing recipients from welfare rolls, and instituting harassing and demeaning programs like "workfare."

Applying Piven and Cloward's analysis of the dynamics of conflict within the welfare system to the more general picture, we can understand more clearly the continuing conflict between the majority, the working people, and the minority, the wealthy owners. On one side of this conflict, we saw in the foregoing section that high levels of collective action are accompanied by a movement toward greater equality. What, then, of the other side of the conflict? What actions appear to maintain or to increase *inequality*?

One that is fairly obvious is legislation (the Wagner Act is countered by the Taft-Hartley Act; tax laws are amended to protect the incomes of the rich) and changes in government policy (the expansion of welfare rolls and benefits is neutralized by restrictive welfare policies; the war on poverty is dismantled). One can think of other notorious examples of governmental actions that clearly reflect the interests of the wealthy: the use of soldiers and police against strikers, subsidies to great corporations, and the close collaboration between the Pentagon and defense contractors. Other government activities that serve as instruments to benefit the rich and to regulate and control workers are less obvious. Two of the most important of these are the maintenance of "law and order" and the continuing intervention of government in economic affairs.

Events within the domain of law and order, or criminal justice, appear at first glance to be almost monotonously consistent and unchanging, lacking the see-saw pattern that characterizes the change in the equality-inequality balance and the changes in the kinds of occurrences that might affect that balance. If we conceive of the major components of the process as crime, police intervention, arrest, and conviction, we find no indication of any rising and ebbing, action and reaction, that correlates with fluctuations in the equality balance. During recent decades we note a fairly steady rise in the crime rate and parallel increases in our relative investment in fighting crime. But our anticrime apparatus shows no improvement in its manifest efficiency. The percentage of crimes that are solved, or as crime statisticians put it, "cleared"—that is, ones for which someone is arrested—remains amazingly constant and shockingly low. Of the major or "index" crimes— murder, rape, robbery, aggravated assault, larceny, burglary, and car theft— the most generous estimate would be that no more than 10 percent are cleared by arrest.[11] Only one variable in the criminal-justice system deviates from this general configuration—imprisonment. The rate at which persons are imprisoned and the proportion of the population in prison at any given time fluctuate dramatically, with marked peaks and troughs. Even though the crime rate and the investment in police activity increase at a steady rate and the ratio between crimes and arrests remains almost constant, we go through some periods when we lock persons up at a furious rate, until the cells are bulging, and others when we dramatically reduce imprisonment. Why do rates of imprisonment fluctuate so markedly and what do changes in those rates have to do with the struggle for equality?

The absence of a correlation between imprisonment and any other element of the criminal justice system suggests to me the interpretation that imprisonment serves some function beyond those ordinarily attributed to it, such as the punishment or rehabilitation of individual offenders, the deterrence of crime, or the disablement of criminals. The additional function I believe it serves is that of societal control and repression. Within the conflict scheme outlined above, imprisonment is an antiequality action, similar to a policy of welfare repression and to legislation like the Taft-Hartley Act.

This interpretation is not an arbitrary one. It coincides with the widespread intuition that, within the realm of political discourse, "law and order" is a code term for antiblack and antipoor sentiments. It is also consistent with the history of our modern criminal-justice system. As the works of Foucault, of Rothman, and of others[12] make clear, imprisonment as a common punishment after conviction for a crime and the widespread development of the penitentiary as an institution are contemporaneous with the beginnings of the modern period of industrial capitalism and related to the need to control the idle poor and the growing class of industrial workers. Indeed, the invention of the professional, full-time, urban police force in the early nineteenth century has been analyzed as a response to the necessity of managing and restraining restless factory workers, who frequently lashed out against their situation by rioting.[13]

If this is a correct interpretation, if one of the major functions of imprisonment is to exert societal control, directly and symbolically, against collective efforts to achieve greater equality, one would expect to find that imprisonment rates fall during successful campaigns for greater equality and rise during the reactions that push us back toward inequality. This is indeed the case. Over time, measures of imprisonment and of equality are negatively correlated. This is most dramatically illustrated in the history of the last twenty years, during which we saw one of the widest swings down and up since such records have been kept. Persons were sent to state and federal prisons at a rate that peaked at about 50 per 100,000 of population around 1960–1961. Beginning about 1964, the rate began to drop rapidly, reaching a low of 38 in 1969 and then, as the counterattack on equality began, rising sharply to a high of over 60 in the late 1970s.[14]

Another weapon available to the wealthy minority in combatting the struggle for equality is unemployment, which is largely controllable by the fiscal and monetary policies of the government. Unemployment has been viewed, at least since the time of Marx, as a mechanism for controlling wages, and it is so defined by economists of varying theoretical persuasions.

There are a number of misconceptions about the relationship between wages, unemployment, profits, and prices. First, there is the common belief that during hard times the pain of unemployment among workers is matched by the pain of low profits for owners. This may sometimes have been true in the remote past, but at least since World War II it no longer is. Periods of high unemployment are almost always periods of *rising* profits, during which the corporations and their stockholders *increase* their shares of overall income. Let us look at the most recent example, the severe recession of the mid-1970s. Unemployment, which stood at 3.5 percent in 1969, had risen by 1975 and 1976 to almost 9 percent. Corporate profits, which had declined from about $82 billion in 1966 to $69 billion in 1970, bounced up during the so-called recession and reached $118 billion in 1976, a 20 percent increase after allowances for inflation have been made.[15]

As we have discovered recently, the sacred relationship between unemployment and inflation (as codified in the famous "Phillips curve") is not an immutable law of God and nature, either. That inflation can be controlled only by allowing unemployment to rise is an article of faith for orthodox economists. Only in this decade, as we experienced zooming rates of both unemployment and inflation at the same time, has this dogma finally been exploded. As is usually the case with such sacred and unquestionable beliefs, the facts beneath the facade tell a quite different and interesting story. The source of the revered Phillips curve is a study by A. W. Phillips[16] that traced out the relationship not between unemployment and *prices,* but between unemployment and *wages* (the gratuitous assumption being that wages determine prices, which may have been valid at one time but certainly is no longer). As unemployment goes up, wages go down, according to Phillips, and vice versa. The real message of his study, then, is not that you can bring down *prices* by raising unemployment, but that you can bring down *wages*—and thereby reduce the shares of income going to those dependent on wages and salaries.

If unemployment is construed as a weapon against equality, we would then expect to find the same pattern that we encountered with imprisonment. (Rising unemployment would be a force tending to stop and reverse movement toward equality.) Again, this expectation fits the facts as we know them. During the advance toward equality in the mid-1950s, the unemployment rate averaged a bit over 4 percent; during the period of slippage in the late 1950s and early 1960s, it averaged close to 6 percent, several times approaching 7 percent; during the spurt toward equality in the late 1960s, it was consistently below 4 percent; and during the most recent assault on equality, unemployment climbed to its highest point in forty years, hovering between 6 and 9 percent.[17]

All these patterns, I propose, mean that the degree of equality at any given time is the result of the interaction between two forces. One is the amount and militancy of collective activity by groups of working people and poor people; the other is the degree of repressive power being exercised by and on behalf of the wealthy minority through such mechanisms as imprisonment and other forms of confinement, restrictive practices in the area of public assistance and other segments of the social-welfare field, and the establishment of economic policies to increase unemployment, reduce wages, and increase profits. At any given time the state of inequality seems to vary with the *relative* magnitude and balance between these two sets of forces. For example, during the Great Depression extremely high rates of unemployment and imprisonment—the antiequality forces—were more than counteracted by even more extraordinarily intense collective action—strikes and union organizing. On the other hand, during the 1960s, a time of high employment and very low imprisonment rates, a substantial advance toward equality was achieved by collective action that was less vigorous than that of the 1930s.

The tension between the two groups and the amount of strength they can bring to bear are very much influenced by what might be termed the ideological climate, the beliefs that people hold about the justness and effectiveness of their activity for or against equality. Efforts to halt movements toward greater equality must be made to seem legitimate in the eyes of the public; in particular, the assault on equality carried out by governmental programs and policies must be made to seem right and justified. The very powerful are not able simply to work their will whenever they please without regard to public opinion. In the long run, "The public be damned" is a losing slogan. Actions that are taken to improve the position and to support the interests of the wealthy minority *must* be viewed by the public as, at least, legitimate and fair or, if possible, "in the national interest" or, best of all, in their own interests. The commonly held values of the people cannot just be ignored. As Barrington Moore, Jr., demonstrates with brilliant scholarship, the response of a people to injustice—whether obedience or revolt— is determined largely by how the people view the process through which the injustice or inequity has occurred.[18] If they believe that common values were adhered to, and the rules of the game were followed, then the injustice is likely to be viewed as unavoidable, and it will be endured. If, however, the injustice is seen to be the consequence of flouting the common values and violating the rules of the game, then it is likely to be resisted, even to the point of open rebellion.

The task of legitimizing assaults on equality is shouldered by those who undertake to shape the belief systems and perceptions of the public. In our time these are the writers and scholars who preach the Fair Play doctrine in the pages of magazines and newspapers. Let me try to describe in some detail this ideological assault on equality from about the summer of 1971, when Richard Herrnstein's article "IQ" appeared in the *Atlantic Monthly.*[19] At this time, I remember, my wife and I and a number of our friends and colleagues in the civil rights and welfare rights movements, among others, had been talking uneasily about what we felt was a reaction to the modest but significant successes that had been achieved during the 1960s. What we perceived dimly then is what I have been formulating more specifically in this section: a series of government actions designed to wipe out the advances that had been made in civil rights and economic equality, accompanied by polemical magazine articles that paved the way for antiegalitarian government policies and provided them with a veneer of scholarly justification. The author of the introduction to Herrnstein's article clearly laid down many of the themes that made up what we soon began to call the "assault on equality." More important, he stated explicitly that Herrnstein's work could best be understood as part of a series, beginning with Moynihan's *Negro Family*, and including the *Coleman Report*, Banfield's *The Unheavenly City*, and Jensen's long article in the *Harvard Educational Review* reasserting the time-worn proposition that blacks were genetically inferior to whites in intelligence.[20]

Articles of a tone and style similar to those of Banfield, Herrnstein, and company had begun to appear regularly, mostly in *Commentary* and the *Public Interest*, but also in the *Atlantic*, the *New York Times Magazine*, and the *New Republic*—significantly, all publications that were at that time generally labeled as "liberal." To many of us, there seemed to be an almost coordinated effort to establish a new, antiegalitarian consciousness in the minds of those who thought of themselves as "liberal intellectuals," to provide a set of prestigious academic rationalizations for waves of reactionary governmental activity. We even, half jokingly, spun out fantasies about a giant conspiracy. It was at that time, I remind you, that full employment was beginning to be redefined as 5 percent unemployment. It was in the same month that Herrnstein's article appeared, August 1971, that Richard Nixon instituted phase one of his "new economic policy," which was clearly anti-labor. Though designated a wage-price freeze, it focused on holding down wages while allowing the freeze on prices to melt. This was the beginning of the erosion of real wages that was to continue over the next years.

To be fair, those of us originally involved in naming and criticizing this most recent assault on equality (myself, George Wiley, S. M. Miller, Frank Riessman, Alan Gartner, James Breeden, Richard Cloward, and Frances Fox Piven, among others) could be identified as leaning more or less to the left politically. It could be thought that our perception of these events was colored by our own political prejudices, particularly since so many of us had been involved in specific criticism of individual work by those whom we defined as the "assaulters."

But our perception was by no means unique, even at the time. As early as November 1972 the political columnist Joseph Kraft (who can hardly be considered anything more dangerous than a moderate conservative) made the same observation we had made,[21] involving many of the same people, whom he identified approvingly as "a group of conservative thinkers." He cited Daniel Bell, Daniel Patrick Moynihan, Seymour Martin Lipset, James Q. Wilson, and James Coleman as members of this group, all of whom were, he pointed out, associated with the quarterly *Public Interest*. (These men also had ties, as did Norman Podhoretz, Irving Kristol, Nathan Glazer, and others, with the monthly *Commentary*. Together with such like-minded colleagues as Ben Wattenberg and Jeane Kirkpatrick, they were more recently active in establishing the Committee for a Democratic Majority, and many of them are associated with the American Enterprise Institute, particularly with its publication, *Public Opinion*.) Kraft praised their work as a "reaffirmation of their belief that a certain inequality is inevitable, even beneficial." He was particularly taken with the "new conservative thinkers," because "having asserted the basic case for inequality . . . Bell and the others go on to point out ways in which the inequality can be tempered . . ." This lauda- tory analysis of the same phenomena that had so alarmed us at least con- firmed for us that we were correct in perceiving what these people were up to, although our evaluation obviously differed from Kraft's.

This outpouring of writings that we identified as the intellectual arm of the pincer movement against the drive for more equality was, and still is, based more or less directly on the Fair Play thesis. In fact, a number of the articles originally dealt directly with this issue, attacking the principle that they called "equality of results" and that I have been calling the idea of Fair Shares.

In Chapter Two, I quoted from the writings of some members of this "neoconservative" group on the subject of equality itself, identifying the main themes of the Fair Play perspective. These writers have not limited their criticisms simply to the principle of "equality of results" but have extended them to the specific issues that had emerged as most salient during the sixties. Thus, for example, we find old friends Glazer and Moynihan attacking welfare programs, while at the same time, on the state level, Gov- ernors Reagan and Rockefeller were instituting the most repressive kinds of welfare regulations and cutbacks and indecent treatment of welfare re- cipients.[22] Jensen and Herrnstein proposed the theory of genetically deter- mined, internal intellectual deficits to explain the educational conditions of the black and the poor. Their work, along with that of Coleman and Moyni- han, provides ammunition for those opposed to school desegregation and to the use of busing in order to achieve it. Glazer has been one of the leaders of the attack on affirmative action; he laid out the intellectual arguments on the primacy of individual merit and ability that I discussed in Chapter Six. The retreat from governmental programs to provide decent housing for the poor and moderate-income families of America is undergirded by the work of second-rank members of the neoconservative fraternity like Roger Starr, who redefines the housing problem as something caused by the individual deficiencies of tenants.[23] One current theme—increased imprisonment, man- datory sentencing, Senator Kennedy's reactionary revision of the federal penal code—rests to a large extent on the writings of such members of the group as James Q. Wilson, who is its crime expert. Wilson deals with the crime problem in predictable individual-internal-difference terms by singling out as the greatest problem the so-called repeat offender or career criminal involved in what Wilson calls "predatory crime." As one might expect, he sees this as an issue of individual deviance: "some persons will shun crime even if we do nothing to deter them, while others will seek it out even if we do everything to reform them. Wicked people exist. Nothing avails except to set them apart from innocent people."[24] To sum up, the task of legitimizing antiegalitarian actions has been undertaken by the ideological troops of the assault on equality, the group most commonly called "neoconservatives." The exposure and neutralization of their work are key components of any new effort to resume our advance toward equality.

IV   THE BIGGER THEY ARE

When we consider the success the neoconservatives enjoy in placing before the public their attacks on the movement toward equality, the smooth integration of these ideological attacks with parallel actions by the government, and the obvious weight of the economic and political forces behind these actions, we come face to face with the issue of power and its exercise. There is an almost complete consensus among students of inequality and social stratification that power and wealth are highly correlated. Domhoff, Mills, and others have traced out in detail the interrelationships between the wealthy elite in the private sector and those in the public sector who exercise governmental and quasi-governmental power.[25] And we have seen that every move in the direction of equality by groups from the vulnerable majority has been countered by repressive reactions reflecting the interests of the wealthy and powerful. If the wealthy few have such disproportionate influence in the daily affairs of our lives, what can be done? How can such overwhelming power be successfully opposed? Is it necessary to adopt the position of those who sit and suck their thumbs, patiently awaiting some magical day that will produce a spontaneous, apocalyptic revolution? I think not. I suggest keeping in mind three thoughts when we tremble overmuch at the power of the wealthy.

First, we know that collective action has produced gains. When faced with enough instability and turmoil, the mighty and powerful do make concessions. They can add and subtract as well as we can, at least, and it is often to their advantage to give in and to back up a little. As an example of the power of direct action by large groups, I always recall the great "stall-in" by CORE on the opening day of the New York World's Fair in 1964.[26] As a major protest against racial discrimination, Brooklyn CORE, with the support of other New York chapters, announced that its members would enter the traffic on the throughways bound for the fair and deliberately stall their cars, thus tying up traffic for miles and disrupting this important event. The fair's managers, civic leaders, and newspaper editorial writers reacted with outrage and indignation to the announcement, condemning the demonstration as dangerous, excessive, unfair, reckless, and counterproductive. There are probably still many persons in New York who could work up a sense of outrage at the thought of this most dramatic of demonstrations.

The "stall-in," however, resembled Sherlock Holmes's "curious incident of the dog in the nighttime" in *Silver Blaze*. As Holmes fans will remember, Watson noted that the dog did nothing in the nighttime, and Holmes replied that that was the curious incident. The "stall-in" never happened (it was, in fact, opposed by national CORE, and, to the best of my knowledge, it was never seriously planned), but the mere announcement, the mere threat, of such disruptive action had a powerful effect. Everyone who was in the civil rights movement can tell similar stories, involving smaller incidents. And, of course, the scenario of every collective-bargaining session between union and management is effective and believable only to the extent that there exists the possibility of a strike as the last act. Every time there actually is a strike, the strikers are denounced for doing more harm than good to themselves and society, and they are cajoled and wheedled into ending their troublesome activities, reforming, and going back to work. The 1978 coal miners' strike taught this lesson most clearly. Relying on the legendary solidarity among miners, rank-and-file union members, braving the wrath of everyone, from some union officers to the president himself, twice rejected unsatisfactory contracts and finally won most of their demands.

This kind of power, the effective force of people in numbers, not as individuals, but as cohesive collectivities, has been demonstrated over and over again. A dramatic example occurred recently in the revolution in Iran. Setting aside for a moment the consequences of the revolution, which is, to be sure, an entirely different kind of political problem, the final answer to which is not yet in, we can still vividly remember that, until his last few months on the throne, the Shah was pictured by most people as virtually omnipotent and untouchable, his singular power resting on the firm foundation of a huge army and police, completely under his control. Yet, within a matter of weeks he was brought down by the power of sheer numbers, cohesive collective action by the overwhelming majority of Iranians, through widespread strikes in financial and industrial institutions, supported by massive street demonstrations by unarmed citizens. Acting together, essentially without firing a shot, the people brought the country to a standstill and put an abrupt end to the reign of the once invincible Shah. The power of masses of people, acting cohesively to obtain a collective goal, should not be underestimated.

Second, we should remember that, imperfect as it may be, the United States is still a political democracy. It is fashionable in progressive and left-wing circles to pooh-pooh democratic and electoral processes as mere window dressing. But, despite the disgraceful distortions of the process and the enormously exaggerated influence of the wealthy minority over it, the democratic process has from time to time produced events that have facilitated movement toward equality or that have fixed in law egalitarian principles and programs, from the abolition of slavery and the enactment of child labor laws to the establishment of social insurance, and to the guarantee of the voting rights of black citizens. In the past, greater equality has been achieved through electoral and legislative means, and there is no reason to doubt that still more equality can be achieved by these often scorned means.

Third, there is the intangible factor that I have referred to as the decline of the credibility of the Fair Play doctrine. In an admiring discussion of the themes running through the work of those he calls "Irving Kristol and friends," Robert Bartley, chief editorial writer of the *Wall Street Journal*, points out that, in addition to advocating their more specific programmatic positions, they constantly deplore the "collapse of values" in America.[27] In my view, they are referring to the particular values of the Fair Play view-point. As I shall demonstrate shortly, the American public also expresses concern about ethics and values, but I believe it has something broader in mind.

In the America of the 1980s, those who wish to persuade people to remain attached to the Fair Play set of ideas are having greater and greater difficulties. One problem in maintaining a belief system that is plainly at odds with reality is, as Pooh-Bah said, that of "giving artistic verisimilitude to an otherwise bald and unconvincing narrative." For example, in order to give credibility to Schumpeter's notion of progress by virtue of the prodigious work of "supernormal" entrepreneurs, it is helpful to have on hand for display some persons who could pass for performers of extraordinary feats. Few such persons are to be found. In the nineteenth century one could plausibly make such a claim and say, "Look at Carnegie! Look at Morgan! Look at Frick!" But in the ninth decade of the twentieth century, where is one to find individuals from the great wealthy families, or among the chief executives of the great corporations, who could be passed off as "supernormal" even under the most casual scrutiny? With some exceptions, most of them avoid the role of public figures, successfully and wisely. John D. Rockefeller, when he showed himself off and talked about his great accomplishments, was accepted by the multitudes as a very clever millionaire. When his grandsons appear on the public stage, it is their millions rather than their cleverness that is most evident, and they tend to be viewed simply as lucky heirs of a multimillionaire.

The fact that the wealthy elite stay out of sight, that nobody knows their names, is probably good for them, but their very anonymity means that there is no cast of characters to enact the illusion of the "supernormal" individual entrepreneur. The plot of the wondrous capitalist miracle play is still a great story, but when the curtain goes up in the theater of today, there is no one to play the role of the miracle worker. The stage is empty.

Owners and managers of the great industrial corporations, even if they had a taste for the limelight, would probably be unable to extol, with a straight face, the virtues of individualistic competition in a free market, since they have found forms of cooperation and collective action (fixing prices, dividing up the market, destroying small competitors) that are far more efficient as methods of producing great wealth for themselves. In fact, many of them appear to sense that the principles of Fair Play, if actually put into practice, would be subversive of their interests. The paradoxical result is that a Ralph Nader, raising his voice in defense of the free-enterprise values of the age of John D. Rockefeller, is denounced as some kind of "socialist or anarchist."[28]

Another source of danger to the believability of Fair Play is the growing phenomenon of what might be called the college-graduate cab driver—the young person whose education has not "paid off" economically the way it should have, according to the rules of the game. Now, in a rational world there is no reason to expect any great correlation between education and occupation, except in the case of jobs requiring highly technical or professional training. From a social perspective the idea of a cab driver with a liberal education can hardly be considered a bad thing, and one would like to see more butchers with M.A.'s in Greek philosophy. Theoretically, education is a good in itself, and, socially, the consumption of education is not all that different from the consumption of, say, opera or symphonic music.

But the dominant American value system has attached a price tag to education as an investment. Four years of studying history and literature and social thought, rather than being perceived as an opportunity to expand and liberalize and enrich one's mind and soul, is defined as an "investment in human capital." For the individual young men and women and their families who have bought this arid conception of learning, who have expended a great deal of time, money, and energy—often at the cost of great deprivation—this is a case of outright fraud. According to the implicit, sometimes almost explicit, contract, a college education was a ticket to a good job, that is, one paying a high salary. To the extent that this contract appears unenforceable, insubstantial, and perhaps actually fraudulent, institutions of higher education stand in great peril, and the ideology they sustain and exemplify must sooner or later be called into question.

Particularly dangerous, from a Fair Play perspective, is the readiness to defect shown by some members from what one would normally consider the upper-middle class, particularly some well-educated and high-salaried professionals, academics, scientists, and public administrators. Such people have become the objects of a new critical fad among neoconservatives, who castigate them as the so-called new class.[29] The new class is said to consist of a coalition of intellectuals and bureaucrats who are trying to seize more power for themselves and who use insincere slogans about egalitarianism to hide their own self-interest. While I agree that something unusual is clearly going on in this stratum of society, the connotation of the term "new class"—calling to mind the work of Djilas and others analyzing the role of party leaders and bureaucrats in the Soviet Union and other socialist countries—seems to me quite inappropriate. First of all, only a minority of persons whose occupation and education, among other things, fit the objective criteria of the new class show a strong interest in equality or even in anything vaguely "liberal." The majority retain their traditional conservative attitudes and attachments. This is most obviously true of the neoconservatives themselves, whose own criteria for deciding who belongs to the new class—intellectuals, grant-grubbers, advisers to and sometimes participants in government, seekers of power—lead to remarkably accurate self-portraiture.

A second reason to doubt that we are seeing the formation of a new class is that there is no evidence of such a social entity in terms of new groupings or in the thinking of the supposed members themselves. On the contrary, we find the unusual phenomenon of high-status professionals recognizing themselves primarily as workers and, consequently, showing signs of a desire for unionization. It is not uncommon nowadays to see a hospital being picketed, not by unskilled ward workers or even by technicians, but by nurses and physicians, residents and interns employed as house officers. We have grown accustomed to the sight of public-school teachers on strike, but lately we have also observed college professors learning to picket. I would suggest an interpretation quite opposite to that which sees a new class emerging. It seems plausible to me that many of these intellectuals and professionals have begun to detect the reality behind the facade of Counterfeit Equality (many of them have excellent vantage points from which to view it) and are discarding the tenets of Fair Play from their belief system. They are beginning to realize that they are not, and are not likely to become, members or even favorite allies of the ruling class and that their own long-term interests are similar to those of others who work for a living and make up the vulnerable majority.

To return to the theme of "collapsing values," something is, I believe, happening in the minds of the American public that leads the Fair Players to this conclusion. But I don't believe they have gotten an accurate reading of what it is. Not that any of us can lay claim to a definitive interpretation, but let me describe a sample of some recent findings from public opinion surveys and give my tentative assessment of what is going on. I draw most of my examples from the convenient "Opinion Roundup" section of *Public Opinion*, the neoconservatives' own journal.

1. There is a strange and contradictory mixture of attitudes toward and beliefs about government. People view government as it is actually functioning very negatively, but they appear to think that its proper goal is providing

more help to meet the basic needs of citizens and to protect them from harm and exploitation.

In 1958, 25 percent of the people thought that the government could not be trusted to do what is right. Twenty years later, 70 percent thought so. Only 18 percent of the respondents in 1958 agreed that the "government is run for a few big interests" compared to an overwhelming 74 percent in 1978.[30]

We are quite familiar with reports that people believe that the government is too big, that it wastes tax dollars, and so forth; but, at the same time, we find that people are strongly in favor of government regulation of almost all industries and that approximately half of them favor *increased* regulation of the drug, oil, and food industries. Furthermore, 81 percent of the people agreed in 1978 that the government "ought to help people get doctors and hospital care at low cost," and 74 percent agreed that it ought to guarantee them jobs. (In 1956 only 60 percent agreed with the medical-expense statement, 62 percent with the jobs question.)[31]

Patrick Caddell reports data that throw some light on these contradictions. In a 1978 survey he asked whether people believed the government *could* do a lot to solve certain problems and whether it was likely that it *would* do a lot. On the problem of curbing inflation, 46 percent thought it could do a lot; on unemployment, 38 percent; on health care, 45 percent. As to whether the government *would* in fact do a lot, the comparable figures were 10 percent, 9 percent, and 13 percent.[32]

There is, then, a disparity between government as people judge it to be in reality and what they wish it would be like. People want government to be helpful and protective. They think it could be much more effective than it is. But the reality that they see is a government that they have no confidence in, that they think neglects ordinary people in favor of a few big interests.

2. Although this complex of beliefs and attitudes is often summed up with terms like alienation, cynicism, malaise, and crisis of confidence, it is noteworthy that people themselves often focus on the role of decaying values and morals (the germ of truth in the Fair Players' alarm about "collapsing values").

To get some sense of specifics, we can turn to a Roper survey which asked people about possible causes of the problems in this country. Fair Players worried about the "collapse of values" would presumably be looking for items such as the decay of the work ethic, and the decline of individual responsibility. In fact, the list was headed by a value item of a rather general nature—"letdown in moral values," named by 56 percent. "Selfishness, people not thinking of others" was seen as a major cause by 50 percent; "too much emphasis on money and materialism" by 41 percent.[33]

A case can be made, then, for the argument that people are not simply cynical and alienated, and that they do not appear to be remarkably alarmed about the decline of traditional Fair Play values like individualism, self-reliance, and ambition. Rather, they appear to be deeply concerned about the growth of selfishness and greed and the decay of more traditional "love thy neighbor" values.

3. Finally, and most important to my case, it is abundantly clear that the belief in the reality of the traditional American dream is eroding:

Agreement with the statement "People who work hard and live by the rules are not getting a fair break these days" rose from 44 percent in 1974 to 53 percent in 1977.[34]

A statement reflecting one of the core beliefs of the Fair Play ideology—"Hard work will always pay off if you have faith in yourself and stick to it"—elicited agreement from 58 percent of those surveyed in 1968. By 1978, the figure had fallen to 44 percent.[35]

Between 1966 and 1977 agreement with the statement "The rich get richer and the poor get poorer" rose from 45 percent to an overwhelming 77 percent.[36]

These and similar data suggest quite strongly that the majority of the American people no longer believe in the validity of the prevailing rules for success. They think that following them doesn't pay off and that the rich are the beneficiaries of this change in affairs. They doubtless continue to feel that hard work and adhering to the rules *should* lead to success, but they appear to be reaching the conclusion that someone is fixing the game.

Paradoxically, even movements that appear to be quite reactionary and regressive—such as those for cuts in taxes and government spending—contain a hidden but potent threat to the Fair Play ideology. Those movements seem to have rooted themselves most deeply among persons who have best learned and most closely followed all the Fair Play rules of the game. They are becoming deeply frustrated as they realize that the promised prizes are being withheld from them. Their hard work, their striving, their conscientious adherence to all the models of independence, self-reliance, and industriousness are getting them nowhere, and they find themselves feeling as poor on an income of $20,000 a year as they did on $10,000. Things are not working out right. Something has gone wrong. Someone, somehow, somewhere, is not playing by the rules. It is their deep faith in Fair Play, in fact, that generates their sense of being cheated out of their just rewards.

Their resentment is not, of course, directed into egalitarian channels. They look for answers, for causes, within the framework of the ideology they have been taught so well, and they are more than ready to seize on the formulations of the intellectual assault on equality. They take up the cry of mandatory sentencing and capital punishment to stop the tide of crime, which they attribute almost completely to the work of a small band of hardened individual deviants, called variously "habitual felons," "repeat offenders," and "career criminals." They want protection from the supposedly lazy, immoral individuals who are consuming welfare dollars. They are easily persuaded that social problems reflect intractable traits of evil, stupidity, and moral turpitude in certain individuals. They are skeptical that the government can do anything about the problems in which such individuals are involved; at the same time, they view many government services as good and beneficial and think that more of them should be provided. They seem to want to cut budgets and taxes but not services, to pare down and enfeeble big government, while expecting government to accomplish big tasks. One detects, above all else, a ballooning sense of impotent frustration and a panicky feeling that America is going to hell in a hand basket. Their intense distrust of their leaders is manifest at the polling booth. Every two years we see that fewer and fewer voters think it worthwhile to vote, believing that the candidates are neither distinguishable from one another nor truthful.

How long, one must ask oneself, can the American people go on believing that their society is operating on the principles of Fair Play? Even if they believe in these principles—indeed, especially if they believe in them—they will become more and more aware that the principles have somehow been sabotaged, leaving them out in the cold, exposed and vulnerable to—who knows what?

It would be foolish to deny that all this dismay and unrest is equally dangerous to the principles of Fair Shares, probably more so. Left unguided, or guided only by the prophets of Fair Play, these unstable, explosive forces will probably move in the direction of reaction and greater inequality. Currently this danger is evident in such phenomena as the organizations of the "New Right," the Moral Majority, and the resurgent Ku Klux Klan.

But the very confusion and anger and sense of injustice that infuse the tax-cut movement reveal it to be the fruit of crisis. In addition, there are within this movement threads of populist, antielitist thinking. One might even think of it as an inverted, perverse parody of what I have called collective efforts to achieve collective benefits. These unwitting members of the vulnerable majority are having the facts of their vulnerability forced upon them. What makes them so potentially dangerous is that they misidentify the minority that is responsible for their troubles. Still, they remain a threat to the Fair Play ideology. If, as they thrash about trying to get life back on the track it is supposed to be on, trying to get the rules reestablished and obeyed, they continue to see greater benefits for others and new grief for themselves, then their loyalty to the basic principles must ultimately be shaken.

And what of those who reap the benefits? What will happen as the economically secure but not wealthy, and even some of the wealthy themselves, lose their grip on the ideology that justifies their position? What then? Without that ideology to comfort and justify them, what are they going to do? They can try for a while to accept themselves as successfully greedy persons.

In fact, we are currently experiencing an avalanche of books praising greed, extolling deceit and chicanery, and singing paeans to selfishness. But the well-to-do are human beings, no less than you and I. They are not, for the most part, willful villains, but are, by and large, decent human beings, also the "work of His hands." The heartless plutocrat exists mostly in cartoons. As long as a person can persuade himself comfortably that what he is doing can be put under the heading of ambition, achievement, accomplishment, and individual excellence, he can feel pretty good about himself. But if he arrives at a point where he has to admit to himself that what he is really doing is exploiting and impoverishing his fellow creatures, then he can in no way feel that he is doing the right thing.

As we move further and further away from the actual social conditions that provided some plausible basis for it, the Fair Play ideology becomes more hollow, more vulnerable. It is antiquated now, shot through with cracks and fissures, crumbling around the edges, and ready to be brought down. There is a substantial minority of Americans who no longer believe in its axioms. Others among the majority are growing confused and feeling betrayed. With appropriate experiences and the proper interpretation of them, they, too, would abandon those axioms.

The "ruling ideas" are ripe for dethronement.

8

Toward Equality

FAIR SHARING IN AMERICA

I EQUALITY AS SHARING

Trying to imagine what equality would be like, without actually experiencing it, is a task that can be accomplished only in part. Lacking appropriate experiences, we are bound to be in some measure mistaken as we try to construct a vision of a Fair Shares future. We cannot avoid carrying over in our imaginations certain assumptions that have become ingrained in our minds and that are beyond the reach of conscious efforts. This is not simply a self-serving plea for tolerance on the part of the reader who perceives flaws in this chapter; in a larger sense, it is a plea for more tolerance among all of us who are trying to achieve greater equality. None of us know how to do it. All of us have to move in such a way as to create new experiences consistent with equality, to learn from these experiences, and then to move again. This will require patience and constant resistance against despair. Let me, then, try to put forward certain partial insights, with the understanding that they are offered as contributions to a process, with the expectation that my own blind spots will be seen and corrected by others.

To give a common example of how unexamined assumptions distort our thinking about equality, I recall being persuaded at a very early age that equality was impossible, and the argument as to why this was so seemed to

me unanswerable at the time. The proposition was that, if you divided up all
the money in the country equally, it wouldn't be long before the clever ones
would begin getting rich again and the rest of us would go back to being
poor.

I feel sure everyone recognizes the general structure of that argument; it is
an old refrain, and I have since heard it many times. It is usually phrased in
a more sophisticated way, and it almost always seems to be persuasive. It is,
of course, a perfect example of what I discussed in Chapter One as the Fair
Play parody of equality, what Tawney called the fallacy of "equality as long
division."

The primary theme of Fair Shares equality is emphatically not division,
but aggregation, not separating resources into small portions for individuals,
but holding and using resources in common—sharing collectively, rather
than dealing out individually. In Chapter One, I tried to suggest briefly that
collective ownership and sharing, both as an idea and as a practice, is neither
alien nor incomprehensible to Americans. We are familiar with the idea of
the public ownership of resources such as libraries, schools, sewer systems,
protective services like fire and police, roads, public transportation systems,
and even, here and there, public utilities. We are also familiar with the
completely free use of many of these resources—free, not in the sense that
they do not cost anything, but in the sense that they are equally open to use
by all. In other cases, we are familiar with publicly owned resources that are
heavily subsidized but not "free" in the same sense—public transportation is
a good example. There is nothing immutable about this arrangement. Forty
or fifty years ago, virtually all transit systems were privately owned. The
time came when it made more sense for them to be owned publicly. There
was no uproar about this ownership or about the obvious need for subsidizing transit. One can conceive of further changes—for example, making public transportation free the way a library is free, that is, not charging any fares
at all. Is there any logical reason that we must pay to ride the subway but
not pay to borrow books from the library? Certainly it would be simpler and
cheaper to operate buses and subways without the bother of fares. There
would be no need for change booths or policemen to guard them, no need
for fare collectors, turnstile repairmen, or money counters. Buses could keep
to a much faster schedule without the delays occasioned by the collection of
fares.

Or go to the other extreme. Suppose you had a fire and the firemen
clanged up to your house and quickly put the fire out, but the next day you
got a bill from the fire department. What would you think? The private fire
department that charged for services was once quite common but is now
almost extinct. Virtually everyone who lives in an organized municipality
takes it for granted that it is a general right for a person to have his property
protected against the unchecked ravages of fire. We don't question that

right, and everyone in town contributes to a common fund, through taxes, to pay for firefighting services that are used by only a few. One might reasonably ask why we are so committed to the safety of houses and stores but not, for instance, to the health of our fellow citizens. Or, as another example, why are we quite willing to have a tax-supported, government-operated enterprise called a fire department or a sewer department but would have trouble accepting the existence of a parallel department to assure decent housing for all of the city's residents?

Now, while it is an unquestionable fact that the kind of governmental services and institutions I have mentioned are really publicly owned, belonging collectively to the citizenry as a group, it is equally true that very few of us *feel* any sense of collective ownership. There is, of course, some variability in this sense of participation. In many communities citizens talk about "our" schools and act as if they were responsible for, and capable of influencing, what goes on in the classroom. In other communities such a sense may be limited, for example, to "our" high school football or basketball team. But there are very few people who would talk about "our" sewer department, "our" post office, or "our" public transit system. These seem quite alienated from us, and we tend to perceive them in pretty much the way we do private businesses. In fact, there is often something of an antagonistic, adversary relationship between a public institution and the citizens who "own" it. The city or county or state is seen, not as a collectivity made up of its residents, but as a separate entity, not unlike a department store or a car dealer. Most of us lack the feeling that we are sharing in the use and cost of service for all of us. More typically, we feel that we are, so to speak, buying services with our tax dollars. Buying from whom? From the officeholders who have acquired at least temporary possession of the city's apparatus. It is not unusual to hear a citizen object to paying taxes for schools on the grounds that he does not have children of school age, or to paying taxes for public transportation on the grounds that he always travels by car. This is consistent with the sense that taxes are equivalent to payment for city services viewed as commodities, in the same way goods and services are paid for in the private sector. His protest is based on this sense of equivalence—he is being billed for commodities he did not order and never received.

There are, I think, three reasons why what is really public ownership and sharing is not often perceived as such. The first is that, with respect to the proprietorship of government, some persons are more equal than others; the government operates largely at the behest and in the interests of the rich, and the average working person is aware of this fact. The second is that governmental services assimilate their organizational structure and style to those prevailing in the private sector. They are hierarchically structured on the pattern of large corporations; public employees see themselves as working "for" their bosses, not for the public; and, consequently, they deal with citizens as "customers"—and customers who are poor credit risks, at that. The third is that we have no vocabulary and no set of mental categories to conceptualize public ownership and sharing in any different way, even though many of us might recognize in an inarticulate way that public institutions and private corporations are actually quite different. For example, we say bitterly, "Go fight city hall" far more readily than we say, "Go fight General Motors," even though most people probably feel that they are more able to influence city hall than General Motors and even that one resource with which to fight General Motors is to be found in the machinery of government itself.

Despite all this, the underlying sense of public ownership often breaks through and becomes visible and relevant. The movements for community control of such public institutions as schools, for citizen and consumer representation on the boards of public agencies, and for turning away from at-large municipal elections and returning to district representation are examples that come to mind. Or, to cite a fairly universal phenomenon, compare the reaction to an announcement that a public elementary school will be shut down with the response to the closing of the local A & P. Both events might arouse anger, but in the first instance outraged citizens from the neighborhood in which the school is located will almost certainly form an organization and militantly agitate to save *our* school. I have yet to hear of such a movement to save *our* A & P.

Nevertheless, even though we have no readily available means to think about them, or any words to describe them, the basic ideas of government ownership and public sharing are really quite well established. This becomes clear if we try to think of private-enterprise alternatives to public institutions. Very few persons are so addicted to the dream of free enterprise that they would propose, for example, a return to the days of privately owned toll roads and bridges. Nor are there very many who would advocate closing down the Postal Service and throwing the task of mail delivery into the hands of private business. And if an eccentric right-winger got upset about the idea of a public sewage system and campaigned for city councilman on the platform of abolishing sewer socialism, most people would probably decide that he was some kind of nut.

In the abstract, then, public ownership and sharing are not political problems. They are problems of shaping ideas to fit realities, but they become political issues when we ask questions about where we draw the lines. What should be public and "free"? What public and subsidized? What services, if any, should be reserved only for some "eligible" minority? What should be left completely in private hands, perhaps regulated to a greater or lesser extent, perhaps not? The current debates about tax and budget cutting refer precisely to these boundary-drawing issues.

The goal of those who advocate the Fair Shares system of equality is the continual expansion of these boundaries, so that more and more of life's essential resources and amenities are consciously shared within the sphere of public enterprise, rather than being held for ransom by private producers. The aim is definitely not simply to reshuffle and to deal out all the resources evenly among all the individuals playing the game. The idea that equal rewards to each individual defines equality adequately, as Tawney pointed out so eloquently, demonstrates a dense misunderstanding of the views of most egalitarians and is a naive or disingenuous trivialization of the issue. Such a limit on the idea of equality reveals an unreconstructed trust in the idea of the just and efficient marketplace, where atomized individuals come to exchange what they have for what they want. This may be an effective method for *allocating* many goods and services efficiently, but it ignores both the social nature of production and the inability of the market alone to guide the production of what is actually needed by the people as a whole.

For example, the market apparently cannot produce many of the basic necessities of life at prices that are not beyond the means of millions of people. That this is true in the area of housing has been grudgingly recognized for decades by the existence of tiny federal programs to subsidize shelter. Recently, with the wild inflation of land prices and of the costs of building materials, larger segments of the population are being priced out of the sales segment of the housing market. Meanwhile, rental housing is rapidly disappearing through the combined effects of abandonment, condominium conversion, and clearance of low-rent neighborhoods for the construction of expensive commercial developments. A rental-housing crisis is around the corner, and we are reaching a point where even real estate and building interests are recognizing that the market cannot provide rental housing for the majority of those who need it. The realm of food is another one in which market forces apparently lead to the degradation of quality, the inflation of prices to the consumer, and the lowering of prices to primary agricultural producers other than the huge enterprises of agribusiness. In a partial and inadequate response to this crisis, the government provides food stamps to millions of families that cannot afford to maintain a reasonable level of nutrition and, at the same time, price supports and other payments to those who produce the food. In order to maintain the illusion that the exchange of money for food takes place in a free market, we spend billions irrationally subsidizing both the consumers and the producers.

Finally, no market mechanisms can even be rationally imagined for meeting the need for vital services like foster care, protective services for the elderly and children, and elementary education. No one has discovered a way of transforming these services into commodities that can be bought and sold and profited from, and therefore the market cannot deal with them.

For all these reasons, Fair Sharing requires that we go far beyond any kind of primary reliance on market mechanisms and that we think of equality in terms far different from the oversimplification of merely giving everyone the same wages.

II THE QUESTION OF REDISTRIBUTION

When reformers talk about moving toward greater equality, they often use some such slogan as "Redistribute income, wealth, and power." At this point, the reader may well wonder if I am, perhaps, renouncing this slogan; he may have noted some discrepancy between my description of inequality and my effort to sketch the outlines of a society based on Fair Shares equality; that is, I have tended to use differences in money income as the primary index of inequality, yet have not urged complete equalization of money income either as a solution to or a definition of equality. To understand this apparent contradiction is to grasp an important contrast between the Fair Play principles that guide the norms and standards of our society and what I have labeled the Fair Shares perspective.

In the United States, how much money you have and get is almost the sole determinant of your standard and style of living, access to resources, services, amenities, and so on. Virtually everything in our society that one might need or want—tangible or intangible, from meat to music, from health to political influence—is treated primarily as a commodity to be bought and sold. As commodities, then, health, education, culture, and recreation are dealt with as if they were cabbages, CB radios, or blue jeans. The one with the most money gets first choice; the one with the least gets what's left over—if anything is indeed left over. So, if everything one needs or wants must be bought, inequality of income automatically produces inequality in all other areas of life.

One of the crucial differences between Fair Play thinking and Fair Shares thinking hinges precisely on the question of what should or should not be dealt with as a commodity. Fair Shares equality means removing from the category of commodities the basic necessities of life, as well as significant services such as health care and education, and redefining them as resources to be held in common and shared in such a way that everyone has an equal right of access to them. Given such an arrangement, money income, and differences in it, becomes far less important.

This is all the more true since a greater reliance on social income and equal access to resources implies a substantial reduction in emphasis on the individual. Individuals, as we have seen, are neither the most relevant producing units nor, in general, the most relevant consuming units, and there is no good reason to stake everything on the single dimension of money income to individuals.

Perhaps paradoxically, breaking the exclusive linkage between income and equality reduces the significance of income inequality itself. Nowadays, the meaning of the difference between a family income of, say, $15,000 and one of $60,000 is almost incalculable. The $15,000 is all but completely devoured in paying for the crucial necessities of life. If anything is left over for optional purchases—what is called "discretionary income"—it might be close to nothing and will scarcely ever be more than $500 or $1,000. The family earning four times that amount may spend only one-third of its income on actual necessities and have many thousands of dollars available for discretionary purchases, which can include quite a few luxuries. A ratio of four to one in absolute amounts of income becomes magnified tenfold or twentyfold or more when income is translated into standards and amenities of living.

The changes that we would look for as the marks of a Fair Shares society would drastically alter the meaning and consequence of money income as such. With a vastly expanded program of social insurance, a reformed and steeply progressive tax structure, and a greatly enlarged public role in the provision of basic needs and services, differences in income from labor would result above all in relatively equivalent differences in discretionary income, allowing for both modest variations in standards of living and great diversity in the consumption of the nonnecessities of life. One family might want to save for an automobile, another for a sailboat, a third for a piano. One might want to spend money on recreation, another on better home furnishings. Given a high level of social income, this transformation in the meaning of labor income becomes quite feasible, and a range of differences in money income of, say, three to one would probably be tolerable and reasonably consistent with the sense of justice of most persons.

The distribution of wealth, however, presents a very different problem. A Fair Shares society, by definition, cannot exist while most resources are controlled by a relative handful of persons. The holdings of the wealthy minority must be substantially reduced. Technically, this can be accomplished largely through an aggressive tax program—one that raises drastically the effective taxation rates on the rich, that includes in the category of ordinary income all capital gains, undistributed profits, and other forms of protected income from wealth and that boosts gift and inheritance taxes at the top levels to quasi-confiscatory levels. Such a program to "soak the rich" is possible within the framework of our present governmental system, but it presents serious political problems of pace and timing. No one knows how fiercely the rich will fight to keep every penny they now own. No one knows how far they will be willing to go in choosing means of resistance. Therefore, no one knows how long such a process will take—a decade or two, or a generation or two—or how difficult or disruptive it will be. Such a goal must be approached cautiously, sensitively, with complete determination, but with a will to avoid violence, and with the understanding that we must learn as we move. I don't believe anyone can predict accurately the details of such a process. I certainly will not attempt to do so.

Finally, it should be underlined once again that the purpose of removing the control of most resources from the hands of the very rich is neither to fritter it away on immediate foolish consumption nor to scatter it broadside among the vulnerable majority. In our interdependent industrial society, the wealth of the rich—however socially unjust—does serve an enormously important social purpose. It is the major source of funds for capital investment in the production system of the country. (Of course, we now have no assurance that this investment will be wise, in the national interest, or sufficient. Eagerness for short-term profit can overcome prudent awareness of the need for long-term reinvestment and modernization. We are learning more and more about this problem as we confront the crisis growing out of the neglect and aging of our industrial plant over the past several decades.) When funds for capital investment are transferred from private vaults to public treasuries, they will be needed for the same purpose. The principal difference is that, having removed the need for personal profits to support extravagant living and social power for a few, we can make investment decisions in a far more democratic, rational, and humane manner, guided by the criterion of the common good.

III   FIRST STEPS, BABY STEPS

Assuming that a Fair Shares society would roughly resemble what I sketched out above, how do we get from here to there? What are the appropriate mechanisms for moving toward a more firmly grounded equality? Given my fundamental assumption that there is a significant degree of concordance between the prevailing belief system in a society and the manner in which that society is structured with respect to equality or inequality, it would seem to me that one cannot reasonably expect to move suddenly toward change in societal structure without some parallel change in the prevailing ideology. I would argue further that changes in ideological assumptions *follow*, and conform to, changes in social reality. This seems to me to imply that movement toward Fair Shares equality must take place in a stepwise manner—first a moderate social change, followed by an adaptive shift in belief systems, then more social change, followed by more ideological change, and so forth.

If this is true, then it follows that we must begin with relatively moderate changes, which may seem like baby steps to some who are impatient for a more immediate transformation. There are, I think, three appropriate areas upon which activity can be focused immediately: (1) social insurance; (2) an expansion of the public sector in the provision of services; and (3) an expansion of public activity—including direct operation, subsidies, and various levels of regulation—in order to provide everyone with an adequate, decent, and assured supply of all the necessities of life, such as housing, fuel, and food. I am persuaded that a properly informed public, provided with a consistent, reliable interpretation of the realities of inequality, would be prepared to support firm governmental action to insure that everyone had those necessities. Not many Americans are prepared to fight for a color television in every home; damned few, indeed, would knowingly and willingly let a child go hungry in an unheated slum apartment.

Social insurance Our Social Security system requires considerable revamping, beginning with the jettisoning of all the vocabulary and procedural trappings that imply, falsely, that social-insurance programs are modeled on private-insurance plans, such as life insurance and annuities.[2] They are not. The average Social Security recipient, for example, gets two to four times as much income as he would if his contributions to the system had been invested in actual annuities or pension funds. The difference between what he "has coming to him" and what he gets—that is, somewhere between 50 and 75 percent of his check—comes from other people's money, from tax money, exactly as public assistance does. This is, I think, as it should be and has to be. Parents support children, and then children support parents. The difference between trying to do this adequately within each family and doing it through Social Security is that the latter spreads and socializes the risk and equalizes the payoff. That is the "insurance" feature. It is something like a mammoth version of old-fashioned burial and benevolent associations.

If the politicians were willing to let the general public in on these facts, a number of rational changes could probably be made without too much protest. First, we could put an end to the absurd and grossly unfair system of deducting FICA "contributions" from our paycheck. They aren't contributions; they're taxes and should, as such, be subject to the principles of progressive taxation. As it is now, the Social Security system is heavily subsidized by ordinary working people while the well-to-do get a practically free ride. If we compare the effect of the federal income tax with that of the Social Security tax, we can see how unfairly the latter is imposed. The income tax is based on the widely accepted principle of ability to pay: those with higher incomes pay a greater *proportion* of it in taxes. Moreover, deductions and exemptions make the amount of taxable income less than the amount of total income. In contrast, the Social Security tax is applied to the first dollar of wages, with no allowance for exemptions. Even worse, it is applied only on a portion of the wages (currently approximately $23,000). Everything above that is tax free. In other words, a worker earning $18,000 a year pays Social Security tax on all of his income, a rate of over 6 percent;

the executive earning $45,000 pays Social Security tax on only *half* his income, an effective rate of only 3 percent. When we add together the deductions for Social Security tax and income tax, we find that the worker earning $18,000 has approximately the same proportion of his wages taken out of his paycheck as does the person earning $30,000 (about 20 percent).[3] This is obviously a gross violation of the principle that the rate of taxation should be based on ability to pay, and it adds up to an unfairly heavy tax burden on lower- and middle-income persons.

At the other end of the process, the inequity continues. The person who has been earning a high income all his life will receive a much higher benefit when he retires (perhaps $750 a month, compared to the average of about $500 a month).

If the $45,000 executive paid Social Security tax on all his income instead of only half of it, and if the rates were progressive, as income tax rates are, he would be paying about 8 percent of his income and the $18,000 worker would be taxed at a rate of about 5 percent. How much difference would that make? The former would be paying $3,600 rather than $1,400; the latter, $900 instead of $1,100.

As for the really low-paid worker, who earns $8,000 and pays $500 in Social Security tax—usually a significantly *larger* amount than his income tax—the rate of his Social Security tax would drop to about 3 percent, and his "contribution" would be halved, to about $250.

Once we admit that the "contributions" are really taxes and deal with them as we do with income taxes, we can do away with other pieces of the masquerade, such as maintaining each person's separate "account," as if he had a real insurance policy, and basing eligibility for benefits on an intricate analysis of these accounts. At that point, eligibility could be made universal, based simply on a particular status—reaching the age of sixty-five, being disabled, and so on—rather than on work history, and benefits would be determined by presumptive need rather than by counting "contributions."

Three additional social-insurance programs would take care of most of the problems of severe income deficit and would, if benefit levels were set high enough, eliminate virtually all official poverty in America. The first provides for children's allowances, which are fixed monthly sums paid to parents, to be used for the benefit of children. (Every major industrial nation except the United States has such a program.) The second is an expansion of the disability segment of Social Security to include temporary disability as a basis for benefit payments. A few states now operate such programs, on a very limited basis, but the majority of American workers who are temporarily disabled for more than a few weeks have no assured source of income during the period of their disability. Now only extended total disability makes one eligible for Social Security payments. The fact that a disabled person can look forward to recovery and return to work within a period of a few months is, of course, a source of great comfort, but meanwhile expenses continue just as if he were working and are often increased as a result of the illness or accident that caused the disability. The loss of income for several months during such a period is one of the principal reasons that so many members of the vulnerable majority fall into periods of poverty. The third program I would propose calls for universal unemployment benefits, that is, an extension of these payments to all who are legitimately jobless regardless of their work histories (including new entrants into the labor market who cannot, after some reasonable period, find work). Such a program would, in passing, I suspect, reduce most objections to a real government commitment to full employment.

Public services   In Chapter Four, as an example, I derived from the principles of Fair Shares a concrete proposal for the form and content of an effective national health service. Similar ones could be generated for a number of other services, among them higher education, counseling services, child welfare programs, protective programs for children and other vulnerable members of society, mental health services, and day care. (I would vote for including cultural services and sports as well.) In the attempt to implement these proposals the same basic principles would apply: These services should be tax supported, the full operating responsibility vested in a governmental entity. They should be made available to all who need them, regardless of income and with no limitation on eligibility. A prominent component of all of them should be activity that is preventive or promotive rather than remedial. Services should be organized nationally to insure uniformity of quality and an equitable geographic distribution, but should, at the operating level, be guided and supervised by representative, elected citizen boards. A full network of such public programs would contribute to the attainment of equality in much the same way that a national health service would, that is, it would equalize access to these services and would reduce the economic burden that they involve.

Necessities of life   There are many examples of existing public programs directed to the problem of assuring the necessities of life: federal housing subsidies and municipal authorities operating publicly owned housing; food stamps and school breakfast and lunch programs; regulation of public utilities; and publicly owned or subsidized transportation, such as Amtrak and regional transportation authorities. While these programs are consistent in theory with the Fair Shares approach, in practice they do not move us very far along the road to Fair Shares, because they are underfunded, organized in an ineffective manner, and, most important, unnecessarily squeezed out of the mainstream by restrictive eligibility requirements that effectively label them as second-class enterprises for the needy. As someone once said, programs for the poor are usually poor programs.

In order to transform these types of programs into effective levers for achieving more equality, it is necessary to meet three requirements. First, small-scale piecemeal programs should be replaced by large-scale, comprehensive ones aimed at a specific and universal goal, e.g., the provision of a standard dwelling unit for every American family at a cost no greater than 20 or even 25 percent of family income. The Housing Act of 1949 contains language encompassing such a goal, but does not provide any means for achieving it. Second, such programs must not be sabotaged at the outset by highly selective eligibility requirements, particularly by income limits. If our supposed goal is standard housing for every family, for example, we can guarantee failure by adding phrases like "over sixty-five" or "with incomes below the poverty level." Since millions of families belonging to the vulnerable majority live in homes that are substandard, overcrowded, or too expensive, it is neither just nor workable to pick out some small subgroup to which housing services will be offered. This produces, on the one hand, resentment among those excluded and guarantees, on the other, that the action will be aborted in some way, so that the housing produced will not be "too nice for them."

Third, the public enterprise must operate right in the middle of the arena, not in some corner reserved for charity cases. It must have the acknowledged capacity to influence the relevant forces at work. For example, a public agency cannot be taken seriously in its commitment to a decent home for every family at an affordable price when it is severely bounded and limited to a few marginal subgoals, such as providing a handful of housing units for the poor. It must have the capacity to occupy a large area of the field and to act so as to rationalize overall policy. Let me illustrate this last point. Theoretically our national housing policy is to stimulate housing production in order to move toward the goal of a decent home for everyone, but our tax policies in regard to housing overwhelm our meager production efforts. Over one-third of all state and local taxes are sucked out of real estate; this creates an enormous drain on the average working family.[4] At the same time, we allow these property levies to be taken as income tax deductions, which is significantly advantageous only for well-to-do homeowners. (The minority who rent get nothing, of course.) The combination of heavy property taxes at the local level and tax deductions at the federal level amounts to an incredible sleight-of-hand trick to swindle the average family in order to enrich the well-to-do. To all intents and purposes, moreover, right and left hands are utterly ignorant of each other's carryings-on: the right hand is taking almost $30 billion in local residential-property taxes, mostly from the pockets of the average family, while the left hand is shoveling, by means of tax deductions, about $8 billion in what are essentially *tax rebates*—mostly into the checking accounts of the well-off (60 percent of these tax benefits go to 10 percent of the homeowners; the majority of them get little or no benefit).[5] A very simple shift in policy—eliminate property-tax deductions and channel the additional revenue right back to local taxing authorities specifically earmarked for property tax relief—could cut property taxes by at least 20 percent and, in the process, redistribute billions of dollars down the income scale.

It is not possible or appropriate here to develop a full list of specific remedies, but consider some of the possibilities: If food stamps, why not fuel stamps? If food stamps for some, why not food stamps for all? If state liquor stores, why not state food stores? If telephone, telegraph, and mail are all handled by a single public agency in other countries, why not here? If subsidized public colleges, why not subsidized public theaters, concerts, sports events? If children's allowances, why not homemakers' allowances? I will not go on. We do not lack *ideas* pertaining to greater equality, to what a world of Fair Shares might be like.

All of these tools for achieving greater equality are quite familiar to us in theory and, in a very limited way, in practice. And we are also theoretically committed to the proper method of paying the costs—sharply graduated taxes on income and wealth. What we lack is the vision of equality that would make such ideas desirable to the majority and thus readily achievable.

The basic idea of Fair Sharing implies two other issues that should be mentioned briefly (although they cannot be discussed adequately in this context). The first has to do with the extent of redistribution. Obviously, the kinds of programs that are needed to achieve equality require broad taxation not only of high incomes but of basic wealth as well. Does such a degree of redistribution necessarily imply that capitalism must, for all practical purposes, be wholly replaced by socialism? I'm not sure, and I'm not sure anyone really knows. Certainly I can't imagine how we could achieve anything resembling equality and still permit a relatively small handful of persons to exploit our resources and our population—that is, *us*—purely for their own profit and desire for wealth. So it seems that equality can be attained only if we are prepared to see our society and our economy transformed into some kind of more socialistic form.

What type of socialism? To what extent should socialism be carried? What should our models be? Do we want the United States to be like Sweden or Rumania or Yugoslavia? To the last question, I believe most Americans would say, No. I think most of us want the United States to be like the United States. To the extent that socialism does develop here, it will have to be American socialism, growing out of American history, responding to the conditions in this country and to the needs of the American people.[6]

The second issue that should at least be mentioned derives from the obvious truth that one could have something called socialism without necessarily attaining equality. Even if many of the goals that I have suggested and those that others have put forth were to be achieved, it is possible that a small group of authoritarian public officials and an unresponsive bureaucracy could *control* resources, without technically owning them, and become functionally equivalent, in some sense, to our own wealthy owning class. This appears to have happened in some socialist countries and is, at the least, a constant danger to be guarded against.[7]

The equalization of power presents special problems, because in a complex society one cannot equalize the *exercise* of authority; that is possible only in some kind of imaginary utopian anarchy. There must exist social norms and means of enforcing them; decisions must be made about the planning and implementation of policy. There is always the possibility that those who exercise authority will in fact accumulate personal power.

One would hope that in a nation with a two-hundred-year history of political democracy and with a constitution based on the principle of the separation of powers and the limitations on government power by a Bill of Rights, the more obvious dangers of excessive concentration of power would be foreseen and avoided. Beyond this, the general principles of the Fair Shares ideology can be applied as directly to the problem of power distribution as they can be to that of resource distribution. Just as the Fair Play doctrine could be used to justify the concentration of power on the basis of extraordinary internal characteristics of individuals, so the general principle of collective participation in decision making by those who are similar to one another and who attend primarily to external situational factors leads to a set of principles regarding the exercise of authority and power consistent with a Fair Shares outlook. They can briefly be summarized as follows:

• Decision making, the establishment of policy, the legislative function—as distinguished from the administrative execution of policy decisions—would have to be established as falling solely within the domain of collective democratic processes. With reference to the kinds of changes proposed above, this would imply the necessity of establishing citizens' boards and policy committees at several levels—neighborhood, region, and so forth—to direct and oversee all the specified functions, such as the provision of health care, social-insurance programs, and governmental housing.

• The principle of similarity translates directly into the established idea of one man, one vote and indirectly into the rule of election, rather than appointment, to all positions of decision making.

• The principle of external emphasis dictates that the processes of democratic decision making be directed only to the situations, problems, and needs that confront the nation and its citizens outside the skin, so to speak. This means that internal processes, thoughts, and beliefs would be off limits and that persons could not be excluded from participation on the basis of real or assumed internal characteristics, such as antisocial thoughts, unpopular values, or emotional deviance.

After this overly brief review of these important issues, it is time to turn to the next questions. (Unfortunately, we no doubt have plenty of time to ponder the twin issues of socialism and the exercise of authority in a significantly more equalized society.)

IV LEARNING WHAT'S GOOD FOR US

I suppose if I were asked to pick out the point I most want to get across to the reader, it would be that the ideology of inequality is an enormously potent barrier to the achievement of equality. The concept of internal individual characteristics that differentiate the best of us from the worst of us both shapes our social institutions and warps our own consciousness so thoroughly that every move toward equality seems to swerve away from the goal or fizzle out into nothing. Even those of us who consciously set out toward the goal of equality must expect to get mired down in the swamps of our own mistaken assumptions and to lose our way. The process is slow and sometimes discouraging. Let me give a personal example. As I was completing this book, I reread my previous book *Blaming the Victim*, published ten years ago, and was painfully aware that phrase after phrase and paragraph after paragraph clearly revealed my own attachment to the Fair Play ideology. I am resigned to having the same experience ten years hence when I reread this one. Even R. H. Tawney's *Equality*, arguably the best book available on the subject, even though it was written over fifty years ago, contains numerous manifest indications of the author's commitment to ideas like equality of opportunity (although he was acutely aware that preexisting inequality negated its possibility) and individually differentiated merit. He was even taken in by the ideas of Cyril Burt, one of the great charlatans in the history of psychology, on the measurement of intellectual ability. If we have been so blinded, how will we learn to see?

Ideas, concepts, assumptions, and ways of viewing man and his world grow largely out of our own experiences and perceptions. We come to believe those ideas and to hold those assumptions that appear to be consistent with our own experiences or—and this is most important—that someone can *interpret to us* as being consistent with our own experiences. The mystification and misinterpretation of our own experiences blind us and distort our thinking. The more appropriate metaphor, then, is, not that we have been *blinded*, but that we have been unknowingly looking at the world through distorting lenses that have been forced upon us.

Ideologies, fundamental belief systems, are established—and, therefore, might be changed—in the interaction between experiencing and interpreting experience. From the moment of raw sense experience to that of formulating an interpretation of that experience, complicated mental processes take place. Some of them might use prior experience to formulate interpretations;

some of them might use earlier interpretations to shape the experience and its perception.[8] If, for example, an egg slips out of your hand while you are walking from the refrigerator to the stove, you know very well that it will not remain motionless in the air or rise to the ceiling. It will fall to the floor and, with your luck, break. Nor is this expectation, that unsuspended objects heavier than air will drop, limited to the case of eggs. Your experiences and perceptions over the years have established this belief quite thoroughly. The explanation of *why* the egg drops is a different matter. The raw phenomenon, egg drops and breaks, can comfortably fit a number of potential explanations, including Newton's mathematical formulations about gravity. Yet most of us, if asked why the egg fell, would say something about the law of gravity, suggesting, accurately, that we *believe in* the law of gravity. However, there are very significant differences between our belief that the egg will fall and our belief in the law of gravity. The former is much more dependent on raw experience, the latter on interpretation.

In this case, the experience and the interpretation are in harmony. Consider another common experience—that of seeing sunrises and sunsets. Here the belief based on interpretation is contrary to the apparent experience; yet it overrides and invalidates the belief that might be based on the more direct experience. A common-sense interpretation of these visual experiences would be that the sun comes up over the horizon, crosses the sky, and then goes down. That's certainly what it looks like. But it is not difficult to persuade someone that the sun is doing no such thing, that the earth is rotating, instead. While not as intuitively believable, this explanation can be supported by logical argument, and most persons believe it without having studied astronomy.

Now, move on to the situation of the school classroom that I outlined in Chapter Five. The study plan for the day is to teach reading, writing, and arithmetic, but the hidden curriculum is to transmit the belief that all children can be divided up into two groups, the tigers and the clowns, on the basis of their individual internal differences. (This curriculum is elaborated as we move along, of course, to cover the belief that some tigers roar louder than others.) If you were assigned the task of constructing a set of classroom experiences designed to teach that particular lesson, could you improve on the performance of the kindergarten teacher described by Ray Rist?

In the kindergarten case, the structure and process of the human situation—nonverbal perceptions and apparently irrelevant verbal perceptions—tell one story; the apparent content of the teaching process tells another story. Which of the two is more true? Every ounce of *interpretation* brought to bear on that situation focuses on the apparent content of the teaching process, and this is the story that is almost always believed. If you doubt this, try to explain to a group of parents that Miss Morris, that supercompetent, high-class, all-knowing kindergarten teacher, may on the surface be teaching colors and shapes and reading readiness to all the pupils in her class, but just below this manifest surface she is really teaching their children how to be tigers or clowns and how to accept these roles. They won't believe it. (As a matter of fact, Miss Morris won't believe it either; she's not aware of what she's doing.) They *know* what is going on in the classroom. It has been shown and interpreted to them again and again. That's *education* and education is good and children have to get their education. Don't come around here with your crazy ideas about schools' being places for sorting children and stratifying them!

Why is it so easy to convince people that the earth rotates into and out of the sun's light and so hard to interpret the destructive processing of children in public schools? For one thing, whether one believes that the sun goes around the earth or the earth around the sun is of no importance in most people's lives. Hardly anyone ever even gives it a thought or has any particular reason to want to believe one explanation rather than another. It is, in our times, an *ideologically neutral* question, at least compared with its ideological significance at the time of Galileo and Copernicus. The nature and function of schools, on the other hand, is an issue of enormous ideological importance; it is one of the major pillars that holds up the whole mythological structure of meritocracy and equal opportunity. Most people believe that "education" *is* enormously significant in the lives of their children. Of course, they have been misinformed about *why* it's important, and they think that education is the key to upward mobility. After all, who wouldn't prefer to believe that his child is going to school to get a better job rather than to be trained to be a clown?

The good news is that acceptance of this interpretation is not universal. Many of the children in school perceive and interpret what is happening quite accurately, and they resist being trained (often earning the label "troublemaker").

This illustrates the fact that efforts to impose an exceptionalistic, antiegalitarian ideology are far from completely successful. A large minority of the population has not bought it at all. They have managed to resist the "ruling ideas." Large numbers of us *are* more inclined to view human events in collective rather than individual terms, to see similarity more readily than difference, and to believe that external events outweigh internal factors in determining what happens to people. The minority who hold these more universalistic assumptions tend to be far more receptive to the ideas of Fair Shares equality, to reject the popular ideas about meritocracy and equal opportunity, and to favor egalitarian public policies, such as a national health program, a guaranteed annual income, and progressive income taxes.

How is it that some persons are able to do this, to take off the distorting lenses and look at their experiences more directly? At present, we have only a few glimpses into this process of resisting the "ruling ideas" that surround us. Examples of such glimmers include the studies in the United Kingdom that focus on a related issue on what differentiates the working person who votes Labor from the one who votes Conservative.[9] The findings indicate various critical factors: where the person lives (if he lives in a large, homogeneous working-class neighborhood, he is more likely to vote Labor); the size of his place of work (the larger the work force of which he is a member, the more likely he is to vote Labor); and union membership (the union man is more apt to vote Labor). We also found some interesting differences in our Massachusetts survey, which I referred to in earlier chapters. For example, the person who owned his home was more inclined to be antiegalitarian and, in particular, to lean toward the individual end of the individual-collectivity dimension. We found that the size of the household was also a predictor of ideology: those from large households were more likely to see persons as similar and to be proegalitarian; those from smaller households, to emphasize difference and to be antiegalitarian.[10]

All these findings, it seems to me, support the proposition that ideology grows primarily out of experience. Consider, for example, the contrasting experience of two children. One lives in a working-class neighborhood of high density, where rows of three-decker houses on small lots line both sides of the street. On one block, five hundred feet long, there are perhaps sixty families, perhaps 150 kids.

The other child lives in a single home on a one-acre lot in the suburbs. He and his sister occupy as much space as do 150 city kids. He probably goes a month without interacting with 150 kids, whereas the first can scarcely pass a day without doing so. Which of the two children is more likely to interpret his experiences in terms of individualism and difference, which in terms of collectivity and similarity? I would predict that the children in densely populated neighborhoods, in constant contact with dozens of their peers, often forming cliques or gangs, frequently dealt with en masse by neighborhood adults, would have a lesser sense of uniqueness and difference among themselves, and a greater sense that human activity occurs at the level of the collectivity rather than purely at the level of the individual.

Or, more concretely, consider the case of the union member working in an automobile assembly plant. On one level, he might well subscribe to abstract propositions about individual merit and the advancement of the more worthy. But on the concrete, practical level he *acts* as if his economic fate were intertwined with that of five hundred or a thousand other men; as if, with respect to economic well-being, they would all advance together or not at all. He *acts* as if everyone were pretty much the same, as if there were no logical way of determining which man is more talented or meritorious in regard, for example, to the question of advancement to a higher-paying job or to that of who should be laid off first. Among union members, the principle of individual advancement or individual pay increases based on some management criterion of "merit" is thoroughly rejected. When a pay raise is being bargained for, it is specifically defined as a raise of the same amount or percentage for *everybody* in a given unit or occupational group. The wage is attached to the job, not to the individual. Merit-raise systems are anathema and even piece-rate wages are ordinarily frowned upon. Seniority as a basis for job security and for bidding for higher-paying jobs is, correctly, a holy institution.

So, where the unionized factory worker may, on the theoretical level, say, yes, indeed, he believes in individualism and advancement by differential merit, when it comes to the real world, he will fight for collective economic benefits and for the principle of the equal treatment of all members of the work force as essentially similar. And, no matter what laws are passed, unions will not (except, perhaps, for the period of a contract) renounce the right to strike, to take collective action for collective benefits. This is a prime example of ideology that grows out of direct experience and is interpreted in terms of equality. The problem of changing ideology, then, can be analyzed as one of expanding opportunities for the experience of equality and of increasing mechanisms for interpreting those experiences in terms of equality rather than of inequality.

In the case of the union member, his beliefs about the real processes of economic advancement have not had to depend on the interpretations he receives from his employer, on what he learned in school, on what he reads, and on what he sees on the television. A major function of the union itself, first in organizing and then in maintaining itself, is precisely one of reinterpretation, of supporting and encouraging workers in a factory to trust their own experiences and to allow their beliefs to become consistent with those experiences. This is not always done skillfully; sometimes, sad to say, it is not done at all; it is rarely done consciously. But the mark of a successful union is that its members have at least some allegiance to the Fair Shares ideology, even though they might, at another level, embrace contradictory beliefs. However embarrassed they might be about it, they will wave the banner of "Solidarity Forever."

The process of organizing, then, as in the case of labor unions, provides both the experience and the potential for interpretation that can help us learn what is good for us.

How can we counter the propaganda of the intellectual assault on equality? There are serious problems here. In the first place, most of the instruments of communication, particularly those beamed at larger audiences, are pretty much under the sway of the Fair Play party. A single article in *Harper's* or *Commentary* reaches ten people for every one who sees an article in *Dissent*, the *Nation*, or *Social Policy*. The Fair Play ideas also trickle down to the editorial pages and columns in the newspapers, especially the large, influential ones, in a very rapid and sometimes frightening way.[11] In the second place, to counteract a dominant idea system like the ideology of Counterfeit Equality requires a great deal more than words. Belief in the principles of Fair Play comes naturally, so to speak—we have been exposed to them from birth. To learn to discard those beliefs and to believe in Fair Shares is much more dependent on vivid experiences, adequately perceived and interpreted.

We should not, of course, leave the field of the large national media in the hands of the Fair Play propagandists without a contest; every effort should be made to combat the Fair Players in that arena. But it is a one-sided battle, and it would be foolish to rely on such combat as the only, or even the primary, method of communicating the Fair Shares perspective.

A higher priority should be given to learning better ways to help people immediately engaged in collective action to change their beliefs to conform to their experiences. In particular, we should not make the mistake of trying to disguise Fair Shares actions with any of the elements of Fair Play ideology on the grounds of making these actions more palatable or understandable. Such attempts are more likely to bolster the forces of inequality. Successful efforts to achieve greater equality will consist of integrating the actions of organizing, of experiencing, and of interpreting. That's the chief way we'll learn what's good for us.

V   ACTION FOR EQUALITY

Let me repeat at this point my general recipe for achieving equality: collective action for collective benefits. I am doubly convinced that this is the best strategy because it serves two mutually reinforcing purposes. It provides at once a direct method of winning a larger share and the kind of experience that nourishes an egalitarian, Fair Shares ideology and contradicts the antiegalitarian ideology of individual internal differences.

Although the recipe can be stated simply, it cannot be put into effect simply. For example, I suggested previously that a general model for this kind of action is the labor union. We have to admit, however, that the success of the labor movement in achieving a better economic position for working people has been very limited. Today, almost fifty years after the exhilarating early achievements of the CIO, less than one-fourth of the labor force is unionized, and the percentage would be even lower if it were not for the heartening success in recent years of new drives to organize such groups as hospital and municipal employees. How can we account for this dismal showing, and how can the labor movement be regenerated to the point where it can be an effective force for Fair Shares? It would be simple (and the temptation is not always resisted) to blame labor leaders themselves, to say they have grown fat and old, and to scold them for sitting back and leaving the unorganized out in the cold. Unions and their leaders can be and have been criticized for many things, from corruption to collusion, but the idea that Lane Kirkland, Douglas Fraser, and other major union leaders are content with the status quo, that they do not *wish* to organize the unorganized—this strikes me as simply incredible. I am quite convinced that they are keenly aware that the larger the proportion of the work force that is unionized, the more powerful and the better off all workers are (although they may not have persuaded all their constituents of the validity of this principle). Labor leaders of the era of Samuel Gompers may correctly be accused of having limited their concerns to the skilled craft worker, the aristocrats of labor, but, in my judgment, most labor leaders of today would agree with the following propositions: first, that the lot of the American worker, who in recent years has been suffering a steady decline in real wages and standard of living, can best be improved by his inclusion in the ranks of organized labor, and, second, that the responsibility for achieving this goal cannot be reasonably assumed by anyone other than the members of the labor movement itself. If the second point is granted, I would argue further that this responsibility is in fact an obligation that the labor movement owes to all workers who are not unionized. In fact, I would not be reluctant to say that the labor movement has an obligation to the American people to get going again and to organize at least a million new members a year.

Again, however, this is easy to demand, hard to achieve. It requires much more than an investment in the salaries of more organizers. Political barriers to further unionization have been erected, particularly through the Taft-Hartley Act and its encouragement of antiunion "right to work" laws in the individual states. The National Labor Relations Board itself has been hamstrung by the political influence of the big corporations, as evidenced most blatantly by the history of the flagrant and illegal refusal of the J. P. Stevens Company to negotiate with the clothing and textile workers, despite years of repeated orders from the NLRB to do so. Only recently, after years of effort, has the union begun to crack through Stevens's resistances. Worst of all, we find huge numbers of working people who have been completely persuaded by antiunion propaganda and who actually do not want to be unionized.[12]

I would suggest that a regeneration of the labor movement would be facilitated by paying attention to the problem of ideology in relation to the interpretation of experience. One of the great gaps in the activities of labor unions is precisely in this area—a failure to provide an adequate interpretation to workers, both in and outside of unions, of what they are experiencing. Where are the external communications of labor to those for whom I said they have a responsibility—to unorganized workers? Why can't labor newspapers be started in at least a few large cities? Why can't labor unions sponsor television programs that will carry the union point of view and counteract the situation comedies and silly melodramas that consistently purvey the "ruling ideas" of the wealthy?

The second major front in the struggle for Fair Shares is racism. If we seriously want to resume the movement toward racial equality, we must get back into the streets. We can let the assault-on-equality gunmen wipe out affirmative action, for example, with their specious talk about reverse discrimination and the preferential treatment of blacks. Or, we can take some initiative by properly defining the discrimination issue as the continuation of old-fashioned, *unreverse* discrimination and preferential treatment of *whites*, affirmative action providing merely the scorecard with which to judge to what extent the old problem is being eliminated. If we are to do the latter we need to call attention to the issue by methods less genteel than a polite tap on the shoulder or a brilliant legal brief. Being in the streets, making noise, collecting in numbers, insisting—that's how we made progress before; that's how we can make it again. It is time to stop mourning lost leaders and to start doing again what they led us in doing. When Dr. King died, George Wiley, in eulogizing him, echoed Bill Haywood's dying words, "Don't mourn for me, organize," and the same words were a fitting epitaph for George Wiley. Not all the leaders are gone, and new leaders of great promise have stepped forward. The mourning period is over. The organization should begin again.

The resurgence of labor unionism and the resumption of the movement toward racial equality would still be only partial approaches to the equality issue. Something broader is needed. And something broader is becoming available. I refer to the new phenomenon of local and regional organizations made up of a relatively broad spectrum of economic groups, oriented toward concrete economic goals with potential benefits that, although modest, are clear and attainable: the reduction of automobile insurance rates; the reform of the utility rate structures for such necessities as telephones, gas, and electricity; the correction of inequities and injustices in tax practices. There are now such organizations in many states and metropolitan areas.

Two of the earliest such organizations—ACORN, which started in Arkansas and has now spread to other states, and FAIR SHARE, which started in the city of Chelsea and is now organized in chapters all across Massachusetts—are direct descendants of the welfare-rights movement. Inspired by George Wiley, they were organized primarily by veteran welfare rights organizers, led by Mark and Barbara Splaine and Lee Staples in Massachusetts, by Wade Rathke in Arkansas and by Bert deLeeuw in the Washington support office. They reflect the thinking and analysis that George Wiley was engaged in during the last year of his life, critically assessing the successes and failures of the welfare-rights movement and starting to plan the direction of the new organization he had founded, the Movement for Economic Justice. I know that he had identified very clearly one weakness of his past efforts—the narrow constituency represented by the welfare issues. I think, but am not sure, that he had also perceived another weakness—that the welfare-rights organizations engaged in *collective* actions but that, in practice, they reaped *individual* benefits. There were, then, certain built-in inequities and also a failure to counteract completely the problem of individualism, which led to the withdrawal of members after they had obtained some substantial concrete benefits for themselves. Fortunately, many of the new generation of organizations such as ACORN have avoided these two problems. Membership is drawn from a rather broad economic and racial spectrum, and issues are chosen that, if successfully resolved, will lead to some permanent changes in institutions and will produce collective benefits.

I don't believe that I am being unreasonably optimistic in saying that the potential for a new surge toward equality is already with us, that the components are all in place for producing an increased level of widespread and concerted collective action for equality that would be unprecedented in American life—a newly expanding labor union movement, a revived demonstration-oriented civil rights movement, and a national coalition of increasing numbers of organizations like ACORN. That in itself, if history is a guide, should provide a tremendous amount of pressure not only to reverse the assault on equality but also to push closer than we have ever been to the goal of equality. Before the more ambitious programs put forth by advocates of equality could succeed, however, an even greater cohesion of the different segments of the vulnerable majority would need to evolve, and it would have to take a clearly political form. Substantial movement toward equality requires, in other words, the vehicle of a political party dedicated to equality. How that might occur is not yet evident. It is a development that is, to be optimistic, at least five or ten years away. It seems clear by now that the existing parties of the left have no appeal for the American people. On the other hand, the Democrats and Republicans scarcely bother any longer to feign concern about the interests of ordinary working people. A new party, it seems to me, will have to be constructed on the base of existing organizations of working people themselves, if it is to be genuinely dedicated to economic, social, and racial justice and equality. Obviously, the largest and strongest segment of that base is the labor movement. It remains to be seen whether the labor unions, or any substantial number of them, are ready for such an escalation of goals. A party that is so dedicated, however, is a necessity if we are to have any hope of seeing real action for equality.

VI THE IMPOSSIBILITY THEOREM

Like the Mad Hatter crying, "No room! No room!" the apologists of inequality have as their final defense the cry "Impossible!" They tell us that genuine equality is only a utopian dream, impossible to attain in an imperfect human world. It is, they imply, simply inconsistent with human nature or at least with the nature of society.

Regarding human nature, we can ponder the differences between two lost tribes of "Stone Age men" that were recently described—the Ik of the East African highlands and the Tasaday in the Philippines.[13] The Ik, having been relocated to a virtually barren territory, were constantly preoccupied with finding food, each person for himself. They would steal food from children or dying old men—and laugh about it. If this was the core of human nature, stripped of all the veneer of civilization, it was indeed a gloomy picture. Mankind was here apparently selfishness incarnate, driven by a ruthless competitiveness. The Tasaday, on the other hand, lived in a fertile valley where food was abundant; and they were incredibly peaceful and coopera-tive. Their language did not even have words for "war" and "fighting." The image of human nature they represented was one of sharing and consider-ation for others.

The answer is, of course, that neither the Ik nor the Tasaday embody basic human nature. Each tribe's behavior and character traits are more plausibly explained by its relationship with its environment. There is no evidence that man is inherently and irreversibly cooperative or competitive, egalitarian or driven to establish some hierarchy of dominance. That leaves essentially without means of proof those equality pessimists who take a rueful, cynical, world-weary stance and conclude that equality is simply incompatible with the selfish, competitive, callous spirit that is an inseparable component of man's flawed nature.

Members of a second class of equality pessimists appear to be more logi-cal, and they are, therefore, somewhat more dangerous. This class includes technologists, planners, economists, and other social scientists who pore over statistics, indices, and trend lines and conclude, sometimes sadly, that whatever was, will be. They argue that all our enormous social efforts to redistribute income—from tax reform to welfare programs and wars on pov-erty—have been ineffective. This refrain is a high-class variation on the old theme, "After all we've done for them . . ." After all we've done for them, they remain poor. The conclusion they arrive at is that economic inequality is awesomely resistant to all efforts at change, to all means of intervention. It persists because it is mysteriously persistent.

These professionals mistake the amassing of detailed statistics for com-plexity of thought; they confuse the meticulous extension of trend lines on graphs with precise prediction; and they confound exhaustive description with rigorous explanation. The conclusions reached by these analysts are remarkably alike in their confident pessimism: inequality is permanent and unchangeable, a given, virtually a law of nature.

This is the stance of the hard-nosed, computer-wise, pragmatic technician, launching his rational assault on the problems of poverty and inequality from a platform built on the assumption that poverty is permanent and on the axiom that inequality is a stable condition of life. It is in no way surprising, then, that they discover a circular explanation for inequality, just as the IQ experts do for intelligence. Whereas the latter say, "IQ tests measure intelligence, which may be defined as the characteristics reflected in the IQ," the former say, in effect, "Inequality is the result of some people's having more wealth and income than others; it persists because some people have more wealth and income than others do."

The pessimistic technician of inequality may be likened to a learned physicist who watches a man fall out of a thirteenth-story window. He may be horrified and deeply sympathetic. The falling man may curse and scream about his condition, about his falling inevitably down, but the physicist would never be so romantic or unscientific as to hope or pray that the falling man's direction might be reversed, that he would fall back *up*. Shaken and appalled as he may be, the physicist is prepared to the end to offer all takers ten-thousand-to-one odds that the man will hit the sidewalk. And when he does, although the physicist may be moved, perhaps to tears, by the crushed and broken body, he would consider it outright insanity to begin circulating a petition to repeal the law of gravity.

So, the inequality pessimist may have great personal sympathy for the poor; he may consider inequality unfair and unjust at some abstract level of idealism; and he may subscribe to the *idea* of equality as a noble if impossible goal. But he never allows his sentimental wishes to become romantic motivations to action. Rather, he rubs his nose in the eternal verities, sighs, "The poor ye have always with you," and turns his talents to the humane task of trying to make poverty less unpleasant, more endurable.

In the descriptive tradition of the social sciences past participles are used as simple adjectives and their dynamic nature as verb forms is overlooked. The poor are thus often described as "deprived" or "impoverished," as if these words connoted inherent characteristics like "tall" or "redheaded." In reality, to say that a group of persons is "deprived" or "impoverished" is to say that they have been deprived. Then, changing voice, we can say that someone has deprived them, someone has impoverished them. Only after that dynamic process has occurred does anyone benefit from a declaration, with a scientific imprimatur, that the resulting state of affairs is permanent and unchangeable. It is not the lack of elegant models that leads to policy decisions that further deprive the deprived. Such consequences are usually quite obvious—at least to those about to be deprived. A policy choice is an act of will and intention. We must once in a while admit that the poor have been impoverished intentionally.

It is only by the refusal to make such admissions, by the creation of narrow and unrealistic models for ending poverty, and by the enshrinement of pessimistic assumptions that the predictions of inevitable inequality, rolling off the assembly line tended by the inequality technicians, can be given a gleaming coat of scientific respectability.

In the face of the insistence on the permanence of inequality, my mind goes—perhaps capriciously, but I think significantly—to the end of the second act of *Tosca*. Tosca is in the presence of Baron Scarpia, the police chief of Rome in the early nineteenth century. Scarpia is a villainous prototype of the cop as fascist, the fascist as cop, the grand enforcer of decisions made, the great guarantor of the persistence and inevitability of inequality. He has captured Cavaradossi, Tosca's lover, a revolutionary, and offers to trade Cavaradossi's life for Tosca's sexual favors. Scarpia seems omnipotent and invulnerable, now and forever. Nothing can be done.

Then, suddenly, impulsively, Tosca grabs a dagger and stabs Scarpia. He falls. He is dead. He is no more. She is astonished. She is awed. All his power, all his invulnerability have disappeared, fled with his breath, and there is nothing before her but a dead body. Over the lifeless flesh, as the curtain falls, she sings softly, wonderingly, "*E avanti a lui, tremava tutta Roma*." "And before this man, all Rome trembled."

Let me hasten to add that I am not advocating political assassination or violence as a way of achieving equality. Terrorism and random so-called revolutionary gestures will bring only violence and anarchy. They do not sow the seeds of justice and equality.

I *am* trying to point out that those who maintain the status quo are mere mortals. They cannot stop our progress toward equality unless we allow them to. The world of Fair Play can be replaced by a world of Fair Shares. A world that would deemphasize the exaltation of the individual as some kind of disconnected, omnipotent being and that would accept the reality that human accomplishments are the results of the actions of many persons working together. A world that would remind us that all men and women are the children of God, and thus essentially similar to one another; not that we will *become* brothers and sisters, but that we *are* brothers and sisters, here, now, in our time, in our place—like it or not. And a world in which we would learn that the wonders of the human being's inner life—his intelligence, his imagination, his capacity for love, his will, his determination—are only meaningful in relation to what goes on around him in the world.

Thousands of years ago the Psalmist sang, "The earth is the Lord's and the fulness thereof, the world and they that dwell therein." I believe that the earth is the Lord's and that He bestowed its bounties upon mankind, not upon some select few individuals. Believing this gives hope that we can learn—together—to act—together—to share those bounties with one another.

Notes

1 | The Equality Dilemma: FAIR PLAY OR FAIR SHARES?

1. Gary Wills, *Inventing America: Jefferson's Declaration of Independence* (Garden City, N.Y.: Doubleday, 1978). Wills's argument regarding the prevalence in eighteenth-century political thought of the concern for *public* happiness, as it affected Jefferson's use of the phrase, is to be found in chap. 10.

2. U.S., Bureau of the Census, *Statistical Abstract of the United States: 1978* (Washington: Government Printing Office, 1978), table 663, p. 411.

3. U.S., Bureau of the Census, *Statistical Abstract of the United States: 1979* (Washington: Government Printing Office, 1979), table 739, p. 451.

4. Ibid., table 796, p. 487.

5. Andrew Levison, *The Working Class Majority* (New York: Coward, McCann & Geoghegan, 1974), pp. 32–3.

6. *Statistical Abstract: 1979*, table 797, p. 488.

7. Paul A. Samuelson, *Economics*, 11th ed. (New York: McGraw-Hill, 1980), pp. 79–80.

8. *Statistical Abstract: 1979*, table 715, p. 470. These are calculations as of 1972: the figures would, of course, be considerably higher today.

9. Ibid.

10. Ibid. The mean per capita wealth was calculated directly from the 1972 data. For example, the value of all personal assets for all persons was $4,344.4 billion. This sum, divided by the 1972 population of approximately 200 million, yields $21,722 as the estimated per capita wealth. Again, appropriate adjustment for the intervening inflationary years would increase the amount significantly.

11. The enormous literature on social mobility is extremely heterogeneous with respect to such issues as methodology and the central question being addressed. The primary focus of some of it is the relative importance of different determinants of the economic success of individuals within their own lifetimes (e.g., Christopher Jencks et al., *Who Gets Ahead? The Determinants of Economic Success in America* [New York: Basic Books, 1979]); other research is more concerned with the mobility rates between generations (e.g., Natalie Rogoff, *Recent Trends in Occupational Mobility* [Glencoe, Ill.: Free Press, 1953]); still other studies compare mobility rates in different countries (e.g., Thomas Fox and S. M. Miller, "Intracountry Variations: Occupational and Stratification Mobility," in Reinhard Bendix and Seymour M. Lipset, eds., *Class, Status, and Power*, 2nd ed. [New York: Free Press, 1966, pp. 574–6]). Since virtually all studies in this field define social mobility as occupational mobility, it is harder to estimate "mobility" with respect to other indicators of social class from one generation to another. The benchmark study of occupational mobility in the United States, emphasizing factors that contribute to the attainment of status, was Peter Blau and Otis Dudley Duncan, *The American Occupational Structure* (New York: Wiley, 1967). It was replicated with essentially the same results by David L. Featherman and Robert M. Hauser, *Opportunity and Change* (New York: Academic Press, 1978).

While most studies find a fair amount of social mobility between generations, the actual distance traversed in such mobility (that is, the relative position of the pairs of occupations being compared within the occupational structure) is rather limited. Accordingly, findings with respect to the *rates* of mobility are necessarily determined in part by the number of occupational or other categories used. A ten-category scale, for example, would show mobility that would not be picked up in a five-category scale. Another problem, particularly in the measurement of intergenerational mobility, is that of "structural mobility," that is, mobility that can be attributed to changes over time in the occupational structure itself, such as the steady decline of farm occupations since the turn of the century, the general shift in the direction of a greater proportion of nonmanual and smaller proportion of manual jobs, and so on. Individual mobility, strictly speaking, is meaningful only when it refers to mobility experienced by the individual over and beyond what can be explained by structural changes. Some studies have been done using simple two-category scales such as white-collar/blue-collar or manual/nonmanual, and these appear to be most consistent. For example, Parker has calculated from the Blau and Duncan data that only 37 percent of the sons of manual workers move into nonmanual jobs and that only 28 percent of the sons of nonmanual workers move down into manual work. Richard Parker, *The Myth of the Middle Class* (New York: Harper & Row, Colophon Books, 1972), p. 215, table 7. For a similar calculation with similar results, see Milton Mankoff, "Toward Socialism: Reassessing Inequality," *Social Policy* 4, no. 5 (Mar./Apr. 1974): 20–32. Comparable figures from the Hauser and Featherman replication are 32 percent and 37 percent: see U.S., Bureau of the Census, *Social Indicators, 1976* (Washington: Government Printing Office, 1977), table 11/2, p. 545. The Rogoff data for the 1940 generation show 38 percent of the sons of white-collar workers in manual jobs, 28 percent of the sons of manual workers in nonmanual jobs. (One of the problems in using these data is that, even when the most refined scales are used, the proportion of jobs in the highest-ranked category tends to be in the 5 to 10 percent range. There is virtually no evidence with respect to recruitment into the ranks of the very rich 1 or 2 percent of the population of the children of persons not themselves in that category—the very rich do not participate in such studies—but projecting from the available data suggests that the number of such persons must obviously be very tiny.)

In sum, the data seem to show that approximately two-thirds of sons stay in the same general category of occupation (manual or nonmanual) as their father. The specific odds that are quoted in the text with respect to the chances of upward or downward mobility are from Arthur B. Shostak, Jon Van Til, and Sally Bould Van Til, *Privilege in America: An End to Inequality?* (Englewood Cliffs, N.J.: Prentice-Hall, Spectrum Books, 1973), p. 21.

For an extensive discussion of the many methodological problems in the study of social mobility see Otis Dudley Duncan, "Methodological Issues in the Analysis of Social Mobility," in N. J. Smelser and S. M. Lipset, eds., *Social Structure and Mobility in Economic Development* (Chicago: Aldine, 1966), pp. 51–97.

12. *Statistical Abstract: 1978*, table 262, p. 160.

13. Paul Menchik, "Intergenerational Transmission of Inequality: An Empirical Study of Wealth Mobility," *Institute for Research on Poverty Discussion Paper* no. 407-77 and idem., "The Importance of Material Inheritance: The Financial Link between Generations," *Institute for Research on Poverty Discussion Paper* no. 474-78 (Madison, Wisc.: University of Wisconsin, 1977 and 1978). Menchik compared the sizes of the estates of parents and children, using probate court records, in a relatively well-off class (at least one parent's estate amounted to $40,000). He summarizes his data in one way as showing that "if one child's parents are 10 times as wealthy as another's, that child will be 8 times as wealthy as the other." For a review and summary of some of the research demonstrating the transmission of great wealth from generation to generation, see G. William Domhoff, *The Powers That Be: Processes of Ruling Class Domination in America* (New York: Vintage Books, 1979), pp. 6–7.

14. James N. Morgan et al., eds., *Five Thousand American Families: Patterns of Economic Progress* (Ann Arbor, Mich.: Institute for Social Research, University of Michigan, 1974-).

15. Ibid., vol. I.

16. R. H. Tawney, *Equality* (London: Unwin, 1964), pp. 122–3. (This is the fifth edition of this classic, originally published in 1931.)

17. Daniel Bell, "On Meritocracy and Equality," *The Public Interest*, no. 29 (fall 1972): 67.

2 | Knowing What's Good for You: BELIEF AND EQUALITY

1. Barrington Moore, Jr., *Injustice: The Social Bases of Obedience and Revolt* (White Plains, N.Y.: M. E. Sharpe, 1978).

2. Karl Marx and Friedrich Engels, *The German Ideology*, ed. C. J. Arthur (New York: International Publishers, 1970). The earliest and, I think, most accessible formulations of Marx's conceptions of ideology are contained in this work.

3. Karl Marx and Friedrich Engels, *The Manifesto of the Communist Party*, in Robert C. Tucker, ed., *The Marx-Engels Reader* (New York: Norton, 1972), p. 351.

4. Karl Mannheim, *Ideology and Utopia: An Introduction to the Sociology of Knowledge*, trans. Louis Wirth and Edward Shils (New York: Harcourt, Brace & World, Harvest Books, 1956), p. 40.

5. Ibid., pp. xxii–iii.

6. Marvin E. Shaw and Jack M. Wright, in their *Scales for the Measurement of Attitudes* (New York: McGraw-Hill, 1967), present and discuss many of the most commonly used of these scales. For discussions and analyses of the problems arising from the multidimensional nature of these scales, see Jack M. Hicks and John H. Wright, "Convergent-Discriminant Validation and Factor Analysis of 5 Scales of Liberalism-Conservatism," *Journal of Personality and Social Psychology* 14 (1970): 114-20 (Hicks and Wright found four separate factors, which they identified as economic, political, religious, and esthetic); W. A. Kerr, "Untangling the Liberalism-Conservatism Dimension," *Journal of Social Psychology* 35 (1952): 111-25; and William Zimmer, "The Internal Structure of Economic Liberalism-Conservatism Scales" (M A diss., Dept. of Psychology, Boston College, 1974).

7. Despite much professional and amateur opinion to the contrary, the evidence that persons from lower occupational, income, and educational levels are far more "liberal" than those from higher strata is enormous, ranging from Centers's survey in the 1940s to that of Curtis and Jackson in the 1970s. Richard Centers, *The Psychology of Social Classes* (Princeton: Princeton University Press, 1949) and Richard F. Curtis and Elton F. Jackson, *Inequality in American*

Communities (New York: Academic Press, 1977). For a thorough analytic review of the data, see Richard F. Hamilton, *Class and Politics in the United States* (New York: Wiley, 1972). The opposing point of view stems largely from Hans J. Eysenck, *The Psychology of Politics* (London: Routledge & Kegan Paul, 1954); idem., "Social Attitudes and Social Class," *British Journal of Social and Clinical Psychology* 10 (1971): 201-12; and Seymour M. Lipset, *Political Man* (New York: Doubleday, 1960). Lipset introduced the notion of the "authoritarian" working class. Eysenck's work is, I think, simply idiosyncratic. His measures of "liberalism-conservatism" include such items as "The idea of God is an invention of the human mind," "A person should be free to take his own life, if he wishes to do so," "Nowadays more and more people are prying into matters which do not concern them," and "Free love between men and women should be encouraged as a means toward mental and physical health." As for Lipset's concept, it should be noted that he acknowledges that members of the working class are "liberal" on economic issues, showing their authoritarian conservatism on social issues. His formulation was immediately challenged by S. M. Miller and Frank Riessman, " 'Working Class Authoritarianism': A Critique of Lipset," *British Journal of Sociology* #12 (1961): 263-76. The empirical base of this notion was undermined by B. G. Stacey and R. T. Green, "Working Class Conservatism: A Review and an Empirical Study," *British Journal of Social and Clinical Psychology* 10 (1971): 10-26. Andrew Levison marshals a considerable amount of evidence (in his *Working Class Majority*, chap. 4) to show that the working class is not apparently as conservative on social issues as Lipset charges, particularly in its attitudes toward blacks. He also cites data showing considerably greater opposition to the Vietnamese War among members of the working class, in contrast to the prevailing stereotype of that period of "hard hats" beating up "long-haired student radicals."

8. Lloyd A. Free and Hadley Cantril, *The Political Beliefs of Americans* (New York: Simon & Schuster, Clarion Books, 1968).

9. Irving Kristol, "About Equality," *Commentary*, Nov. 1972, pp. 41-7.

10. Ibid., p. 42.

11. Ibid., p. 46.

12. Paul Seabury, "The Idea of Merit," *Commentary*, Dec. 1972, pp. 41-6.

13. Ibid., p. 43.

14. Ibid., p. 44.

15. Ibid., p. 45.

16. Daniel Bell, "On Meritocracy and Equality," *The Public Interest*, no. 29 (fall 1972): 29-69.

17. Ibid., p. 39.

18. Ibid., p. 40-1.

19. Ibid., p. 58.

20. Ibid., p. 65.

21. Ibid., p. 67.

22. See, for example, Robin Williams, *American Society*, 2nd ed. (New York: Knopf, 1960); Vernon Parrington, *Main Currents in American Thought* (New York: Harcourt, 1930); and Kenneth M. Dolbeare and Patricia Dolbeare, *American Ideologies* (Chicago: Markham, 1971). A recent, unfortunately neglected, study by Michael Lewis, *The Culture of Inequality* (Amherst, Mass.: University of Massachusetts Press, 1978), documents the fact that individualism remains an extremely dominant part of American ideology and analyzes its specific relationship to the maintenance of inequality.

23. Some position on the relationship between the individual human and the human collectivity (society, the state, the culture) is a necessary component of any coherent theory of human nature, particularly with respect to the "chicken-egg" aspect, that is, which came first. For example, man in the state of nature existing as a separate individual—either in reality or only conceptually—is the beginning point and common element of all social-contract theories, from

Rousseau to Rawls, and this emphasis on the individual as the primary unit remains a vital part of any social theory that starts at that point. One corollary of this is that historians and social scientists must begin either with that assumption (methodological individualism) or with the assumption that the collectivity can transcend the individual. For an excellent review of this problem, see William H. Dray, "Holism and Individualism in History and Social Science," in Paul Edwards, ed., *The Encyclopedia of Philosophy* (New York: Macmillan, 1967), IV, 53–8. Another common problem around which discussion of this issue revolves is that of so-called feral children. Most of those who have addressed this problem arrive at some variation on the conclusion that the collectivity is paramount. See, as an example, Lucien Malson, *Wolf Children and the Problem of Human Nature* (New York and London: Monthly Review Press, 1972). For an excellent review of the overall question, see Steven Lukas, "Types of Individualism," in Philip P. Wiener, ed., *Dictionary of the History of Ideas* (New York: Scribner's, 1973), II, 594–604. A recent article, incisive but difficult, that illuminates this issue is David Rasmussen, "Between Autonomy and Sociality," *Cultural Hermeneutics* 1 (1973): 3–45.

24. The apprehension and the mental organization of similarities and differences are the core activities of processes variously named abstraction, generalization, categorization, and concept formation. They constitute one of the major themes in philosophy and psychology—Plato's doctrine of forms, various efforts to formulate relationships between the universal and the particular, or between the genus, the species, and the individual, the problem of definition in logic, etc. An interesting analysis of the relative emphasis on similarity and difference (or, in his words, "the age-old distinction between the Same and the Other") is to be found in Michel Foucault, *The Order of Things: An Archaeology of the Human Sciences* (New York: Vintage Books, 1973). Foucault demonstrates a shift in Western thinking at the end of the sixteenth century from an emphasis on resemblances to an emphasis on classification, hence on difference. Another example of the effect of social and historical forces on cognitive processes, including perceptual emphasis on similarity or difference, is provided by Luria's study of the effect on mental processes of the social change in the Asian provinces of the Soviet Union following the revolution. See A. R. Luria, *Cognitive Development: Its Cultural and Social Foundations* (Cambridge, Mass.: Harvard University Press, 1976).

25. Disputes on this axis range from those relating to innate ideas as opposed to the empiricist doctrine that all ideas come from externally produced sensations to those that attempt to identify the source of intelligence, mental illness, and so forth—the nature-nurture or heredity-environment dispute. Most general theories about human behavior can be divided into those that give great weight to instinctual, genetic, or other innate determinants—e.g., Freud, the "sociobiologists"—and those that pay much more attention to such external determinants as the social structure or patterns of reinforcement—e.g., Durkheim, Pavlov. For excellent reviews of several of these issues, see John O. Nelson, "Innate Ideas," *Encyclopedia of Philosophy*, IV, 196–8; Michael Wertheimer, *Fundamental Issues in Psychology* (New York: Holt, Rinehart & Winston, 1972), chaps. 2 and 9.

26. Robert K. Merton, "Singletons and Multiples in Scientific Discovery," *Proceedings of the American Philosophical Society* 105 (1961): 470–86. Merton uses as a springboard formulations from Bacon's *Novum Organum* that relate the standardization of scientific method to the necessary collectivization of the scientific enterprise. Although demonstrating rather conclusively that all scientific "discoveries" are what he calls "multiples," Merton nevertheless reconciles this with the idea of the individual scientific genius by showing that the latter differs quantitatively from the ordinary scientist in that he is involved in a larger number of such discoveries.

27. It should be underlined here that the three ideological dimensions are independent and not necessarily correlated, since they are, of course, dealing with quite different issues. The emphasis on collectivity and difference, for example, is fairly common both in time of war and in situations involving such questions as the defense of "turf" in urban neighborhoods. As another example, the psychological theory of behaviorism strongly emphasizes the individual

and focuses exclusively on external determinants of behavior. Theoretically, the three dimensions could be organized in different ways so as to yield not simply two belief systems (such as Fair Shares and Fair Play), but eight. There is nothing inherently illogical in belief systems that emphasize, say, collectivity, similarity, and the external or the individual, similarity, and the internal. In unpublished pilot work that I have conducted with students to develop methods of measuring the three ideological dimensions, the typical findings are that scales to measure the three dimensions tend to correlate with one another in the .20 to .30 range.

28. Kingsley Davis and Wilbert E. Moore, "Some Principles of Stratification," *American Sociological Review* 10 (1945): 242-9. For an interesting discussion of this issue, which attempts to strike a balance between the functionalist position and a more Fair Shares perspective, see Arthur M. Okun, *Equality and Efficiency: The Big Tradeoff* (Washington: The Brookings Institution, 1975).

29. *Statistical Abstract: 1978*, table 677, p. 417.

3 | Some Hard Answers: THE CASE FOR FAIR SHARES

1. David Wechsler, *The Measurement of Adult Intelligence*, 3rd ed. (Baltimore: Williams and Wilkins, 1944). The original Wechsler-Bellevue scale has been replaced in general clinical use by the Wechsler Adult Intelligence Scale, so the "professional secrets" I will be revealing are, I believe, no longer classified information.

2. Lewis Terman, *The Measurement of Intelligence* (Boston: Houghton Mifflin, 1916).

3. Alfred Binet and T. H. Simon, *The Development of Intelligence in Children* (Baltimore: Williams and Wilkins, 1916).

4. For a review and analysis of this research and related issues, see Frank Riessman, "The Hidden IQ," in Alan Gartner, Colin Greer, and Frank Riessman, eds., *The New Assault on Equality: IQ and Social Stratification* (New York: Harper & Row, Perennial Library, 1974).

5. James Cronin et al., "Race, Class, and Intelligence," *International Journal of Mental Health* 3, no. 4 (1975): 46-132 (see esp. pp. 52-61 for a detailed criticism of the Stanford-Binet and Wechsler Intelligence Scale for Children); David C. McClelland, "Testing for Competence Rather than for Intelligence," *American Psychologist* 28 (1973): 1-14; Jerome Kagan, "What Is Intelligence?" *Social Policy* 4, no. 1 (July/Aug. 1973): 88-94. Jeffrey Blum, *Pseudoscience and Mental Ability: The Origins and Fallacies of the I.Q. Controversy* (New York and London: Monthly Review Press, 1978).

6. See Christopher Jencks et al., *Who Gets Ahead? The Determinants of Economic Success in America* (New York: Basic Books, 1979), for an extensive review of this research.

7. James Fallows, "The Tests and the 'Brightest': How Fair Are the College Boards?" *The Atlantic*, Feb. 1980, p. 40.

8. *Statistical Abstract: 1979*, table 230, p. 144. For an excellent analysis of the many facets of this general issue, see Ivar Berg, with Sherry Gorelick, *Education and Jobs: The Great Training Robbery* (Boston: Beacon Press, 1971).

9. Samuel Bowles and Herbert Gintis, "I.Q. in the U.S. Class Structure," *Social Policy* 3 (1972-3): 65-96.

10. Ibid.

11. U.S., Bureau of the Census, *Social Indicators, 1976* (Washington: Government Printing Office, 1977), table 7/11, p. 299.

12. Ibid., table 7/12, p. 300.

13. John C. Flanagan and William W. Cooley, *Project Talent: One Year Follow Up Studies* (Pittsburgh: School of Education, University of Pittsburgh, 1966), p. 95.

14. Samuel Bowles and Herbert Gintis, *Schooling in Capitalist America: Educational Reform and the Contradictions of Economic Life* (New York: Basic Books, 1976), esp. pp. 119-22 and table 4-4.

15. Leon Kamin, *The Science and Politics of I.Q.* (Potomac, Md.: Lawrence Erlbaum Associates, 1974); N. J. Block and Gerald Dworkin, eds., *The I.Q. Controversy* (New York: Pantheon Books, 1976).

16. Joseph A. Schumpeter, *Capitalism, Socialism and Democracy*, 3rd ed. (New York: Harper & Row, Torchbooks, 1950). See chap. 6 for Schumpeter's exposition of the key role of "super-normal" individual entrepreneurs in the rapid development of industrial capitalism in the nineteenth century.

17. James N. Morgan et al., eds., *Five Thousand American Families: Patterns of Economic Progress* (Ann Arbor, Mich.: Institute for Social Research, University of Michigan, 1974-).

18. Ibid., IV, app. A, pp. 421-8.

19. Ibid., III, 339.

20. Ibid., IV, 421-2.

21. Kingsley Davis and Wilbert E. Moore, "Some Principles of Stratification," *American Sociological Review* 10 (1945): 242-9. The best-known criticism of this article is Melvin M. Tuman, "Some Principles of Social Stratification: A Critical Analysis," ibid. 18 (1953): 387-94.

22. Robert W. Hodge, Paul M. Siegel, and Peter H. Rossi, "Occupational Prestige in the United States: 1925-1963," in Reinhard Bendix and S. M. Lipset, eds., *Class, Status, and Power: Social Stratification in Comparative Perspective,* 2nd ed. (New York: Free Press, 1966).

23. Christopher Jencks et al., *Inequality: A Reassessment of the Effect of Family and Schooling in America* (New York: Basic Books, 1972), esp. pp. 225-6.

24. U.S., Bureau of the Census, *Statistical Abstract of the United States: 1979* (Washington: Government Printing Office, 1979), table 164, p. 108.

25. Ibid., table 249, p. 154.

26. Ibid., table 519, p. 320.

27. Ibid., table 705, p. 427.

28. Ibid. The average percentage difference in unionization rates for the four pairs of states (New York and Connecticut; Michigan and Ohio; California and Oregon; Washington and Oregon) is 25 percent. The range was as follows: Michigan's rate was 4 percent higher than Ohio's, while New York's rate was 49 percent higher than Connecticut's. In all four comparisons, the state with the higher rate of unionization has the higher average salary for teachers.

29. David Halberstam, *The Best and the Brightest* (New York: Random House, 1972).

30. Randall Collins, *The Credential Society: An Historical Sociology of Education and Stratification* (New York: Academic Press, 1979), pp. 54-5.

31. R. H. Tawney, *Religion and the Rise of Capitalism* (London: J. Murray, 1926).

32. I have not been able to find a bibliographic source for this quotation. It is used as an epigraph on materials produced by the National Indian Youth Council, Albuquerque, N.M.

33. Edward Bellamy, *Equality*, 3rd ed. (New York: Appleton, 1897), pp. 88-9.

34. U.S., Bureau of the Census, *Historical Statistics of the United States* (Washington: Government Printing Office, 1975), series P299, vol. II, p. 697.

4 | Help the Needy and Show Them the Way: IDEOLOGY AND SOCIAL POLICY

1. For a detailed demonstration and discussion of this point, see Martha N. Ozawa, "Social Insurance and Redistribution," in Alvin L. Schorr, ed., *Jubilee for Our Times: A Practical Program for Income Equality* (New York: Columbia University Press, 1977), chap. 4. Ozawa also shows that the pensions of high-wage workers are subsidized more than are those of low-wage workers.

2. This figure and the others quoted in this section regarding other income maintenance programs are to be found in U.S., Bureau of the Census, *Statistical Abstract of the United States: 1979* (Washington: Government Printing Office, 1979). For Social Security benefits, see table

538, p. 336; unemployment compensation, table 562, p. 348; SSI, AFDC, and general relief, table 566, p. 352.

3. S. M. Miller and Pamela Roby, *The Future of Inequality* (New York: Basic Books, 1970); Herbert Gans, *More Equality* (New York: Pantheon Books, 1973); Arthur B. Shostak, Jon Van Til, and Sally Bould Van Til, *Privilege in America* (Englewood Cliffs, N.J.: Prentice-Hall, Spectrum Books, 1973).

4. William Ryan and Ali Banuazizi, *Mental Health Planning in Metropolitan Areas*, Boston College, Community Psychology Monograph no. 1 (Boston, 1972), pp. 63-4.

5. Harold L. Wilensky and Charles N. Lebeaux, *Industrial Society and Social Welfare* (New York: Free Press, 1965), esp. pp. 138-40.

6. Richard M. Titmuss, *Social Policy: An Introduction* (New York: Pantheon Books, 1975), pp. 30-1.

7. Roland Warren, *The Structure of Social Reform* (Lexington, Mass.: D. C. Heath-Lexington Books, 1976).

8. George Hoshino, "Britain's Debate on Universal or Selective Services: Lessons for America," *Social Service Review* 43, no. 3 (1969): 245-58; Arthur Seldon and Hamish Gray, *Universal or Selective Social Benefits?* (London: Institute of Economic Affairs, 1967).

9. U.S., Bureau of the Census, *Statistical Abstract of the United States: 1979* (Washington: Government Printing Office, 1979), table 430, p. 258.

10. Henry J. Aaron, *Politics and the Professors: The Great Society in Perspective* (Washington: The Brookings Institution, 1978), p. 25.

11. *Statistical Abstract: 1979*. For federal income tax revenues for these years, see table 426, p. 256; for personal income, see table 722, p. 440.

12. Ibid., table 443, p. 266. Total federal income tax for such a family would be about $3,400, which is about $65 a week. Of the total federal budget, 5.7 percent goes to all forms of public assistance, 23.2 percent for national defense (table 430, p. 258). Applying these figures to the family's income tax payments yields $ 3.73 for public assistance, $15.17 for national defense, per week.

13. Ibid. Annual federal income tax for a person earning $250 a week, using the overall average of 17.6 percent, would be about $2,200 a year. In 1978 federal expenditures for the AFDC program were $10.7 billion (table 567, p. 352), 2.4 percent of the total federal budget of $450.8 billion; 2.4 percent of $2,200 is $52.80 a year, or fourteen cents per day.

14. Alvin L. Schorr, "The Duplex Society," *New York Times*, 4 June 1972, p. 15.

15. U.S., Bureau of the Census, *Historical Statistics of the United States* (Washington: Government Printing Office, 1975), series H28, vol. I, p. 341. (This amount of $41 million includes *all* social-welfare services.) As late as 1929, tax-supported public assistance benefits for the entire country totaled only $60 million (ibid., series H15, p. 340).

16. For a review of the influence of the Social Darwinists in late-nineteenth-century America, see Richard Hofstadter, *Social Darwinism in American Thought*, rev. ed. (Boston: Beacon Press, 1955), which includes many chilling quotations from the writings of Herbert Spencer, William Graham Sumner, and other eminent scientific advocates of the "survival of the fittest."

17. The idea of the opportunity structure as an important issue originated in Richard A. Cloward and Lloyd E. Ohlin, *Delinquency and Opportunity: A Theory of Delinquent Gangs* (New York: Free Press, Macmillan, 1960). For varying viewpoints on the history of the war on poverty, see Peter Marris and Martin Rein, *Dilemmas of Social Reform: Poverty and Community Action in the U.S.* (New York: Atherton, 1967); Sar A. Levitan, *The Great Society's Poor Law: A New Approach to Poverty* (Baltimore: Johns Hopkins University Press, 1969); Daniel P. Moynihan, *Maximum Feasible Misunderstanding: Community Action in the War on Poverty* (New York: Free Press, 1970); and Aaron, *Politics and the Professors*, esp. his discussion of the built-in contradictions of the war on poverty, pp. 27-30.

18. Richard F. Hamilton, *Class and Politics in the United States* (New York: Wiley, 1972). A

recent review of this issue in the "Opinion Roundup" section of *Public Opinion* (1, no. 4 [Sept./Oct. 1978]: 35) shows that agreement with the idea that "government ought to help people get doctors and hospital care at low cost" was 60 percent in 1956, 65 percent in 1960, 58 percent in 1964, and 61 percent in 1968, and that it had risen to 81 percent by 1978.

19. For Senator Moynihan's autobiographical account of this episode, see his *The Politics of a Guaranteed Income: The Nixon Administration and The Family Assistance Plan* (New York: Random House, 1973). For an account from a somewhat different perspective, see Nick Kotz and Mary Lynn Kotz, *A Passion for Equality: George A. Wiley and the Movement* (New York: Norton, 1977), chap. 30. The Kotzes describe the long fight against the Nixon-Moynihan plan, led by George Wiley's "virtuoso lobbying performance that won't be soon forgotten on Capitol Hill." For a brief, journalistic account of the events, see James Welsh, "Welfare Reform: Born, Aug. 8, 1969, Died Oct. 4, 1972," *New York Times Magazine*, 7 Jan. 1973, p. 16.

5 | Dishwashers Trained Here: IDEOLOGY AND EDUCATION

1. U.S., Bureau of the Census, *Historical Statistics of the United States* (Washington: Government Printing Office, 1975), series H599, p. 379; series H755 and H756, p. 385; series H701 and H711, p. 383.

2. Samuel Bowles and Herbert Gintis, *Schooling in Capitalist America: Educational Reform and the Contradictions of Economic Life* (New York: Basic Books, 1976).

3. Colin Greer, *The Great School Legend* (New York: Viking Press, 1973); Michael Katz, *The Irony of Early School Reform* (Cambridge, Mass.: Harvard University Press, 1968); Joel Spring, *Education and the Rise of the Corporate State* (Boston: Beacon Press, 1972).

4. James Conant, *Slums and Suburbs: A Commentary on High Schools in Metropolitan Areas* (New York: McGraw-Hill, 1961).

5. See *Youth in the Ghetto* (New York: Harlem Youth Opportunities Unlimited, 1964).

6. Robert Rosenthal and Lenore Jacobson, *Pygmalion in the Classroom* (New York: Holt, Rinehart and Winston, 1968).

7. Ray Rist, "Student Social Class and Teacher Expectations: The Self-Fulfilling Prophecy in Ghetto Education," *Harvard Educational Review* 40 (1970): 411–50.

8. For examples of the literature on innate differences (either cultural or genetic) between classes and/or races and for discussions of the issue, see Arthur Jensen, "How Much Can We Boost IQ and Scholastic Achievement?" *Harvard Educational Review* 39 (1969): 1–123; Richard Herrnstein, "I.Q.," *Atlantic Monthly*, Sept. 1971; Christopher Jencks et al., *Inequality: A Reassessment of the Effect of Family and Schooling in America* (New York: Basic Books, 1972); James Coleman et al., *Equality of Educational Opportunity* (Washington: Government Printing Office, 1966); M. Deutsch, I. Katz, and A. R. Jensen, eds., *Social Class, Race and Psychological Development* (New York: Holt, Rinehart and Winston, 1968); Donald M. Levine and Mary Jo Bane, eds., *The "Inequality" Controversy: Schooling and Distributive Justice* (New York: Basic Books, 1975); Frederick Mosteller and Daniel P. Moynihan, eds., *On Equality of Educational Opportunity* (New York: Random House, 1970).

9. Rist, "Student Social Class and Teacher Expectations," p. 435.

10. H. S. Becker, "Social Class Variations in Teacher-Pupil Relationships," *Journal of Educational Sociology* 25 (1952): 451–65; A. J. Hoehn, "A Study of Social Status Differentiation in the Classroom Behavior of 19 Third Grade Teachers," *Journal of Social Psychology* 39 (1954): 269–92; T. Good and J. Brophy, "Analyzing Classroom Interactions: A More Powerful Alternative," *Educational Technology*, Oct. 1971, pp. 36–41; B. Mackler, "Groupings in the Ghetto," *Education and Urban Society* 2 (1969): 80–95.

11. Richard Sennett and Jonathan Cobb, *The Hidden Injuries of Class* (New York: Alfred A. Knopf, 1972).

6 | Black Like Them: IDEOLOGY AND RACISM

1. Most students of social stratification agree that there is some castelike quality to the position of blacks in American society, although they differ with respect to extent. For strong argument and persuasive detail on race as caste, particularly in the South of a generation ago, see John Dollard, *Caste and Class in a Southern Town* (New York: Harper, 1937), and Allison Davis, Burleigh Gardner, and Mary Gardner, *Deep South* (Chicago: University of Chicago Press, 1941).

2. U.S., Bureau of the Census, *Statistical Abstract of the United States: 1979* (Washington: Government Printing Office, 1979), table 735, p. 449.

3. Ibid. In 1977, 38.4 percent of white families had incomes of $20,000 or more, compared with only 17.2 percent of black families; conversely, 37 percent of black families had incomes below $7,000, compared with 14.1 percent of white families.

4. William Ryan, "A Survey of Massachusetts Voters," mimeographed (Boston: City Missionary Society, 1975); "Several Racial Barriers Disappearing," "Opinion Roundup" section, *Public Opinion* 1, no. 4 (Sept./Oct. 1978): 37; Philip E. Converse et al., *American Social Attitudes Data Sourcebook, 1947-1979* (Cambridge, Mass.: Harvard University Press, 1980).

5. For a description of the functioning of the Massachusetts state agency at that time (the late 1950s and early 1960s), see Leon Mayhew, *Law and Equal Opportunity: A Study of the Massachusetts Commission against Discrimination* (Cambridge, Mass.: Harvard University Press, 1968). Of particular interest is the distinction he makes between the conceptions of "reasonable treatment" and "equal treatment."

6. Nathan Perlmutter, *You Don't Help Blacks by Hurting Whites*, League for Industrial Democracy, Occasional Paper no. 14 (New York, 1968). This was reprinted from the *New York Times Magazine*.

7. Nathan Glazer, *Affirmative Discrimination: Ethnic Inequality and Public Policy* (New York: Basic Books, 1975).

8. *Statistical Abstract: 1979*, table 650, p. 396.

9. Ibid., table 236, p. 148.

10. U.S., Bureau of the Census, *Social Indicators, 1976* (Washington: Government Printing Office, 1977), table 8/8, p. 376.

11. *Statistical Abstract: 1979*, table 265, p. 161.

12. Ibid., table 268, p. 163.

13. Ibid., table 222, p. 141. From this table it can readily be seen that, for the total age range from fourteen to nineteen, a higher percentage of black than white youths are enrolled in school.

14. Ibid., table 238, p. 148.

15. Joe Dreyfuss and Charles Lawrence III, *The Bakke Case: The Politics of Inequality* (New York: Harcourt Brace Jovanovich, 1979). The authors discuss the role of the "Harvard Plan" in the decision making and describe in detail (pp. 177-89) Archibald Cox's appearance before the Court, where he argued the case for the defendant, the University of California, Davis, Medical School. (The justices seemed interested in learning from Cox more about Harvard than Davis.)

16. See Andrew Levison, *The Working Class Majority* (New York: Coward, McCann & Geoghegan, 1974), for a detailed summary of this point. In the "Survey of Massachusetts Voters," we found no significant differences on questions about racial attitudes; the small differences that appeared indicated that blue-collar workers were *less* prejudiced than were white-collar workers and that those who identified themselves as "working class" or "lower class" were *less* prejudiced than those who identified themselves as "middle class" or "upper class." For an extensive refutation of the idea that working-class whites are more racist than are middle-class whites, see Richard F. Hamilton, *Class and Politics in the United States* (New York: Wiley, 1972), esp. pp. 399-434.

17. For a presentation of the "white flight" thesis, see James S. Coleman, Sara D. Kelley, and John Moore, *Trends in School Segregation, 1968 73* (Washington: The Urban Institute, 1975). For a briefer presentation, see James S. Coleman, "Liberty and Equality in School Desegregation," *Social Policy* 6, no. 4 (Jan./Feb. 1976): 9-13. For criticisms of this thesis, see Thomas F. Pettigrew and Robert L. Green, "School Desegregation in Large Cities: A Critique of the Coleman White Flight Thesis," *Harvard Educational Review* 46 (1976): 1-53; Christine Rossell, "White Flight: Pros and Cons," *Social Policy* 9 (Nov./Dec. 1978): 46-59. Rossell summarizes much of the detailed criticism of Coleman's notion, including her own influential studies.

18. U.S., Commission on Civil Rights, *Racial Isolation in the Public Schools* (Washington: Government Printing Office, 1967). Thomas Pettigrew was the principal author of this report. For a thorough summary of the research on this issue see Nancy St. John, *School Desegregation Outcomes for Children* (New York: Wiley, 1975).

19. For a typical (and influential) presentation of this point of view, see McGeorge Bundy, "The Issue before the Court: Who Gets Ahead in America?" *Atlantic Monthly*, Nov. 1977, pp. 41-54. This is a "well-meaning" argument in *favor* of affirmative action, but it, typically, gives away all the points to critics of "reverse discrimination," talking about the need for special admissions, preferential treatment, and the like, on the grounds that we "owe it" to currently disabled black people, since their difference, their disability, was caused by *past* discrimination. Bundy does not include in his argument—and does not even acknowledge—the fact that discrimination against blacks continues today and requires a remedy in public action.

7 | Making It Happen: THE INVISIBLE CLASS STRUGGLE

1. The problems of estimating income distribution accurately and the additional ones of determining its relative degree of equality or inequality have been a source of difficulty and dispute among economists for decades. (Much of the technical discussion is beyond my reach and, I believe, beyond that of most persons outside the profession; nevertheless, the broad outlines of the data showing historical change seem reasonably clear.) For the data in this chapter, I have relied on the following principal sources: Daniel Creamer, *Personal Income During Business Cycles* (Princeton: Princeton University Press, 1956), (a study by the National Bureau of Economic Research); Gabriel Kolko, *Wealth and Power in America: An Analysis of Social Class and Income Distribution* (New York: Praeger, 1961); studies by the Census Bureau, the National Bureau of Economic Research, and the Office of Business Economics, data from which are published in U.S., Bureau of the Census, *Historical Statistics of the United States* (Washington: Government Printing Office, 1975), series G1-G415, pp. 289-305; and various editions of the *Statistical Abstract*. Several of these sources cite data from Simon Kuznets, *Shares of Upper Income Groups in Income and Savings* (New York: National Bureau of Economic Research, 1953).

There appears to be a clear consensus that inequality of income distribution has significantly improved over the past fifty years, but Kolko and Miller and Roby, among others, argue strongly that the official statistics underestimate the income of the upper stratum by overlooking legal devices (stock options, deferred incomes, expense accounts, tax shelters, undistributed profits, etc.) as well as illegal ones, principally straightforward deceit in not reporting income. (See Kolko, *Wealth and Power in America*, pp. 9-45, and Miller and Roby, *The Future of Inequality* [New York: Basic Books, 1970], chaps. 3 and 5.) These devices make the real income of the wealthy considerably greater than that reported in the literature.

For additional discussion of some of these problems see Robert J. Lampman, "Measured Inequality of Income: What Does It Mean and What Can It Tell Us?" *Annals* 409 (Sept. 1973): 81-91; and Sheldon Danziger, "Trends in Economic Inequality in the U.S. since World War II: A Conference," *Focus, Institute for Research on Poverty Newsletter* 1, no. 2 (winter 1976 77): 5-6, 13.

2. *Historical Statistics*, series H599, p. 379. In the last decade of the nineteenth century, fewer than 5 percent of young persons were graduating from high school; by 1930, the figure was 29 percent. With respect to the slight increase in inequality during this period, see Kolko, *Wealth and Power in America*, table I, p. 14; and Creamer, *Personal Income During Business Cycles*, table 24, p. 82 (taken from Kuznets).

3. *Historical Statistics*, series H599, p. 379. Between 1940 and 1944, high school graduation rates declined from 49 to 42.7 percent; between 1965 and 1968, from 76.3 to 74.2 percent.

4. Frances Fox Piven and Richard A. Cloward, *Poor People's Movements: Why They Succeed, How They Fail* (New York: Pantheon Books, 1977).

5. *Historical Statistics*, series D927, p. 176; U.S., Bureau of the Census, *Statistical Abstract of the United States: 1979* (Washington: Government Printing Office, 1979), table 703, p. 426.

6. *Historical Statistics*, series D972, p. 179; *Statistical Abstract: 1979*, table 708, p. 429.

7. *Historical Statistics*, series G203, p. 297; *Statistical Abstract: 1979*, table 744, p. 454.

8. *Statistical Abstract: 1972*, table 234, p. 148.

9. Studs Terkel, *Hard Times: An Oral History of the Great Depression* (New York: Pantheon Books, 1970).

10. Frances Fox Piven and Richard A. Cloward, *Regulating the Poor: The Functions of Public Welfare* (New York: Pantheon Books, 1971).

11. There are two factors to be considered here: first, the "clearance" (arrest) rate for various kinds of crimes, which varies from very high for relatively rare crimes like murder to very low for most property crimes, and, second, the accuracy of crime statistics. A number of so-called victimization studies have clearly established the fact that two to four times as many crimes are reported by victims as find their way into police statistics. There are twice as many aggravated assaults as the police report to the FBI, more than three times as many robberies, two and one-half times as many burglaries. (For summary data on these points see *Statistical Abstract: 1979*, table 291, p. 177, for official FBI figures, and tables 296 and 297, p. 180, for data from national crime surveys.) This means that the official overall clearance rate, which in 1977 was 22 percent, has to be divided by a factor of at least two or three to get the true rate.

12. David Rothman, *The Discovery of the Asylum* (Boston: Little, Brown, 1971); Michel Foucault, *Discipline and Punish: The Birth of the Prison* (New York: Pantheon Books, 1977); Erik Olin Wright, *The Politics of Punishment: A Critical Analysis of Prisons in America* (New York: Harper & Row, Colophon Books, 1973), esp. chap. 15, which gives a formulation of the role of the prison in social control; Michael Ignatieff, *A Just Measure of Pain: The Penitentiary in the Industrial Revolution 1750-1850* (New York: Pantheon Books, 1978), esp. chap. 7.

13. Evelyn N. Parks, "From Constabulary to Police Society: Implications for Social Control," *Catalyst*, summer 1970, pp. 77-97.

14. *Statistical Abstract: 1979*, table 332, p. 195.

15. Ibid., table 725, p. 441.

16. A. W. Phillips, "The Relation between Unemployment and the Rate of Change of Money Wage Rates in the United Kingdom, 1861-1957," *Economica* 25 (1958): 283-89. In summarizing his findings, Phillips puts it very neatly (p. 299): "the rate of change of money wage rates can be explained by the level of unemployment and the rate of change of unemployment. . . ."

17. *Statistical Abstract: 1979*, table 671, p. 404.

18. Barrington Moore, Jr., *Injustice: The Social Bases of Obedience and Revolt* (White Plains, N.Y.: M. E. Sharpe, 1978).

19. Richard Herrnstein, "I.Q.," *Atlantic Monthly*, Sept. 1971, pp. 44-64.

20. U.S., Department of Labor (Daniel P. Moynihan principal author), *The Negro Family: The Case for National Action* (Washington: Government Printing Office, 1965); James Coleman et al., *Equality of Educational Opportunity* (Washington: Government Printing Office, 1966); Edward Banfield, *The Unheavenly City* (Boston: Little, Brown, 1970); Jensen, "How Much Can We Boost I.Q. and Scholastic Achievement?" *Harvard Educational Review* 39 (1969): 1-123.

21. Joseph Kraft, "Inequality in American Society," *Boston Globe*, 8 Nov. 1972.

22. For examples see Daniel P. Moynihan, "The Crisis in Welfare," *The Public Interest*, no. 10 (winter 1968): 3–29; Nathan Glazer, "The Limits of Social Policy," *Commentary*, Sept. 1971, pp. 51–8; idem., " 'Regulating' the Poor—or Ruining Them?" *New York Magazine*, 11 Oct. 1971, pp. 55–8.

23. Roger Starr, "Which of the Poor Shall Live in Public Housing?" *The Public Interest*, no. 23 (spring 1971): 116–24.

24. James Q. Wilson, *Thinking About Crime* (New York: Basic Books, 1975), p. 289.

25. G. William Domhoff, *The Higher Circles: The Governing Class in America* (New York: Vintage Books, 1971); idem., *The Powers That Be: Processes of Ruling Class Domination* (New York: Vintage Books, 1979); C. Wright Mills, *The Power Elite* (New York: Oxford University Press, 1956); Kolko, *Wealth and Power in America*.

26. August Meier and Elliot Rudwick, *CORE: A Study in the Civil Rights Movement, 1942–1968* (New York: Oxford University Press, 1973), pp. 252–8; Nick Kotz and Mary Lynn Kotz, *A Passion for Equality: George A. Wiley and the Movement* (New York: Norton, 1977), pp. 126–7.

27. Robert L. Bartley, "Irving Kristol and Friends," *Wall Street Journal*, 3 May 1972, p. 20.

28. In an interview in *Public Opinion*, Irving Kristol is quoted as saying, "Nader calls himself, what, an anarchist-socialist of some sort . . .?" See "Is America Moving Right? Ought It?: A Conversation with Irving Kristol and Arthur Schlesinger, Jr.," *Public Opinion* 1, no. 4 (Sept./Oct. 1978): 12. In a subsequent exchange of letters (Nov./Dec. 1978, inside back cover), Nader protests the characterization and Kristol's refusal to retract the statement and describes his work as being "about making the competitive market system operate fairly and safely." Kristol responds by expressing pleasure on learning that Nader is a defender of free-market capitalism.

29. For examples of "new class" theorizing, see Kristol, "About Equality," *Commentary*, Nov. 1972, pp. 41–7; Daniel Bell, *The Coming of Post-Industrial Society* (New York: Basic Books, 1973); Daniel P. Moynihan, "Equalizing Education: In Whose Benefit?" *The Public Interest*, no. 29 (fall 1972): 69–89.

30. "Mounting Frustration with Government," *Public Opinion* 2, no. 5 (Oct./Nov. 1979): 29.

31. S. M. Lipset and William Schneider, "The Public View of Regulation," ibid., 2, no. 1 (Jan./Feb. 1979): 6–13; "But Continued Support for Some 'Big Government' Programs," ibid., 2, no. 4 (Sept./Oct. 1979): 29.

32. Patrick H. Caddell, "Crisis of Confidence: Trapped in a Downward Spiral," ibid., 2, no. 5 (Oct./Nov. 1979): 2–7, 57–60. See esp. p. 52.

33. "Country in Trouble," ibid., p. 28.

34. "What's Your Beef?" ibid., 1, no. 3 (July/Aug. 1978): 22.

35. "The Work Ethic Reviewed," ibid., 3. no. 1 (Dec./Jan. 1980): 36.

36. "Lou Harris Finds Rising Alienation," ibid., 1, no. 2 (May/June 1978): 23.

8 | Toward Equality: FAIR SHARING IN AMERICA

1. For a very clear and perceptive analysis of how inequality itself blocks access to many goods and services for those of lower income, particularly to such goods as housing, medical care, and education, see Mark Kelman, "The Social Costs of Inequality," in Lewis A. Coser and Irving Howe, eds., *The New Conservatives: A Critique From the Left* (New York: Quadrangle Books, 1974), pp. 151–64.

2. For a clear and detailed description of the Social Security system and of the differences between social and private insurances, see Martha Ozawa's chapter in Alvin L. Schorr, ed., *Jubilee for Our Times: A Practical Program for Income Equality* (New York: Columbia University Press, 1977), esp. pp. 151–9.

3. U.S., Bureau of the Census, *Statistical Abstract of the United States: 1979* (Washington: Government Printing Office, 1979), table 447, p. 268.

4. Ibid., table 475, p. 286. In 1977 property taxes amounted to $62.5 billion, or 36 percent of the total of $175.9 billion in taxes collected by state and local governments; approximately half of that was in taxes on residential property. For a further discussion of this tax problem (and others), see Robert M. Brandon, Jonathan Rowe, and Thomas Stanton, *Tax Politics: How They Make You Pay and What You Can Do About It* (New York: Pantheon Books, 1976).

5. *Statistical Abstract: 1979*, table 436, p. 261, shows that in 1979 taxpayers who itemized deductions listed $5.9 million in deductions for property taxes. Of all the tax deductions, 59 percent were taken by taxpayers with adjusted gross incomes of $25,000 or more. This group makes up 10 percent of all taxpayers (table 449, p. 270).

6. For a thoughtful discussion of some of these issues, see Michael Harrington, *Socialism* (New York: Saturday Review Press, 1972).

7. Frank Parkin, *Class Inequality and Political Order: Social Stratification in Capitalist and Communist Societies* (New York: Praeger, 1971). For an interesting case study of this issue, see Zygmunt Bauman, "Economic Growth, Social Structure, Elite Formation: The Case of Poland," in Reinhard Bendix and S. M. Lipset, eds., *Class, Status, and Power*, 2nd ed. (New York: Free Press, 1966), pp. 534-40.

8. For a readable explanation of the processes of visual perception, see Richard L. Gregory, *The Psychology of Seeing*, 3rd ed. (New York: McGraw-Hill, 1978).

9. Frank Parkin, "Working-Class Conservatives: A Theory of Political Deviance," *British Journal of Sociology* 18 (1967): 278-90. Parkin argues that a Labor or Socialist orientation in the United Kingdom is a deviation from the dominant Conservative ideology and that these factors act as "normative 'subsystems' which serve as 'barriers' to the dominant values of the society."

10. William Ryan, "A Survey of Massachusetts Voters," mimeographed (Boston: City Missionary Society, 1975). These are from raw data not published in the report.

11. See Peter Steinfels's *The Neoconservatives: The Men Who Are Changing America's Politics* (New York: Simon & Schuster, 1979), pp. 4-15, for a discussion of how neoconservative thought makes its way from the intellectual journals to the mass media. This book is an excellent study of the history and status of the neoconservative movement, with particular emphasis on Kristol, Bell, and Moynihan.

12. In this connection, it is interesting to note patterns of support and opposition to unions. A summary in the "Opinion Roundup" section of *Public Opinion* ("Confidence in Selected Institutions," vol. 2, no. 5 [Oct./Nov. 1979]:32) shows the pattern of relative trust in various institutions among subgroups in the population. While confidence in "the people running major companies" is about twice as high as in "the people running organized labor" (23 percent as against 12 percent), among nonwhites the proportions are reversed; among the less educated, and presumably, unskilled or semiskilled workers, confidence in the two institutions is about the same, while among college graduates there is much greater confidence in "major companies" than in "organized labor" (36 percent, compared with 5 percent). Among young persons eighteen to twenty-four, as well, there is apparent a slightly higher level of trust in labor than in industry. So, while labor has a tremendous amount of ground to make up with respect to public confidence, its most sympathetic constituency is, it would seem, its natural one. It is also interesting to note that the three groups that show the most confidence in organized labor are the ones with the highest confidence in the federal government.

13. Colin M. Turnbull, *The Mountain People* (New York: Simon & Schuster, 1972); John Nance, *The Gentle Tasaday: A Stone Age People in the Philippine Rain Forest* (New York: Harcourt Brace Jovanovich, 1975).

Index

Aaron, Henry J., 220
abortion, 42
access to resources, 29, 191; black peoples',
139, 141; as equality, 146–47; Fair Play
vs. Fair Shares view, 8, 9; as right, 7, 8, 9,
29. *See also* Fair Shares equality; public
ownership; resources
ACORN, 207, 208
Adult Education, 115
advertising, 3–4, 53
affirmative action, 138, 147–60, 207, 223; effects on education, 151–52, 157–58; and
equal opportunity, 149; individual merit
and group membership and, 155–56;
quotas, 149, 154–58; as reverse discrimination, 147, 148–54; and working class,
149, 158
Aid to Families with Dependent Children
(AFDC), 22, 103, 110, 111, 113; attitudes
toward, 102, 104; size of grants, 102. *See
also* children and child welfare; welfare

Alabama, 79; civil rights movement, 166–67,
169
Alaska, 80
American dream, 183
American Enterprise Institute, 175
American family; economic progress of,
75–76, 162; economic inequities, 11–14,
222; economic vulnerability of majority,
18–25; female-headed, 21, 102–3; socioeconomic mobility of, 16–18; urban,
13–14. *See also* vulnerable majority
American Indians, *see* Native Americans
American myths, 53
American society: central inequality in, 31;
economic inequities, 11–26; equality dilemma, 3–10; foundation documents,
6–8, 9; minority domination in, 84; as
political democracy, 178–79, 199; stupidity problem, 81–85. *See also* American
family
Aristotle, 10, 43

227

ABOUT THE AUTHOR

Dr. William Ryan, a clinical psychologist by training, received his Ph.D. from Boston University and is currently a professor of psychology at Boston College. Since the mid-1960s, he has been active in welfare rights and in prison reform, helping to organize the Citizen Observer program in Walpole Prison in 1973.

His previous books include *Distress in the City* and *Blaming the Victim*.